Equal
Separation

**Recent Titles in
Contributions in Legal Studies**

Death by Installments: The Ordeal of Willie Francis
Arthur S. Miller and Jeffrey H. Bowman

Truman's Court: A Study in Judicial Restraint
Frances Howell Rudko

The Gladsome Light of Jurisprudence: Learning the Law in England
and the United States in the 18th and 19th Centuries
Michael H. Hoeflich, editor and compiler

James Madison on the Constitution and the Bill of Rights
Robert J. Morgan

Lawyers, Courts, and Professionalism: The Agenda for Reform
Rudolph J. Gerber

John Marshall's Achievement: Law, Politics, and
Constitutional Interpretations
Thomas C. Shevory, editor

Affirmative Action and Principles of Justice
Kathanne W. Greene

Unfounded Fears: Myths and Realities of a Constitutional Convention
Paul J. Weber and Barbara Perry

Protecting Constitutional Freedom: A Role for Federal Courts
Daan Braveman

The Employment Relationship in Anglo-American Law:
A Historical Perspective
Marc Linder

The Aristocracy of the Long Robe
J.M. Sosin

EQUAL SEPARATION

UNDERSTANDING THE RELIGION CLAUSES OF THE FIRST AMENDMENT

EDITED BY
PAUL J. WEBER

FOREWORD BY MARTIN E. MARTY

CONTRIBUTIONS IN LEGAL STUDIES,
NUMBER 58
PAUL L. MURPHY, *SERIES EDITOR*

GREENWOOD PRESS
NEW YORK • WESTPORT, CONNECTICUT • LONDON

Library of Congress Cataloging-in-Publication Data

Equal separation : understanding the religion clauses of the first
   amendment / edited by Paul J. Weber ; foreword by Martin Marty.
      p. cm.—(Contributions in legal studies, ISSN 0147–1074 ;
  no. 58)
   Includes bibliographical references.
   ISBN 0–313–26700–6 (lib. bdg. : alk. paper)
   1. Freedom of religion—United States. 2. Church and state-
-United States. I. Weber, Paul J., 1937– . II. Series.
KF4783.E65 1990
342.73′0852—dc20
[347.302852]   89–25777

British Library Cataloguing in Publication Data is available.

Library of Congress Catalog Card Number: 89–25777
ISBN: 0–313–26700–6
ISSN: 0147–1074

First published in 1990

Greenwood Press, 88 Post Road West, Westport, Connecticut 06881
An imprint of Greenwood Publishing Group, Inc.

Printed in the United States of America

∞

The paper used in this book complies with the
Permanent Paper Standard issued by the National
Information Standards Organization (Z39.48-1984).

10 9 8 7 6 5 4 3 2 1

Contents

Foreword

Martin E. Marty

Not often does a single essay cause one to reorient his or her thinking. Nor does one frequently gain from reading such an essay a framework for further thought and inquiry. Usually we look for a life work by a titan to nudge us toward reorientation. We demand at least a book-length argument to be challenged to create a new framework.

Paul J. Weber, however, through a single article on "equal separation" and James Madison, did lead me to think about relations between religious and civil authority and response in fresh ways. And his set of options concerning styles of separation between "church" and "state" has become one that I find so congenial that it has almost become instinctive for me. That is why when he asked if I would take a look at this collection and possibly write a foreword I agreed to do so. My high expectations were by no means denied.

For a quarter century I have been a University of Chicago colleague of Philip Kurland, a law professor who has with great force and clarity argued that the two First Amendment clauses must always be treated as one. Courts should rule with perfect consistency. In effect, his principle would see the Constitution as a document which was and intended to be "silent" about religion. Professor Kurland has always admitted that this did not picture getting his way, but behind the resigned smile with which he did the admitting was a more determined look: it would be good, he keeps suggesting, if the courts and the Supreme Court used *some* such principle, preferably his, to bring some clarity and focus to what now looks like muddling or chaos.

Professor Weber, who earlier had written a more historically minded paper (which I wish could appear as an appendix in this book, and which all readers will certainly want to read), here offers a synthetic and synoptic sort of chapter that refines the Kurland approach. It should achieve the purpose of teasing respondents to reorient their thought or to find a new framework for further pursuits. Just to be sure that we will not think that he plays unfairly, Weber has invited in some critics whose replies to him, which make up most of this book, not only argue back but offer principles of their own.

It is hard to picture a reader who will be fully convinced by Weber or any of the other authors, not because their statements are uncompelling but because the interests the constitutional tradition addresses are so ample, competitive, and tangled. They run through faith communities, legal and philosophical subcultures, and the middle of the mind of many citizens.

To illustrate: Some years ago to enjoy my (hour and) 15 minutes of celebrity that artist Andy Warhol licensed for all citizens, I was on a national television program, Phil Donahue's show, "Donahue." It dealt that day with issues of church and state. In the first 15 minutes a dozen people in the audience spoke up, as did all four panelists. During the first commercial break the host asked us panelists to keep conversation going with the audience members near us, so that the psychological room temperature would not be lowered.

A woman near me volunteered: "Until this morning, I never gave a thought to any side of this issue. Now I have heard a dozen or more 'sides' from as many people—all of whom disagreed totally with each other. My problem is: I agree with all of them!" Most readers of this book will have given thought to the issue and will not be so readily convertible to every position as that audience member was. Yet if their experience is like mine, they will find something of value in chapters they will basically reject, and flaws in those they find more congenial.

Thus while the neatness of the Kurland proposal has always been alluring, I have not been able to go along with it; I agree with its proposer that it would clear the air and give us a refined set of expectations; but I also agree that most of the public would not want such an approach. They do not desire a truly "strict neutrality." The same is the case with the preferable (to me) approach that Weber sometimes lapses into calling "strict neutrality" and on other occasions refers to in terms of his own patent as "equal separation."

No sooner will Weber sink in again than I read Dean Kelley, whose chapters and verses dazzle. Kelley knows all the outs and ins of church-state legality, makes a marvelous case for privileging religion, and helps call into question elements that seemed secure and safe in the mind after a reading of Weber. Along comes "strict separationist" James Dunn, who agrees somewhat more with Weber, but Weber's reply to him in turn throws off balance anyone who found it easy to go along immediately with Dunn.

So with the rest of the book. As an advocate of "pluralism" I found much that was congenial in Steven Monsma the accommodationist, who talks so much good sense in a field where good sense rarely rules. Weber finds some holes to plug, some gaps that will remain. Then there is William Marty; I am glad Weber did his most strenuous opposing there, since if I stated all the disagreements and it became a court case here we would obviously have *Marty v. Marty*. At too many points in his chapter there are hints of theocracy—that's too heavy a word for his benign proposals, but it seems he wants the government to do some of the work churches ought to be doing. Robert Healey knows his Jefferson and presents tantalizing contributions by him even as he presents constructive proposals on the educational front.

The Weber responses are courteous and firm, and they tend to succeed in giving voice to reservations many will have while reading the other authors. Then again, picture this as a Phil Donahue-type show with the criticized getting to return once more to the scene. They would thus contribute to a continuing, I have to and hope to say unending, conversation.

That's the point, or a point: The day will not come when this argument ceases, when all interests have been satisfied. Weber knows this and points to a kinetic scene where change forces constant re-posing of church and state questions. He knows there will always have to be some muddling, but he is opposed to *mere* muddling. He knows that the whole public will not buy the whole "equal-separation" package. But he is certainly right that the effort to produce consistency has a potential payoff in society and in personal expectations. If the courts acted on some consistent principle, we would know better how to respond. If it acted on the one he offers, we would at least have raised the terms of decisions and discussions. No one will act on it, however, unless they give currency to the Weberian scheme. I'll quickly get out of the way so that the reader can discern what that scheme is, and begin to make reply.

Preface

Books sometimes begin in strange ways and take unexpected shapes. This one began on a lazy summer afternoon as I was leafing through a stack of recent law-review articles on the First Amendment religion clauses. All agreed—and lamented—that religion-clause jurisprudence is in disarray. The Supreme Court justices are divided, religious lobbyists and litigators are more aggressive than usual in pursuing their often conflicting goals, and almost daily, or so it seemed, newspaper articles reported another novel church-state piece of litigation. The law-review articles appeared as hopelessly disjoined as the justices and cases they analyzed.

What struck me as I read the articles was that in reviewing possible new approaches, so many authors returned again and again to a 25-year-old theory called strict neutrality. They examine it briefly, then dismiss it as "attractive on its face" but "too harsh" or "not politically feasible," and move on. Having completed a dissertation on the topic a dozen years ago, I knew how very little serious analysis had been done of strict neutrality and how little attempt made to develop the concept. Perhaps even worse, there was even less effort given to sort out and answer the criticisms. What made strict neutrality so clearly attractive and so quickly rejected? And why, if so often rejected, do writers keep coming back to it? Is there perhaps a foundation there, a basically sound structure on which a more compelling theory of the First Amendment religion clauses can be developed? If that were to happen, the pros and cons of strict neutrality would have to be argued in a more focused manner than had yet been done. That was the beginning of the book.

The next step was organizing a panel on strict neutrality at the 1988 American Political Science Association Convention. I arranged to write an initial paper outlining a strict-neutrality thesis. Other panelists were invited to critique the concept, each focusing on a different perspective. The only rule for panelists was that personal attacks were out of bounds. Three scholars accepted the invitation, representing a challenging array of viewpoints.

There is hardly a church-state scholar in the United States as well-known and respected as Dean Kelley, Religious Liberty Director of the National Council of Churches. Both a personal friend and an insightful critic of strict neutrality, he graciously agreed to develop his criticisms focused on a defense of the free exercise of religion.

James Dunn, Executive Director of the Baptist Joint Committee on Public Affairs, who in spite of his claims to be just a "simple country preacher" is a canny and unwavering defender of church-state separation, agreed to take up the gauntlet in defense against what he considers strict neutrality's assault on the establishment clause. We were joined on the panel by Professor Steve Monsma of Pepperdine University, a towering presence, both physically and intellectually, who although not yet as well known as Kelley and Dunn, made his mark originally in evangelical circles. He is now being heard more broadly for his thoughtful defense of accommodation (what he prefers to call a pluralist model). Here he contrasts that pluralist theory with strict neutrality.

The panel was chaired by Professor Booth Fowler of the University of Wisconsin, who added a number of insights of his own, including a suggestion to change the name of the theory from "strict neutrality" to "equal separation." After hearing the criticisms of several of the panelists, I agreed that this would be a clearer, more consistent term to use. In fairness to the other authors who were using the term "strict neutrality," I really did not make the change until the last chapter. I apologize for any confusion this switch in terminology creates for readers.

After the panel it became evident that there were gaps in our coverage of the issues. Professor William Marty of Memphis State University, who attended the panel, was invited to address the issue of strict neutrality and the schools. Finally, since we had all consciously avoided mere recitation of Supreme Court cases, we lacked an overview of the Court's development of the concept of separation of church and state. Professor Robert Healey of the University of Dubuque Theological Seminary was invited to adapt his recent article from the *Journal of Church and State* to fill that gap. All that remained was a final chapter addressing the criticisms and defending the strict-neutrality/equal-separation theory.

As I proceeded with that task I was struck by two things. One was the dedication each author had to religious liberty, despite vigorous disagreement over the conditions required for such liberty and the means necessary to achieve it. The second was the amount of overlap each of the other positions shared with equal separation. Is the overlap enough to make equal separation a viable First Amendment theory? That is for the readers to decide.

Many people contribute to the writing of a book and this one is no exception. I want first of all to thank Professor Philip Kurland of the University of Chicago, who originally proposed the strict-neutrality thesis. I am not certain he will recognize the new equal-separation theory as his own, but he provided the core idea. Next in line are Professor Booth Fowler and the contributors. We had a tough, but genial panel, and responding to their papers over the intervening months has been a challenging task. Dr. Martin Marty has always been an inspiration and I was honored when he agreed to write a foreword. I also want to thank my administrative assistant, Ms. Sherry Allen, for her unfailing good humor and organization while I was preoccupied with this project, the typists, Amy Fey, Sandy Hartz, and Bryan Raymer, and of course, Mildred Vasan of Greenwood-Praeger for her patience and encouragement as I missed deadlines. Finally, I dedicate the book to my wife, Madeline, who lives the struggle to integrate the value of freedom and equality, an ideal central to this book.

Equal
Separation

Neutrality and First Amendment Interpretation

Paul J. Weber

Perhaps no Supreme Court case since *Widmar v. Vincent*[1] supports the neutralist theory of the First Amendment religious clauses as clearly as does *Bowen v. Kendrick*.[2] In that case, a number of groups challenged an act of Congress, commonly known as the Adolescent Family Life Act.[3] Congress, recognizing that the roots of problems leading to adolescent pregnancy and parenthood are multiple and complex, decided that

> such problems are best approached through a variety of in-
> tegrated and essential services provided to adolescents and their
> families by other family members, religions and charitable or-
> ganizations, voluntary associations, and other groups in the
> private sector as well as services provided by publicly sponsored
> initiatives.[4]

It may be that "neutrality" is now the dominant theory of religion-clause decision-making on the Supreme Court, but neither the philosophical underpinnings nor the constitutional implications of that theory have been adequately worked out.[5] It is the purpose of this chapter to propose a constitutional foundation for strict neutrality which locates it within the traditional language of separation of church and state yet responds to contemporary values.

The author's personal and constitutional objectives can be stated up front. I am committed to a defense of religious liberty in as broad a range of activities as is possible consistent with public safety and health, *and* to the extension of that liberty to all similar groups and individuals. I am equally committed to nonestablishment, by which I mean no privileges, no advantages, no exceptions, no supports extended by government based on religious belief, affiliation, or organization that is not extended equally to all similarly situated groups or organizations. I accept the three-pronged *Lemon* test with one minor exception.

To understand the strict-neutralist position it is helpful to begin with two presuppositions. First, when the Founders wrote the First Amendment they did not write with either the clairvoyance or the specificity that would make it easy to apply their principles to problems arising in contemporary church-state relations. There are various strands in the Founders' thought which allow not only for conflicting interpretations but for contemporary adaptation. Second, we live almost 200 years since the First Amendment religion clauses were penned and enormous changes have taken place, changes far beyond what the Founders could have imagined.

Granted these presuppositions, the challenge in constitutional theorizing is to create a principle of interpretation which (1) remains as faithful as possible to the language of the Constitution and the intent of the Founders, (2) respects case-law development in this area, (3) respects contemporary constitutional values such as due process and equal protection, (4) is realistic, that is, acknowledges the political, social, religious, and economic facts of life, and (5) resolves problems in a manner seen by as many citizens as possible as just and fair.[6] Before undertaking that challenge, further reflection on the presuppositions may be helpful.

VARIETIES OF SEPARATION

The term "separation of church and state," although never appearing in the Constitution, has become so embedded in American consciousness that it seems to sum up what is meant by the First Amendment religion clauses. Small wonder. The term is so broad it can embrace a wide variety of beliefs and practices, and allows groups espousing any one of several policy agendas to wrap themselves in the mantle of the Constitution. Our first task is to sort out the divergent meanings of the term "separation" and determine which best meet the challenges of constitutional theorizing.

Separation, in the First Amendment context, is a *generic* term which has at least five distinct meanings.[7] The most fundamental is *structural separation*, which distinguishes most Western systems from such organic systems as exist in Iran, Saudi Arabia, and other Muslim countries. The characteristics of structural separation are independent clerical and civil offices, separate organizations for government and religions, different personnel performing different functions, separate systems of law, independent ownership of property, and the absence of any officially designated church or religion. Jefferson, Madison, and most of the other Founders accepted the need for structural separation, and where they found remnants of organic relationship, as in parts of common law, they worked to remove them. It may be that this is as far as their thought had progressed at the time, although there are clues that they wanted something more.

Absolute separation is a type vigorously pursued by some interest groups in this country. It is usually considered in terms of financial separation, holding that no aid of any kind should flow from government to religion or churches, and no financial support should flow from religion or churches to the government. Absolutists would take as normative Justice Hugo Black's description of the establishment clause in *Everson v. Board of Education*.

> The "establishment of religion" clause of the first amendment means at least this: Neither a state nor the Federal Government can set up a church. Neither can pass laws which aid one religion, aid all religions, or prefer one religion over another. Neither can force nor influence a person to go to or to remain away from church against his will or force him to profess a belief or disbelief in any religion. No person can be punished for entertaining or professing religious beliefs or disbeliefs, for church attendance or non-attendance. No tax in any amount, large or small, can be levied to support any religious activities or institutions, whatever they may be called, or whatever form they may adopt to teach or practice religion. Neither a state nor the Federal Government can, openly or secretly, participate in the affairs of any religious organizations or groups and vice versa. In the words of Jefferson, the clause against establishment of religion by law was intended to erect "a wall of separation between Church and State."[8]

The difficulties facing the advocates of absolute separation are twofold. First, it is by no means clear that the Founders intended such a specific meaning of separation.[9] Second, historical practice in the United States, including contemporary practice, has included enormous amounts of aid, both direct and indirect, flowing to religion from government in return for enormous amounts of mostly indirect aid from religion.[10] This is a political and economic reality absolutists may rally against, but it is so embedded in law and practice that it is unlikely to change in the foreseeable future. Absolutists are left in the awkward position of claiming as a constitutional principle—a law to be obeyed—something that has never existed and is never likely to. Absolute separation is an ideal for some, but certainly not a reality.

Unfortunately for absolutists, the Constitution, unlike the Declaration of Independence, has the force of law and is meant to be obeyed as well as admired.

Transvaluing separation is less understood in the United States, but does have a devoted following. It holds that one objective of government is to secularize the political culture of the nation, that is, to reject as politically illegitimate the use of all religious symbols, or the appeal to religious values, motivations, or policy objectives in the political arena. Transvaluing separation would deny all aid to religious organizations under any circumstances. It is this type of separation that is touted in the Soviet constitution and law.[11] One statement from an American group that seems best to express this position is that of the American Humanist Association:

> To promote the "general welfare," a particular measure may be favored by church interests, and consequently pressure and influence are brought to bear on the state's political machinery to assure its passage. Or a measure may be viewed with disfavor by the church with a resultant pressure on the state's political machinery to assure its defeat. This type of activity by the church harks back to pre-Revolutionary days both here and in Europe, where there was "cooperation" between government and church. But it was just that sort of religion-political interplay that the Founding Fathers tried desperately to prevent on American soil by adopting the First Amendment and the corresponding state laws.[12]

Thomas Jefferson's desire to provide access to the University of Virginia for neighboring schools of divinity is prima facie evidence that he did not favor this type of separation.[13] I have argued elsewhere that Madison's "Memorial and Remonstrance" shows his opposition to this type of separation.[14] In any event, the Supreme Court has rejected transvaluing separation (although not under that name) and it does not appear to have much promise as a constitutional principle in the United States.

What has traditionally been called "accommodation" I would call *supportive separation.* Those who hold this position acknowledge the need for structural separation but would not drive the principle to the extremes of the absolute or transvaluing types. To the contrary, supportive separationists favor aid and support for religion, holding only that government may not support one religion over another.[15] This position takes as normative Justice William O. Douglas's dictum that

> we are a religious people whose institutions presuppose a Supreme Being. We guarantee the freedom to worship as one

chooses. We make room for as wide a variety of beliefs and creeds as the spiritual needs of man deem necessary. We sponsor an attitude on the part of government that shows no partiality to any one group and that lets each flourish according to the zeal of its adherents and the appeal of its dogma. When the Government encourages religious instruction and cooperates with religious authorities by adjusting the schedule of public events to sectarian needs, it follows the best of our traditions. For it then respects the religious nature of our people and accommodates the public service to their spiritual needs.[16]

Unfortunately for advocates of supportive separation the history of the battle for religious liberty in Virginia and of the framing of the First Amendment undermines any claim that this is what the Founders intended. In addition, a whole series of decisions indicate very clearly that the Supreme Court does not believe this is what the Constitution requires. Finally, there has been strong political opposition to such a position throughout American history.

Equal separation rejects all political or economic privilege, coercion, or disability based on religious affiliation, belief, or practice, or lack thereof, but guarantees to religiously motivated or affiliated individuals and organizations the *same* rights and privileges extended to other similarly situated individuals and organizations. It provides protection to religion without providing privilege. It treats the right to religious belief and practice as a human right to be protected along with other human rights in an even-handed manner. It protects the right of religiously motivated groups and individuals to participate in the political process and the economic system in the same manner and to the same extent as it protects the rights of other similar groups and individuals to participate.

A difficulty facing proponents of equal separation is that it is a concept only recently developed and therefore unfamiliar to most Americans. It has been viewed suspiciously by advocates of other types of separation who fear that it will lead to a decrease in protection for religious liberty or an increase in aid to religion. Nonetheless it is the basis for the strict-neutrality approach to the religion clauses and will be further developed below. I have argued elsewhere equal separation is most consistent with the thought of James Madison.[17]

HISTORICAL DEVELOPMENTS

Several developments of enormous proportions have made it difficult to apply the original First Amendment religion clauses to contemporary problems in any generally acceptable fashion and still meet the requirements for constitutional theorizing posited above.[18] The first development is the application of the religion clauses to the states through the due process clause of the Fourteenth Amendment by the Supreme Court. The free exercise clause was applied to the states in *Cantwell v. Connecticut* in 1940[19] and the establishment clause in *Everson v. Board of Education* in 1948.[20] This development alone altered in a fundamental and radical way the intent of the Founders who wrote the First Amendment.

The First Congress and the legislatures of the states which ratified the amendment fully anticipated that states would aid religion and even establish particular religions if they saw fit. They also anticipated that states could and would regulate religious activity limited only by their own constitutional provisions. Only the federal government was prohibited from making laws establishing religion or infringing on its free exercise. Separation of church and state originally meant only separation of church and *national* government. It was the Supreme Court which began to require states to apply the Bill of Rights through incorporation under the due process clause of the Fourteenth Amendment. This device, first utilized in 1925, dissolved the very distinction which the Founders envisioned would free both the federal government and the churches from troubling entanglements.[21]

A second unforeseen development is the transformation of both federal and state governments from passive-protective, minimalist governments to active-expansive, pervasive administrative bureaucracies. This change from a laissez-faire to a bureaucratic state with broad taxing, regulatory, and spending powers has enormous implications for church-state relations. In a complex, heavily populated society whose members demand equity, due process, accountability, and a high level of product performance, "the inclination to administer, to standardize, to regulate, to reorganize, to define—and therefore constrict—personal activity and private choice is endemic."[22] When governments regulate everything from seat belts on buses to exit signs in public buildings to commercial TV to the sale of bonds, should only church buses, buildings, TV empires, and bonds be exempt?[23] That constitutes a uniquely privileged position in society, the very essence of establishment.

On the other hand, regulation of church activities in such areas has been seen as an infringement on religious liberty.[24] Unless some principle is developed which both clarifies and limits the allowable type of regulation, this will become an increasingly difficult area of controversy.[25]

Parallel to the expansion of government has been the expansion of religious organizations in population, physical institutions, activities undertaken, and sheer variety of denominations, sects, and cults. While TV programs such as "The 700 Club" and, until recently, "PTL" are the most visible symbols of the size and vigor of religion, churches currently run day-care centers, retirement homes, hospitals, schools at all levels, research centers, settlement houses, halfway houses for prisoners, sports facilities, theme parks, publishing houses, and even nightclubs. They sponsor low-cost housing projects, bus tours, and travel agencies. Many of these activities rely heavily on state and federal funding.

Religion is, from one perspective, big business. In each of the areas mentioned, religious organizations complement and compete with commercial enterprises. The line between many types of activity undertaken by religious groups and secular activity has become irretrievably blurred.[26] The interaction and potential entanglement of religion and government are both substantial and inevitable. Should religious activities be held to the same standards as other enterprises or should there be a double standard?

A fourth major change is the invention of technologies which make possible such new activities as mass education, mass communication, massive impersonal solicitation of funds, the fabrication of mind-altering drugs, and in the very near future, genetic manipulation. When used by religious groups, how much regulation should government exercise? Less than that exercised over other similar groups? To explore one very real problem, do the American people want the government to allow fraud in the solicitation, investment, or expenditure of funds by religious groups? Do even religious groups want religious organizations to have such "freedom," especially when they no longer accept such a caveat emptor attitude for other organizations? The headlined escapades at PTL in the 1980s and the conviction of Rev. Jim Bakker indicate not. Yet to protect against such fraud requires administrative accountability and an ongoing reporting-auditing relationship between church groups and government agencies.

Fifth, the sheer growth in population density, mobility, and diversity has profoundly altered the environment within which religious organizations and activities exist and the laws affecting them are made. Density and mobility are significant because it is no longer easy for individuals to live solely among their own kind or to shelter their children from exposure to competing values. The result is severe disagreement over what laws should require, permit, or prohibit. An even greater difficulty exists in making a principled defense of laws that deal specifically with religious organizations or activities.[27]

Finally, in the last two decades there has been a religious awakening of enormous proportions, the results of which are only beginning to be felt. Particularly acute have been the proliferation of values and theologies which reject many values taken for granted by traditional mainline American Christianity and Judaism, values such as the private nature of religion and the very concept of separation. Fundamentalism has been adequately pilloried elsewhere and is the example most used to support this assertion. Other approaches are Liberation Theology,[28] the so-called New Age Cults,[29] the Christian revisionism developed in Dominican priest Matthew Fox's *Original Blessing*,[30] and to some extent, Process Theology.[31]

None of these new religious thrusts, if I understand them correctly, finds traditional struggles between separationists and accommodationists either relevant or important. Establishment is not seen as a contemporary problem nor separation as a virtue. They tend to support a social-political-economic-cultural vision variously called integration, holism, monism, or "a higher unity."

Taken together, these six developments since the First Amendment was written pose such difficulties in terms of potential conflict, discrimination, and entanglement that legal theories which ignore them are doomed to failure. The task of the original Founders was to protect religious liberty *from* government. The contemporary task of constitutional scholars is to protect religious liberty *in the midst of* government, and prevent establishment in the face of indifference.

THE THEORY OF STRICT NEUTRALITY

Strict neutrality was proposed a quarter century ago by Philip Kurland of the University of Chicago:

> The thesis proposed here as the proper construction of the religion clauses of the first amendment is that the freedom and separation clauses should be read as a single precept that government cannot utilize religion as a standard for action or inaction because these clauses prohibit classification in terms of religion either to confer a benefit or to impose a burden.[32]

The thesis has been developed since then and some clarifications may be helpful. First, the purposes of the religion clauses can be summed up as freedom, separation, and equality. The application of the clauses in conjunction is both possible and necessary. It can be done by reading the clauses as an equal-protection doctrine, or as Kurland explains:

> For if the command is that inhibitions not be placed by the state on religious activity, it is equally forbidden the state to confer

favors upon religious activity. These commands would be impossible of effectuation unless they are read together as creating a doctrine more akin to the reading of the equal protection clause than to the due process clause, i.e., they must be read to mean that religion may not be used as a basis for classification for purposes of government action, whether that action be the conferring of rights or privileges or the imposition of duties or obligations.[33]

The equal-protection doctrine is a well-developed component of constitutional law and can provide a firm foundation for dealing with current controversies in the church-state area, providing both consistency and flexibility. Acceptance of strict neutrality is not a denial that religion can be used as a classification to identify and protect a significant personal interest or social unit. It would be incongruous to hold that the Constitution could recognize the existence of religion but that the government based on that Constitution could not. Recognition of an objective fact of personal value preference or of social organization would not be a violation of the neutrality principle.[34] Examples of the former might be wearing a skull cap or scapular and of the latter might be recognition of the presence of a church or synagogue when planning traffic-control signals or assigning personnel to expedite traffic.

Such recognition implies that in relevant secular aspects, individual religious interests and social groups are similar to other interests and groups, not based on religious content, but on the other public and secular aspects of a religion's social organization. Put in other words, strict neutrality is committed to the proposition that there is seldom a *legally significant* characteristic of religion so unique that it is not shared by similar nonreligious individuals and groups. The conclusion to be drawn is that in most aspects, religious individuals and interests are subject to the same laws as other similarly situated individuals and groups.

But what happens when there is a claim based on a uniquely religious belief, such as when an Adventist cannot work on Saturday and requests unemployment compensation? Or when a Mennonite refuses to have her picture on a driver's license? Or when a Baptist church requires all its employees to be members of the church? Or what happens when a seemingly neutral law in fact imposes a significant burden on a religion or even prohibits a religious activity, for example, an ordinance that prohibits door-to-door solicitation on weekends? In such cases religion may be treated as a *suspect classification* subject to strict scrutiny by the courts. A suspect classification is one in which there is "a presumption of unconstitutionality against a law implying certain classifying traits."[35] If religion is considered a suspect classification, any statute utilizing religion or specifically impacting on religion is automatically suspect, will demand a very heavy burden of justification, and will be subject to the most rigorous scrutiny. More than just a rational connection to a legitimate public purpose will be required. Nevertheless, if the standards of proof are met, the religious interest will be protected.

The suspect-classification concept is used most frequently to prohibit racial and sexual discrimination, but it can equally well be used to preserve government neutrality in respect to religion. The question immediately arises: What are the principles that justify such a classification and define its limits? Several years ago Donald Giannella offered two such principles. The first is the principle of free-exercise neutrality that "permits and sometimes requires the state to make special provision for religious interests in order to relieve them of both direct and indirect burdens placed on the free exercise of religion by increased governmental regulation."[36] Such a provision is consonant with the "protected civil right" nature of religious liberty, but in accordance with the general neutralist position such provisions must be extended to other similar groups if there are any.

The second principle is that of political neutrality. Its aim is "to assure that the establishment clause does not force the categorical exclusion of religious activities and associations from a scheme of governmental regulations whose secular purposes justify their inclusion."[37] The grants contested in *Bowen v. Kendrick* would appear to be of precisely this sort. Several other examples might clarify the concept: If a local government is distributing excess cheese and bread to the poor through neighborhood organizations, church groups could neither be given exclusive rights to distribute the foodstuffs nor excluded from doing so. If government rents neighborhood buildings as polling places, churches could be neither preferred nor excluded from participation. Obviously, equal-access legislation fits within the strict-neutrality concept. At the same time, if a church does participate in secular programs, under the neutrality principle it would have to keep the same records, maintain the same standards, and follow the same regulations as other participants.

OBJECTIONS TO THE STRICT NEUTRALITY PRINCIPLE

A number of objections have been raised to the neutrality principle and we now turn to them. First is the objection that strict neutrality "guts" the religion clauses of any substantive meaning. This objection argues that if religious groups, individuals, and interests are to be treated equally with others, then the religion clauses are irrelevant—surely not a situation the Founders intended.

My response is that very much of religious activity and all of religious thought are fully protected in the speech, press, and assembly clauses of the First Amendment, as well as by the due process and equal-protection clauses, etc. Double protection serves no additional function. Unlike the speech, press, and assembly clauses, however, the religion clauses are twofold, prohibiting the establishment of religion as well as guaranteeing its free exercise. The recognition of an independent liberty must be such that it offends neither one nor the other.

Classification in terms of religion may tend to discriminate either by favoring religious interests at the expense of other similarly situated interests or by burdening religious interests in such a way as to have a "chilling effect" on religious liberty. The most equitable solution to this dilemma is to treat religious groups and interests like similar groups and interests. For example, a religious group seeking funds for its projects would have to conform to the same fund-raising rules and accounting standards as other nonprofit groups. This is the clear implication of *Bowen v. Kendrick*.

But, precisely because religious liberty is an independent, substantive right, it functions as an indicator of the need to protect other groups and limit government intrusion into their affairs as well as into its own. Religious liberty is a protected legal right but not a uniquely privileged one. That is, it gives no rights on the basis of religious commitment that do not extend equally to similar interests. In that sense it is a qualified legal right—qualified by the establishment clause.

A second objection holds that strict neutrality will limit religious liberty, that is, religious groups will be required to live under the same government regulations, abide by such things as affirmative-action goals, file informational tax returns, etc., in the same manner as other not-for-profit organizations. That objection is partially valid, and designedly so. There is a cost to be borne for living in an organized society and while that cost is not borne equally (that is, we tax businesses differently than individuals, rich differently than poor) under the neutrality principle, churches and other religious groups ought to be paying the same price and sharing the same burdens as other *similar* groups. If they do not, they are in a uniquely privileged position, which is not something the Founders intended and avoidance of which is a major objective of the establishment clause. Does this mean churches would have to pay taxes under this principle? No, so long as other not-for-profit groups do not.

But there is another side to this. Bureaucracies can be burdensome; regulations can be unreasonable. Religious groups often may find themselves resisting government intrusions, opposing new regulations or reporting requirements, etc. Their input into the policy process is useful and healthy; churches and religious interest groups can act as a brake on unnecessary government expansion and protect not only religious interests but the interests of others in society as well. Strict neutrality does not limit religious liberty; it only removes religious privilege. It also respects the reality that religious interest groups are a vibrant, vital, and effective political force.[38]

A third objection is that strict neutrality is only a smokescreen behind which to usher in massive aid to religious schools at the expense of the public schools. Several considerations are relevant. Religious schools seeking funds would need to conform to the same hiring, certification, accreditation, admissions, and attendance standards, the same curriculum and textbook requirements, and submit to inspections and oversight the same as other publicly funded schools. This is not at all the Religious Right agenda or that of the parochial schools.[39] Under the above conditions there is unlikely to be a rush for funding.[40] The real advantage, if there is one in this area, is to stimulate competition and innovation in education by groups willing to accept government regulation, a competition many public schools desperately need.[41]

A fourth objection is that acceptance of strict neutrality would undermine decades of court precedents and open the floodgates to a torrent of cases testing the limits of neutrality. The Supreme Court has increasingly been using the language of neutrality (although not consistently) and many of its holdings are consistent with the principle. Acceptance would not, for example, undermine the three-pronged test for establishment clause cases, except that entanglement would need to be refined.[42] One advantage, if the principle were accepted, would be more consistently decided cases, a major dividend.

A fifth objection is that "similarly situated" is a vague term fraught with potential conflict and abuse. Similar in what? How broad must the category be? Who gets to decide? One model is nonprofit organizations under the IRS 501(c)3 category, which includes charitable, literary, recreational, fraternal, scientific, social, and educational groups. The neutrality principle is built on the realization that in most legally significant dimensions religiously motivated individuals and groups are similar to their secular counterparts. Unfortunately the use of a strict neutrality principle will not do away with lawsuits, but testing the contours of similarity and difference is precisely what courts do best.

THE VALUES OF NEUTRALITY

Having attempted to spell out and counter the major objections to strict neutrality, it may be appropriate to end with a brief list of the perceived values of adoption of such a principle. They appear to be the following:

1. The integration of free exercise and nonestablishment clauses into a coherent, consistent, comprehensible principle which is faithful to the intentions of the Founders, responsive to contemporary constitutional values of due process and equal protection, cognizant of current political and economic realities, and defensible as a fair and equitable rule of law.
2. Equal protection for nonreligious groups and individuals that are similar to other religious groups and individuals.
3. Establishment of a principled reason for bringing the secular components of religious activities into conformity with the standards and procedures required for other not-for-profit groups and activities.
4. A stimulus for religious groups which currently seek to influence government policy to undertake protection of the rights of others in society while they protect their own.

Whether the courts will accept a neutrality principle depends in large measure on whether it is understood, analyzed, critiqued, developed, and ultimately accepted or rejected by the intellectual community which deals with church-state issues. For that to happen the principle must be given far more attention than it has yet received.

NOTES

1. 454 U.S. 263 (1981).
2. 108 S.Ct. 2562 (1988).
3. Public Law 97–35, 95 Stat. 578, codified at 42 U.S.C. §300z *et seq*. (1982 ed. and Supp. III).
4. §300z (a)(8)(B).
5. A number of recent articles have been exploring the neutrality concept, such as Michael McConnell, "Neutrality Under the Religion Clauses," 81 *Northwestern University Law Review* 146 (1986); Arnold Loewy, "Rethinking Government Neutrality Towards Religion Under the Establishment Clause: The Untapped Potential of Justice O'Connor's Insight," 64 *North Carolina Law Review* 1049 (1986); Douglas Laycock, "Equal Access and Moments of Silence: The Equal

Status of Religious Speech by Private Speakers," 81 *Northwestern University Law Review* 1 (1986); and Michael Paulsen, "Religion, Equality and the Constitution: An Equal Protection Approach to Establishment Clause Adjudication," 61 *Notre Dame Law Review* 311 (1986).

6. The fascinating and complex intellectual jousting over how to interpret the Constitution is beyond the scope of this chapter. However, one's value commitments in the area of constitutional interpretations do have an impact on First Amendment analysis, so it may be useful to explore the problem, if only in a footnote. Schools of constitutional interpretation can be roughly classified as believers in (1) the plain meaning of the text, (2) the intent of the Founders, (3) measured historical development through case law [the scholarly tradition], (4) adaptation with the spirit of the Constitution, and (5) adaptation to support the manners and morals of contemporary society. While the author's personal commitments are in the (3) to (4) range, the neutralist position itself is not incompatible with any schools of interpretation.

7. The following typology is adapted from an earlier article, "James Madison and Religious Equality: The Perfect Separation," *The Review of Politics*, vol. 44, no. 2 (April 1982), p. 163.

8. *Everson v. Board of Education*, 330 U.S. 1 at 15–16 (1947).

9. For a credible discussion of this point, see Michael Malbin, *Religion and Politics: The Intentions of the Authors of the First Amendment* (Washington, D.C.: American Enterprise Institute, 1978).

10. For a discussion of the types and amounts of aid from government to religion, see Paul J. Weber and Dennis Gilbert, *Private Churches and Public Money: Church-Government Fiscal Relations* (Westport, CT: Greenwood Press, 1981).

11. See Paul D. Steeves, "Amendment of Soviet Law Concerning Religious Groups," *Journal of Church and State*, vol. 19 (1977) p. 37.

12. American Humanist Association, "In Defense of Separation of Church and State," in Joseph L. Blau (ed), *Cornerstones of Religious Freedom in America* (Boston: Beacon Press, 1949), p. 309.

13. See 19 *Writings of Thomas Jefferson* 413–16 (1905), Report of the Rector and Visitors of the University of Virginia, Oct. 7, 1822; 7 *Works of Thomas Jefferson* 266–67 (1861) (Letter to Dr. Cooper, November 2, 1811).

14. "James Madison and Religious Equality," pp. 168–73.

15. A contemporary example of an accommodationist argument is the *amicus curial* brief filed by the Rutherford Institute in *Bowen v. Kendrick* (87–253). The author(s) of that brief unfortunately (and inaccurately) use the terms accommodation and neutrality interchangeably.

16. *Zorach v. Clausen*, 343 U.S. 306 at 310 (1952).

17. "James Madison and Religious Equality," pp. 168–73.

18. For an elaboration of the following section, see Paul J. Weber, "A Wavering First Amendment Standard," *The Review of Politics*, vol. 46, no. 4 (October 1984).

19. 310 U.S. 296 (1940).

20. 330 U.S. 1 (1948).

21. This distinction, too often forgotten in today's controversies, accounts for the rather odd wording in the First Amendment, "Congress shall make no law *respecting* an establishment of religion. . . . " Congress was not allowed to inter-

fere with already existing establishments in the states. See Chester J. Antieau et al., *Freedom from Federal Establishment: Foundation and Early History of the First Amendment Religious Clauses* (Milwaukee: Bruce Publishing Co., 1964).

22. John Lukacs, "The Age of Bureaucracy Has Replaced the Era of Democracy," *U.S. News & World Report*, vol. 97 (August 13, 1984) p. 70.

23. For example, on May 14, 1988, a church bus was struck by a drunk driver near Carrollton, Ky., 27 people were killed, and several others maimed for life. While no one blames the church bus driver (who was among those killed), an investigation is being conducted to determine whether a better trained driver could have avoided the accident.

Currently in Kentucky all public school and commercial bus drivers are required to undergo a fairly extensive training and certification process. Drivers for private groups—such as churches—need only be 18 years of age and have a valid driver's license. Should states require all aspiring bus drivers to be certified, including church bus drivers? The National Transportation Safety Board has actively supported this position since 1979, and it is the position most consistent with strict neutrality. See the [Louisville] *Courier-Journal*, July 24, 1988.

24. Dean M. Kelley, "Uncle Sam: Church Inspector," *Liberty*, vol. 79 (May-June 1984).

25. For example, a recently decided case, *Nally v. Grace Community Church of the Valley*, 253 Cal. Rptr. 97 (1988); Cert. denied 109 S. Ct. 1644 (1989), was a "clergy malpractice" suit growing out of the 1979 suicide of a Mr. Kenneth Nally, who had sought counseling from Grace Community Church, a nondenominational church in the Los Angeles area. Although some 1,577 churches and religious organizations are helping to appeal a trial court ruling that the church can be held liable *if* there is a finding of "negligence and outrageous conduct," there is a legitimate question of responsibility and legal liability that needs further discussion. Assuming a judge or jury finds negligence and outrageous conduct, are only church groups and counselors to be found immune? I raise this question not because I think the answer is clear; quite the opposite. It may be that liability should be limited to those, whether religious or not, who charge for their services and are qualified to accept insurance payments. This would be the strict neutralist position. Indeed this was the holding of the California Supreme Court.

26. For a thought-provoking article on not-for-profit hospitals and the challenge to their tax-exempt status, see "Putting Money Ahead of Mission?" *U.S. News and World Report*, May 16, 1988, pp. 25–26.

27. See "Pluralism in America," *Law Quadrangle Notes*, vol. 28 (Winter 1984), p. 14 (University of Michigan).

28. See Ricardo Planas, *Liberation Theology: The Political Expression of Religion* (Kansas City: Sheed and Ward, 1986).

29. See Fergus M. Bordewich, "Colorado's Thriving Cults," *New York Times Magazine*, May 1, 1988, p. 37.

30. Matthew Fox, *Original Blessing* (Santa Fe, NM: Bear Publishing Co., 1983).

31. See John B. Cobb, Jr., *Process Theology as Political Theology* (Philadelphia: The Westminster Press, 1982).

32. Philip B. Kurland, *Religion and the Law* (Chicago: The Aldine Press, 1962), p. 18.

33. Ibid.

34. Recognition of this fact is one major difference between the author's argument and that developed in the otherwise excellent argument by Michael McConnell in "Neutrality Under the Religion Clauses," 81 *Northwestern Law Review* 146 (1986).

35. Joseph Tussman and Jacobus TenBroeck, "Equal Protection of the Laws," *California Law Review*, vol. 37 (1939), p. 354.

36. Donald Giannella, "Religious Liberty, Nonestablishment and Doctrinal Development, Part II: The Nonestablishment Principle," *Harvard Law Review*, vol. 81 (1968), p. 518.

37. Ibid.

38. Alan Hertzke, *Representing God in Washington* (Knoxville: University of Tennessee Press, 1987).

39. William K. Steven, "Fundamentalists Pledge to Press Drive on Schools," *New York Times*, August 29, 1987, p. 1.

40. If there appears to be some "fudging" in this area it is because I have not fully worked out a strict neutralist position in this critical area. In outline form, I believe that within the public schools, strict neutrality would permit equal access, moments of silence (stripped of any religious overlays), and teaching about religion in an objective fashion. It would not allow prayer in any form, religious services, proselytizing, etc.

In the religious school realm there are two public-policy values to be preserved: religious liberty and quality nonreligious education. Religious liberty would seem to require that schools be free of government regulations beyond those necessary for safety and health. In the secular education component strict neutrality would appear to support tuition tax credits and educational vouchers which would necessarily be accompanied by the full panoply of state certification, regulation, etc. In other words, I do not believe religious schools could be forced to accept government funds, but if they voluntarily did so, regulation would necessarily follow.

41. An article in the *New York Times*, April 26, 1988, page 1, reports that "the key to efficient public services is not replacing government agencies but pitting them against companies in continual competition." "It is not the private sector or the public sector which is better; it is the competition between the two of them that works," says John D. Donahue, a public-policy expert at the Kennedy School of Government at Harvard. It may well be that a voucher system, particularly if it were designed so private, for-profit businesses could compete, would be an excellent stimulus for public education.

42. See Paul J. Weber, "A Wavering First Amendment Standard," p. 483ff. The suggested refinement in the nonentanglement clause is simply that administratively religious organizations voluntarily participating in government programs would be required to accept the same accounting, oversight, reporting, etc., procedures as apply to nonreligious participants, no more, no less.

2

"Strict Neutrality" and the Free Exercise of Religion

Dean M. Kelley

It is no small accomplishment that Paul Weber has managed to set forth clearly and succinctly a proposal for applying a consistent and "principled" theory of the religion clauses of the First Amendment, since there is probably no more intensely controverted area of constitutional interpretation than that of the so-called "separation of church and state." Somehow most scholars of constitutional law can discuss the separation of powers and other themes of the Constitution without elevating others' blood pressure or their own. But the establishment clause and the free exercise clause seem to be fraught with the makings of apoplexy. Therefore, Weber's discussion is doubly welcome, not only for its content but also for the reasonable and irenic way in which he has presented it.

I am largely in agreement with Weber's personal and constitutional objectives as stated in his third paragraph. I simply believe the means he has chosen to advance them to be singularly misguided for three reasons to be set forth in this critique. He has already intimated the gist of these in his outline of objections to the theory, but his refutation of these objections I do not find persuasive. Those reasons are:

1. The strict-neutrality theory would have the admitted result of largely nullifying the religion clauses of any independent effect.
2. It would cut back on several significant protections of the free exercise of religion that have been defined by the Supreme Court.
3. It is predicated upon a serious misperception and undervaluation of the uniqueness and *secular* importance of religious interests, activities, and organizations. There are no other groups in society that are "similar" to religious groups with respect to their basic

function, which is the most "legally significant" fact about any organization.

Philip Kurland's ingenious thesis—that the free exercise and no-establishment clauses "should be read as a single percept" that "religion may not be used as a basis for classification for purposes of government action . . . either to confer a benefit or to impose a burden"[1]—made a small stir in "the intellectual community which deals with church-state issues"[2] when it appeared in 1962. At first glance, it seems commendably fair and even-handed, but it did not carry the field before it, then or since. The Supreme Court has often used the term "neutrality" to characterize the government's role with relation to religion, and some of its decisions are not inconsistent with the Kurland thesis, but the same could be said of various alternative theses as well. The Court has never embraced the Kurland thesis in any systematic way nor any of the other ingenious theories that academic theorists have propounded. The Court seems to prefer to muddle through on its own, and any occasional congruence with one academic theory or another seems to be more an accidental artifact cast up by the interplay of diverse views within the Court itself than a conscious tracking of any outside intellectual *system*.

I

The first reason that Kurland's thesis has not caught on may be that it would have the result of whittling back on the scope and force of the religion clauses to the point that they would have little independent effect. Weber does not deny that this would be the result. He admits that "very much of religious activity and all of religious thought are fully protected in the speech, press, and assembly clauses of the First Amendment, as well as by the due-process and equal-protection clauses" and that "double protection serves no additional function."[3] He points out, however, that the establishment clause is not redundant and thus would serve to prevent religion from enjoying any "special privileges" (such as the *press* might presumably enjoy, since there is no prohibition of "establishment of the press").

He offers similar cold consolation to the criticism that strict neutrality will limit religious liberty: it will do so *only* to the extent that churches and other religious groups are not "paying the same price and sharing the same burdens as other groups." If they are not doing so, he contends, "they are in a uniquely privileged position which is not something the Founders intended and which is a major objective of the Establishment Clause to avoid."[4] (Here an empirical demonstration of just what the Founders did intend might be helpful, but that is not easy to ascertain, since there were quite a few of them, and they didn't all agree on these matters any more than Supreme Court justices—or academic theorists—do today.)

To correct that deplorable condition of supposed privilege, the strict-neutrality doctrine would collapse the Founders' explicit and intentional references to *"religion"* into the neighboring speech, press, and assembly clauses so that religious activities and organizations would be treated just like "other similar groups"—whatever *they* may be (a question to which we shall return in Section III)—a gratuitous "improvement" on the Founders' apparent verbal ineptness that will need more than simple *ipse dixit* to justify. To sum up this proffered improvement, Weber assures us that "strict neutrality does not limit religious liberty; it only removes religious privilege"[5] (another plausible but specious formulation).

By way of compensation for the loss of any supposed "special privilege," the strict-neutrality doctrine would enable religious schools and other religious agencies to participate more fully in government-funded programs that provide secular services to the public, thus similarly (and admittedly) reducing the scope and force of the establishment clause. But that will be justified, says Weber, by making the recipient religious schools and institutions conform to "the same hiring, certification, accreditation, admissions, and atten-dance standards, the same curriculum and textbook requirements . . . " and the same "inspections and oversight" as other publicly funded schools and agencies. The advantage of this change "is to stimulate competition and innovation in education . . . , a competition many public schools desperately need."[6]

While I would applaud that outcome, I doubt that it will be achieved by subjecting religious schools and other agencies to the same stand-ards and requirements as their public counterparts. What meaningful "competition" or "innovation" will they be able to offer if they are to be wired into the very same matrix of bureaucratic regulation, lowest common denominator standards, and public funding overly regulated with red tape that have created or contributed to the problem proposed to be resolved?

The effect of strict neutrality, then, would be to cut back on the unique provisions for free exercise of religion and to reduce the supposed asperities of nonestablishment so that religious entities could move up to the "public trough" along with other private social service providers. It would result in "leveling out" the constitutional treatment of religion to the degree that "religion" would cease to be an operational term in the Constitution—and that revision is advo-cated as an *improvement*! If that is what the Founders really wanted, why did they put the word "religion" in the Constitution in the first place? In the first place!

In devoting two clauses—or two parts of the same clause—to religion, the Founders were stating, not two opposing thoughts that would cancel each other out, but two complementary thoughts that would apply in different ways in different circumstances. Sometimes they might seem to have the effect of giving religion an *advantage* in relation to other activities and entities in society—as in the case of military chaplaincies, exemptions for conscientious objectors to military service, and exemptions from various inspection and reporting requirements (see Part II below). Sometimes they might seem to have the effect of putting religion at a *disadvantage*—as in the case of disqualification for public subsidy. In either case, the objective would be to enable religion to do its important work with a minimum of governmental interference (see Part III below). The idea that the free exercise clause and the no-establishment clause should in effect cancel each other out and throw the interests of religion onto the dubious protection of other clauses designed to meet other needs is a radical revision of the actual wording of the First Amendment and a nullification of the plain *textual* intention of the Founders.

Laurence Tribe has commented in his authoritative treatise, *American Constitutional Law*:

> To most observers . . . strict neutrality has seemed incompatible with the very idea of a free exercise clause. The Framers, whatever specific applications they may have intended, clearly envisioned religion as something special; they enacted that vision into law by guaranteeing the free exercise of *religion* but not, say, of philosophy or science. The strict neutrality approach all but erases this distinction. Thus it is not surprising that the Supreme Court has rejected strict neutrality, permitting and sometimes mandating religious classifications.[7]

What are some of the religious classifications the Supreme Court (and lower courts and legislatures) employed, permitted, or mandated that might be wiped out if the strict-neutrality thesis were adopted? (Of course, the Court might apply the idea of strict neutrality only prospectively and leave existing decisions as they are insofar as possible, but that does not seem to be what the proponents of strict neutrality have in mind; much of their quarrel is with existing case law, and that is precisely what they appear to want overruled.) Let us scan the uneven terrain of church-state law to see what seemingly settled landmarks might be swept away.

The following catalog is based on the needs and interests of religion. The first major category pertains to church autonomy.

A. *The Autonomy of Religious Bodies to Govern Their Own Internal Affairs.*
   That autonomy has been characterized by one commentator as an essential element of free exercise: Churches have a constitutionally protected interest in managing their own institutions free of government interference.

> One category of [rights under the free exercise clause] is the bare freedom to carry on religious activities: to build churches and schools, conduct worship services, pray, proselytize, and teach moral values. . . .
> Second, and closely related, is the right of churches to conduct these activities autonomously: to select their own leaders, define their own doctrines, resolve their own disputes, and run their own institutions. They exercise their religion through religious organizations, and these organizations must be protected by the clause.[8]

1. *Church Property.* One of the earliest affirmations of the autonomy of religious bodies was expressed with regard to disputes over the ownership and control of church property in case of schisms within hierarchical churches. Such disputes, as Justice Felix Frankfurter astutely observed, are not just squabbles over property; "What is at stake here is the power to exercise religious authority,"[9]—the ability of a religious group to decide for itself at what level(s) decision-making authority is to be exercised: local, regional, national, or international. Civil courts are often asked by one or more factions in such internal disputes to decide the scope and effect of such religious authority. In one of its early and definitive church-state decisions, the Supreme Court said in 1872:

> The right to organize voluntary religious associations to assist in the expression and dissemination of any religious doctrine, and to create tribunals for the decision of controverted questions of faith within the association, and for the ecclesiastical government of all the individual members, congregations and officers within the general association, is unquestioned. All so

unite themselves to such a body do so with *an implied consent* to this government, and are bound to submit to it. But it would be a vain consent and would lead to the total subversion of such religious bodies, if any one aggrieved by one of their decisions could appeal to the secular courts and have them reversed.

Therefore

whenever the questions of discipline or of faith, or ecclesiastical rule, custom or law have been decided by the highest of these church judicatories to which the matter has been carried, the legal tribunals [of the state] must accept such decisions as final, and as binding on them, in their application to the case before them.[10]

Under strict neutrality, presumably, there would be no such deference by civil courts to religious authorities. As a matter of fact, we can see just how such an approach would work by looking at the most recent church-property decision of the Supreme Court, *Jones v. Wolf* (1979), in which a majority of the Court adopted an alternative method of resolving such disputes based on the doctrine of "neutral principles of law"—a doctrine similar to strict neutrality in that it views religious interests, considerations, and commitments as nugatory and of no effect. Under that method courts would examine only the secular instruments of property ownership—real-estate deeds, title conveyances, trust documents, and church charters of incorporation—to determine ownership of the disputed property, irrespective of the decisions of any ecclesiastical tribunals or the locus of authority within the particular church polity recognized by the parties before their dispute.

Under "neutral principles" the implied consent is "vain," and aggrieved parties *can* appeal to the civil courts to have ecclesiastical decisions reversed, leading to the "total subversion" of hierarchical religious bodies. (Courts were left the option by *Jones v. Wolf* of pursuing the older practice of deference to ecclesiastical tribunals, but several states have adopted the "neutral principles" approach for use in all church property disputes, *viz.*, New York,[11] Missouri,[12] and South Dakota.[13] Others have chosen to stick with the deference principle of *Watson v. Jones*: Maryland,[14] Washington,[15] and Iowa.[16])

What difference does it make? Since property ownership in this country is usually registered locally in the name(s) of local trustees, it is usually those trustees or their successors whose names appear on the deeds and who thus—under "neutral principles of law"—are said to "own" the local church property in the absence of any explicit trust in the real-estate instruments for the general church. So when a local congregation wants to break away from the denomination that previously had governance over it in all matters (including control of property), a court looking only at the property deeds and disregarding the rulings of superior church judicatories on that case could find that the local trustees were the owners of the church, so the schismatic congregation gets to keep the property, contrary to the structure of religious authority agreed to in that church before the dispute. That is exactly what happened in the two most recent church property decisions of the Supreme Court.[17] What that means is that the Supreme Court has by judicial fiat *congregationalized* the polity of the Presbyterian church by letting three dissident congregations break away and steal the church property, contrary to what had been recognized in earlier court decisions as the hierarchical polity of that church.[18] Would that not also be the effect of strict neutrality? (It would also wipe out the entire Religious Corporations Law of New York State, which is one long "religious classification" carefully tailored to each denomination's polity and which the Supreme Court has recognized as one way to accommodate religious liberty.[19] Restructuring churches by judicial fiat is the opposite of religious liberty.

2. *Church Employment*. One of the core elements of church autonomy is the right to hire, supervise, promote, demote, and fire the employees of the church, including its clergy. Lower courts have held that, in setting up sanctions against employment discrimination, Congress did not intend to interfere in the relationship between a church and its clergy[20] nor did it intend to require a church's seminary to have to report to the Equal Employment Opportunities Commission the statistics on its employment practices with respect to clergy, faculty, and administrators, though it would have to report on its support staff.[21] The Supreme Court has held that Congress had not explicitly authorized the National Labor Relations Board to have jurisdiction over union or-

ganizing among teachers in Roman Catholic parochial schools, since that could interfere with the church's control over its schools.[22]

Congress has determined that churches may discriminate on the basis of religion in hiring their own members for secular jobs as well as religious ones.[23] That provision was struck down by a federal district court as an establishment of religion, but the Supreme Court unanimously reversed that decision.[24] All of these provisions are religious classifications and would be swept away under a regime of strict neutrality, thus severely undercutting the ability of religious bodies to manage their own internal affairs—a serious setback for religious liberty.

3. *Confidentiality of Internal Communications.* (This claim can refer to a wide range of internal messages, utterances, and records, but we shall focus on only the most central and generally recognized at law.) One of the clearest and most universal "privileges" afforded on the basis of a religious classification is the "seal of the confessional," an evidentiary privilege similar to the attorney-client privilege. It is protected under the statutes of every state but West Virginia in some form such as the following (from the Vermont statute, chosen because of its brevity): "A priest or minister of the gospel shall not be permitted to testify in court to statements made to him by a person under the sanctity of a religious confessional."[25]

Some states have more elaborate provisions; some extend it to religious counseling as well as confession, but all predicate it upon a religious classification. It has long been settled policy in this country that the cure of souls is of secular importance to the health, safety, and well-being of the civil community, that the cure of souls cannot be carried out without confession of sins, and that the penitent will not confess sins (especially those that are also crimes) unless assured of the confidentiality of the confession. That is the rationale of the priest-penitent privilege. Strict neutrality would presumably sweep away all laws on this subject. The attorney-client privilege would survive, the husband-wife privilege would survive, the physician-patient privilege would survive, but not the priest-penitent privilege. That would seem to be a curious way to honor, not only religious liberty, but the concern of legislatures for the cure of souls.

The general pattern having been indicated above, the remaining sections will be set forth in outline form only.

B.   *Outreach Activities of Religious Bodies*
     1. *Evangelism/Conversion/Solicitation/Fund-raising*
        a. Supreme Court decisions involving Jehovah's Witnesses in the 1940s protected religious activities at first under the free speech and press clauses, but then began to protect religion *per se*, especially colporteuring (*Cantwell v. Connecticut, Murdock v. Pennsylvania, Jamison v. Texas,* etc.). These religious activities might continue to be protected by the speech and press clauses in a strict-neutrality doctrine, but why should it be necessary for religion to take a back seat to speech or press? It did not do so in the minds of those who wrote the First Amendment; why should it in ours?
        b. *U.S. v. Ballard.* This case stands for the teaching that:

        > Men may believe what they cannot prove. They may not be put to the proof of their religious doctrines or beliefs. . . . If those doctrines are subject to trial before a jury . . . then the same can be done with the religious beliefs of any sect. When the triers of fact undertake that task, they enter a forbidden domain.[26]

        Would strict neutrality mean that people *could* be required to persuade a jury of the verity of their religious beliefs?
        c. "Religious Gerrymandering" (*Larson v. Valente*).[27] Minnesota attempted to regulate religious solicitations by groups dependent upon nonmembers for more than 50 per cent of their income. The Supreme Court struck that down as a "religious gerrymander." Would such gerrymanders be permissible under strict neutrality? Legislatures need show only a rational relationship to a legitimate public purpose in order to discriminate between *non*religious voluntary associations (for example, between veterans' groups and public-interest lobbying groups[28]); should they be able—under strict neutrality—similarly to discriminate between, say, popular and unpopular religious groups, as Minnesota tried to do?
     2. *Influencing Public Policy*
        Strict neutrality seems already to be dominant in this area: religious leaders, religious bodies, and their members have as much right to participate in political action in the public

arena as anyone else[29] (though churches, like other nonprofit private, exempt organizations, may lose their tax exemptions if they do so corporately to any "substantial" degree). But a new religious group in New York City was denied real-estate tax exemption because a large part of its activities was said to be "political" and "economic" rather than religious. The highest court in the state reversed that denial on the ground that it is not the business of government to determine what is religious and what is not within the operations of a religious body; that is for the religious body to determine without governmental second-guessing—a ruling that would certainly not apply to a commercial enterprise or a secular voluntary organization.[30] Would religious bodies be granted the same degree of self-definition and self-direction under strict neutrality?

C. *Inculcation of the Faith by Religious Bodies*
   1. *State Regulation of Religious Schools*
      a. Religious schools exempted from state regulation. State efforts to regulate religious schools of general instruction on the same basis as private secular schools have been curtailed by courts in some states—Ohio, Vermont, Kentucky, and Maine—and upheld in others—Michigan, North Dakota, Nebraska.[31] Some states have exempted by statute religious schools, day-care centers, homes for delinquent youth, and residential treatment centers run by churches.[32]

      The theory of such exemptions may be that, since churches were in the education, nurturing, and charitable care business long before the state ever took any interest in such matters, they may be as well able to carry on such work as the state and therefore do not need state supervision. Or the exemptions may be simply accommodations of church autonomy. In any event, would they survive under strict neutrality?

      b. Religious nurture immune under compulsory-attendance laws. In 1972 the Supreme Court held that the State of Wisconsin had not shown a sufficiently compelling state interest in requiring Amish children to attend ninth and tenth grades of public school to justify criminal penalties for truancy, since such public schooling would interfere with the Amish community's historic mode of inculcation of its faith and agrarian way of life and might jeopardize the survival of the unique Amish community itself. The

Court explained that this exception to a law of general application was unique to claims of free exercise of *religion*:

> A way of life, however virtuous and admirable, may not be interposed as a barrier to reasonable state regulation of education if it is based on purely secular considerations; to have the protection of the Religions Clauses, the claim must be rooted in religious belief.[33]

This is probably the outstanding example of a religious classification and would be the first to go under strict neutrality—another great loss for religious liberty!

2. *Religious Inculcation in Public Schools*
3. *State Aid to Parochial Schools*

Most of the cases in these two categories were decided under the establishment clause, and Weber writes that strict neutrality would not generally alter the *Lemon* test of establishment; therefore, we may proceed to the next major category.

D. *Protecting the Practice of Religious Faith in the World*

This category pertains mainly to conflict between individual conscience and the public order, plus various exemptions and government proprietaries in religion designed to protect the practice of religion.

1. *Conscientious Objection to Military Service*

Statutory exemptions to conscription have been provided in various ways throughout the history of the United States. There is no conscription in effect at present, but the most recent statute—the Selective Training and Service Act of 1940 and its successors—exempts from combatant service any person "who, by reason of *religious* training and belief, is conscientiously opposed to participation in war in any form."[34] The Supreme Court has considerably broadened the definition of "religious training and belief" to include many systems of thought that might not be readily recognized in any historical definition of "religion." Still, that phrase remains a religious classification in the law that would not withstand the purge of all such under strict neutrality—a great loss for the rights of conscience.

2. *Legal Prctection for Sabbath Observers*

In 1972 Senator Jennings Randolph, a Seventh-day Baptist, introduced an amendment that was included in Title VII of the Civil Rights Act of 1964 to protect (Saturday) Sabbath observers like himself. It required employers "to reasonably accommodate an employee's . . . *religious* observance or practice" unless it would cause "undue hardship on the conduct of the employer's business"[35]—a religious classification if there ever was one. However, the Supreme Court has largely vitiated the Randolph Amendment by holding that any cost to the employer beyond a *de minimis* level (= trifling) would be "undue hardship,"[36] so perhaps strict neutralists may take some comfort from that, though advocates of religious liberty will not.

The Court has repeatedly held, however, that *religious* obligations which prevent an employee from holding or finding work must be treated like those causes of joblessness that are beyond the applicant's control (such as illness, physical handicap, etc.) in qualifying for unemployment insurance.[37] Thus, the free exercise clause was held to require the addition of a religious classification to existing laws, and a *"strict scrutiny" test was set up for free exercise.* If state action was shown to impose a burden upon religious practice, the state was obliged to justify it by a compelling interest that could be served in no other way. That is the opposite of the way Weber's use of strict scrutiny would work. He would place the burden on the person or group seeking protection for religious practice to justify that protection by showing more than a rational connection to a legitimate public purpose.[38] Since religion would be a "suspect classification" by definition, it is hard to see what kind of a justification by appeal to a "legitimate public purpose" could be offered. That is surely turning the Founders' view of things on its head.

3. *Others Acts of Conscience*

The Supreme Court has upheld an individual's refusal to serve on a jury for reasons of conscience,[39] and upheld by an equally divided Court a circuit court's ruling that an individual for religious reasons could refuse to carry her picture on her driver's license.[40] The Ninth Circuit Court of Appeals upheld the right of an individual for religious reasons to refuse to use a Social Security number in applying for public assistance,[41] but the Supreme Court muffed a more muddled case of the same kind, a majority holding that the individual could not control what government did in assigning and using a Social Security number for that individual, while a different majority seemed to hold that the government could not require the individual to supply that number when applying.[42]

Some people (chiefly Seventh-day Adventists) refuse for religious reasons to belong to or support financially any labor union, though they are usually willing to pay an amount equal to the costs of labor representation to a suitable charity. When most labor unions refused to accept this modification of the union-shop principle (despite urging to do so by the Executive Council of the AFL-CIO), Congress adopted another amendment proposed by Senator Randolph, this one to the National Labor Relations Act, *requiring* unions to do so.

> Any employee who is a member of and adheres to established and traditional tenets or teachings of a bona fide religion, body or sect which has historically held conscientious objections to joining or financially supporting labor organizations shall not be required to join or financially support any labor organization as a condition of employment; except that such employee may be required . . . to pay sums equal to . . . dues and initiation fees to a nonreligious, nonlabor organizational charitable fund.[43]

That is clearly a religious classification written into law and has been upheld as a legitimate accommodation of free exercise interests by two circuit courts of appeals.[44]

Some religious groups object to certain kinds of medical treatments or therapies or to medical care in general. Christian Scientists have obtained exemptions in the laws of several states for spiritual healing carried on by Christian Science practitioners for adherents of that faith, and those exemptions are religious classifications such as would offend the principle of strict neutrality. Nevertheless, those exemptions would seem to be important safeguards for the religious liberty of those who believe that spiritual healing is God's will, and that obeying God is more important than earthly survival—at least for themselves, if not for others.

The courts of several states have vacated convictions of American Indians for use of peyote, a hallucinogenic cactus prohibited by law, when such use is carried on as a sacramental practice of the Native American church.[45] That is a religious classification, yet most commentators consider it a legitimate accommodation of venerable religious practice among American Indians.

4. *Religious "Matching" in Foster Care of Children*
A number of states have statutory provisions designed to protect the continuity of a child's religion when custody moves from the natural parent(s) to others. A typical example is found in the 1921 Constitution of New York State:

> Whenever a child is committed to an institution or is placed in the custody of any person by parole, placing out, adoption or guardianship, it shall be so committed or placed, when practicable, to an institution governed by persons, or in the custody of a person, of the same religious persuasion as the child.[46]

Sometimes the phrase "when practicable" has been interpreted to mean "whenever possible," but the original intent was to give religion equal or commensurate attention with other factors in determining the "best interests of the child." In a recent case in which racial and religious discrimination in child-care placements in New York City was sought to be corrected, the city reached a settlement with the plaintiffs and several private child-care agencies which includes an elaborate religious classification to secure continuity of religion (where desired by the parents) without loss of quality care:

> Children are to be placed on a first-come, first-served basis, with preference for religious matching honored only to the extent that it does not give a child greater access to a program appropriate for his needs over other children for whom the program is also appropriate but who earlier became candidates for placement . . . If the parents express a preference for a religious matching placement, the City will be required to place the child in the best available program of an agency with the preferred religious affiliation, provided there is a vacancy. If no vacancy exists, the parent then has a three-fold option: (a) having the child wait until there is a vacancy in the best "in-religion" program; (b) having the child placed in the next best

"in-religion" program, or (c) having the child placed in the best available "out-of-religion" program.[47]

There also is a provision for the designation of special agencies to which could be assigned the care of children "whose religious beliefs pervade and determine the entire mode of their lives, regulating it with detail through strictly enforced rules of the religion" (such as Orthodox Jews), independent of the rest of the stipulation. In these instances, religion would be almost the sole consideration.

Although this settlement—approved by the district court and the Second Circuit Court of Appeals—greatly attenuates the effect of religious "matching," it could hardly be called an example of strict neutrality, since religious classifications still abound. Yet one would hardly want the state to be totally "religion-blind" when acting *in loco parentis*, that is, disregarding religion entirely when assigning a dependent child to an institution or foster parents. Rather than relying on intuition in weighing religion among other factors in determining placement, the settlement spells out precisely how religion will apply.

5. *Religious Classifications in the Internal Revenue Code*
   The tax code is one example of a major federal statute that is riddled with religious classifications. Some may be consonant with strict neutrality, such as Section 501(c)(3), which characterizes the primary category of exempt nonprofit organizations as those which are "organized and operated exclusively for *religious*, charitable, scientific . . . (etc.) purposes." But others confer unique treatment on religious organizations:
   a. Churches are given a "mandatory exception" from the requirement that new organizations must apply for recognition of tax exemption and the presumption that they are private foundations. Sec. 508(c)(1)(A).
   b. Churches are given a "mandatory exception" from the requirement that Sec. 501(c)(3) organizations must file annual information reports (Form 990) with the Internal Revenue Service. Sec. 6033 (a)(2)(A)(i).
   c. Churches are the subject of a special limitation on the ability of the IRS to examine or audit them, called the "Church Audit Procedures Act" at the time Congress adopted it in 1986. Section 7611.
   d. Clergy are permitted to exclude the rental value of a parsonage or any cash housing allowance from their tax-

able income—a privilege they share only with certain military personnel. Section 107.

e. Notwithstanding the exclusion, they may count the excluded amount in the net earnings from self-employment upon which they pay Social Security tax (no boon) and on which their Social Security payments will be based at retirement (an important benefit). Sec. 1402(a)(8).

f. Clergy may be exempted from payment of Social Security taxes entirely (and from receiving any benefits) by filing a declaration of conscientious objection to such taxation (and benefits) at the beginning of their ministry, which then is irrevocable. Sec. 1402(8).

g. Members of certain religious faiths who are self-employed and have conscientious objection to Social Security (mostly the Amish) may likewise be exempted from such payments and benefits. Section 1402(g).

h. Clergy are classified as "self-employed" and thus have to pay their entire Social Security tax themselves rather than sharing the obligation with an employer, even if they receive a salary from a church and are thus indistinguishable from other employees, which (as I can testify) is a *dis*advantage costing several thousand dollars a year! Sec. 1402(c)(4).

There are other specific rules for religious orders, church pension plans, and certain church employees' income, etc., but this much should be sufficient to show an array of religious classifications adopted by Congress in what it presumably thought to be the public good, particularly to protect free exercise interests and to avoid relationships between religious bodies and the taxing authority that might create constitutional problems under the religion clauses. Religious bodies, clergy, and adherents have proceeded for many years in reliance upon these provisions, and they should not now be changed without good reason.

6. *Chaplains and Chapels at Prisons, Hospitals, and Military Facilities*

A final and very extensive provision for the free exercise of religion is the Chaplain Corps in the Army, Navy, Air Force, Coast Guard, in federal and state prisons and jails, and in state hospitals and institutions for the emotionally disturbed and mentally retarded, as well as veterans' hospitals. The rationale for these governmental proprietaries in religion is that when state action has removed persons from their normal civilian environments and placed them in artificial, government-operated environments where they do not have ready access to their customary religious leadership and institutions, government has a responsibility to remedy this lack by providing surrogates for the same in order to enable the constitutionally protected free exercise of religion.[48] That is one of the vastest examples of religious classification, and its elimination would produce resounding reverberations in Congress and throughout the country.

These are but a few of the innumerable religious classifications in federal and state statutes and municipal ordinances from coast to coast, too numerous to catalog. Some may be wise, some unwise, some indifferent. But the idea that none of them should mention "religion"—either to impose a burden or confer a benefit—is so far from prevailing practice as to require more than an abstract theory for justification. Together they constitute a large body of accepted practice that stands as a considerable obstacle to change in constitutional theory of the kind suggested. Among that body of practices are some that represent significant provisions for the free exercise of religion that would be lost in a shift to strict neutrality.

To recapitulate, we have noted above several serious cutbacks on free exercise that strict neutrality would bring about:

- The congregationalizing of connectional church polities;
- Elimination of right of a church to hire its own members;
- Nullification of the priest-penitent privilege of confidentiality;
- Restrictions on religious proselytization and fund-raising;
- Scrutiny of religious claims and beliefs by finders of fact;
- State evaluation of church teachings as basis of tax exemption;
- Abandonment of strict scrutiny of burdens on free exercise;
- Impairment of conscientious objection to military service;
- Loss of Randolph Amendments (accommodation of Sabbatarians and conscientious objectors to union membership);
- Reversal of *Sherbert, Thomas, Hobbie, Yoder, Amos*, etc.
- Elimination of chaplaincy programs in government institutions.

III

The third and last and most weighty reason for rejecting the strict neutrality proposal is that it seriously misconceives and undervalues the secular importance of religious interests, activities, and organizations. To the proponents of strict neutrality, it seems, religious entities are just another kind of club or social circle. (Too many of them may—alas!—be just that, but they are merely poor specimens of an essential genre. Fortunately, the legal character of institutions does not turn on the inadequacies of their least impressive members.) Our author makes clear his presuppositions on this point:

> Strict neutrality is committed to the proposition that there is seldom a legally significant characteristic of religion so unique that it is not shared by similar nonreligious individuals and groups. . . .
>   In most legally significant dimensions religiously motivated individuals and groups are similar to their secular counterparts . . . [and should be] subject to the same laws as other similarly situated individuals and groups.[49]

This perspective may come easily to those who have never lived in a religionless society, which is all of us, because there is none. (Not even Albania. Even in ostensibly atheistic societies there are vigorous underground religion(s) and surrogate religion(s) in the ideology of the Party.) Every known society has one or more systems/structures/folk-faiths performing the function of religion. As one sociologist has written:

> It is widely held by students of society that there are certain functional prerequisites without which society would not continue to exist. At first glance, this seems to be obvious—scarcely more than to say that an automobile could not exist, as a going system, without a carburetor. . . . Most writers list religion among the functional prerequisites.[50]

Another noted sociologist, Talcott Parsons, has written: "There is no known human society without something which modern social scientists would classify as a religion. . . . Religion is as much a human universal as language."[51]

Because most people have only a mild need for religion most of the time, and some people may feel no need for it at all, we often tend to think of religion as an optional, and even dispensable, sort of activity. For (some) individuals it may be, but for society, it is not. It serves a function essential to the survival of society itself, which is why there is no human society without one or more ways of performing the essential function of religion.

Why is religion important? Why is it not just another club or voluntary association? What is the essential function it performs? Some might say that religion is the name we give to the means by which human beings relate themselves to their Creator and seek to do their Maker's will. From that standpoint, there is no other human enterprise to compare with it, and it alone offers struggling human beings the Pearl of Great Price: *Salvation*. But our author might reply that, though this view might be dispositive for those who hold it, it is not "legally significant," and it might be "sectarian" in the sense that not all religious people would express it in the same terms, and nonreligious people wouldn't express it in any terms at all, or recognize its reality when expressed by others.

It may perplex us that such terms, which may be as real and urgent as any human thought can be, and which would resonate with a large proportion of the population, including many legislators, lawyers and judges, not to mention a number of the Founders, are thought not to be "legally significant." After all, convictions about the realities pointed to by those terms have stirred some of the most massive movements of history, led to the shedding of rivers of blood (for religion is not always a "tame" enterprise), the building of cathedrals, the composing of some of the world's greatest music, and the painting of some of the world's greatest art. They also brought many of our forebears to this land, looking for ways to follow their faiths in freedom.

But let us look for language that may be more "legally significant," that may be recognizable across all faith groups and even pertinent to those who do not identify with any faith group. The language of sociology may be helpful here, if not of political science. In that language, religion may be said to be performing the survival function of *explaining the ultimate meaning of life*. Regardless of its particular content—rites, structures, symbols, doctrines—or what Deity or deities (if any) it may worship, it is telling its adherents about the nature of Reality and the purpose of existence—why we are here and what we are to be and do—and acting out the embodying dramas of earthly pilgrimage, aspiration, and attainment.

Why is that important? Because it answers the second oldest question of human experience. If the oldest question is "How do I survive?" the second oldest is "Why do bad things happen to me/those I love?" Every human being confronts experiences that are both unsatisfactory and technologically unmanageable: failure, handicap, defeat, loss, illness, bereavement, the prospect of one's own death. Those are the experiences that press upon us the need to know "what is the reason for it all?" Religion tries to provide answers to that question, offering the widest and deepest concepts the mind can grasp, so that the suffering of the moment can be seen in a broader perspective of greater good or longer purpose or firmer reality.

Such "explanations" of the ultimate meaning of life may be theistic or nontheistic, naturalistic or supernaturalistic, activistic or quietistic, ascetic or orgiastic, arcane or prosaic, conventional or bizarre. If they help believers to rise up each morning with hope, to get through the day somehow with purposiveness and resilience, to lie down at night with some sense of satisfaction and fulfillment, they are performing— for those believers—the function of religion, whatever nonbelievers may think or however implausible those beliefs may appear to outsiders. Not all churches, synagogues, mosques, or temples perform that function well for all believers all the time, and many people may get what snatches of ultimate meaning they may have from other sources, including some that may not be conventionally religious. Yet whatever the source, the *function* being served is still essentially *religious*.

Unless a society provides moderately effective ways of meeting its members' meaning needs, it will be in peril. Persons who cannot find some kind of more or less satisfying answers to their deepest inward pangs of spiritual hunger are apt to succumb to despair, bitterness, resentment, anomie, or fall into one or another of the escapisms, derangements, and addictions which are the increasingly prevalent maladies of meaninglessness besetting our society today. Such persons are often a hazard to themselves and others, sometimes resorting to impulsive or desperate acts of violence, crime, or suicide.

Some people in this plight get caught up by a religion that relieves their distress and provides the needed structure for their lives; others do not. The same mode of "explanation" does not work for all. Some resonate to a mystical appeal, others to an emotional one. Some want to escape from "the world" while others want to "save" it. Fortunately, there are many varieties of religion in our society, and almost anyone should be able to find one that suits. That is one reason for religious liberty: to foster as wide a range of religious "answers" as possible. It is not the content or the initial appeal of a religion, however, that makes it functionally effective, but its *cost* to the believer, not so much in money (which is cheap in this market) but in exertion, devotion, commitment. The more a religion *demands* of its adherents, the more convincing it seems to be to them. The less *effort* it requires, the less *effect* it will have—in their lives and in others.

So it is of important practical secular concern to any society to optimize the conditions under which one or more effectively functioning religions can flourish. In the past that was usually done by setting up one favored faith as the official religion, showering its leaders with prestige, prerequisites, and emoluments, requiring all subjects to adhere to that persuasion (or at least profess to do so), and suppressing all rival faiths. That arrangement was called Establishment, and it didn't work very well, for at least five reasons:

1. The people who set up the established religion, and whose own religion is usually the one so favored, are invariably the "haves" in that society—the people on top. The people who have the greatest need for religion because they have the largest proportion of experiences that are both unsatisfactory and unchangeable are the have-nots—the people on the bottom. The established religion is of little use to them because it doesn't "explain" *their* lives.
2. In fact, the very act of "establishing" it as the official, respectable, "required" faith that embraces and endorses the status quo makes it part of the problem that needs to be "explained" to the have-nots.
3. In addition, the established religion loses much of its persuasiveness even among the haves, since the quality of religion that makes it convincing is its *cost*, and the effect of establishment is precisely to take the cost out of religion, to make it *easy*, respectable.
4. Furthermore, the effect of prosperity, security, and deference upon the functionaries of the established religion seems to be to make them pompous and indolent. As a result, the established faith begins to alienate its adherents, who turn to competing faiths that have not (yet) lost diligence and zeal—the new cults that invariably spring up among the have-nots.
5. The response of the establishment to such competition from below is seldom increased vigor and productivity but rather suppression and persecution, which produce resentment and greater vigor in the suppressed groups, but in the suppressors that characteristic blend of arrogance and debility that "establishment" fosters.

Force is of little avail in trying to spread religion or to stop its spread, and often generates resistance and emigration. After centuries of costly trial and error, some governments have concluded that the best way to handle the problem of religion is to *leave it alone*, neither preferring nor suppressing, neither helping nor hindering (since for government to try to "help" is still to hinder). *Mirabile dictu*, that was the tack taken by the Founders of this nation—among the first in the world to do so. They made, admirably, gingerly provisions for the propagation of the religious function without government sponsorship, favoritism, entanglement, or duress, and they set forth those provisions in the religion clause(s) for the First Amendment.

So religion is not just another voluntary association like the Society for the Prevention of This or That. It is the bearer of a powerful and socially essential function that is of great *secular* importance to everyone, whether they need it or realize its importance themselves.

If that is not "legally significant," it is hard to think what would be. And the conditions necessary for the effective performance of the religious function are precisely those at stake in the puzzle over "strict neutrality." There are no other groups in society that *are* "similar" in this sense to religious bodies. They are *sui generis*—unique. They are doing vital work in their sometimes inept, flaccid, or blundering ways, and the condition for their doing it well is that they be left alone by government, spared the temptations or distractions of government favor, support or interference, free to "sink or swim" in proportion to their ability to attract and retain adherents by their effectiveness in meeting religious needs.

This understanding of the nature of the religious function has some significant corollaries for our discussion.

1. The most significant contribution that religious bodies make to society is not their social service undertakings—schools, child day-care centers, shelters for the homeless, hospitals, orphanages, etc.—meritorious as these may be; they can also be distractions and diversions from the religious function, and at best they are auxiliary to and derivative from it. The most significant contribution of religious bodies to social utility and the chief justification for their unique treatment under the First Amendment is their central function—*religion*: explaining the ultimate meaning of life to their members, acting out that meaning in rite and symbol, embodying it in a supportive and continuing community. As an "outsider," government is not able to discern which religious bodies are performing this function well and which are not, so it must treat them all alike, but not necessarily like other, non-religious organizations.

2. From this perspective, it is not of urgent importance to society that religious bodies be afforded an equal chance to obtain government aid for their social service undertakings, since others can do those things as well or better and since the conditions of government aid generally, and perhaps necessarily, dilute the distinctive contribution that religious groups can make to society, even in and through their social service works. That is, government should not assist religious bodies to promulgate their faith (though it should get out of their way and let *them* do so[52]), nor should it aggrandize their real estate or their deployable personnel.[53] They are entitled to do that with their own money, but not with tax money drawn by force of law from people of all faiths and none. So if social service activities of religious bodies are aided by

government, they are legitimately subject to government regulation.

Such efforts have historically made their most significant contribution to education, health care, and social welfare when they have relied on their own resources and therefore could shape their own mode of mission without government support or control. Even when unaided by government, these activities are still subject to some governmental regulation—more than the central meaning-promulgative activities—because they are of a "mixed" character, a mingling of religious and secular functions. Government invariably tends to overregulate, so in both "pure" and "mixed" activities the free exercise clause may provide some shielding from such overregulation.

3. That shielding should take the form of maximization of church autonomy, as described in the opening section of Part II above. Religious bodies should be free of governmental interference in managing their own internal affairs, that is, setting the locus of their internal decision making—local, regional, national, or international—without civil courts second-guessing those decisions at the behest of disaffected members; hiring, supervising, and discharging their employees in accordance with their own faith requirements; maintaining confidentiality of internal communications necessary to preserve a relationship of confidence and trust within the organization; not having to justify or "prove" their beliefs or rites to outsiders, particularly civil administrators or courts; setting and enforcing their own standards of membership and church discipline.

4. In relations with outsiders, religious bodies should be able to engage in evangelizing, solicitation, and fund-raising without government supervision (churches have resisted disclosure requirements accepted by nonreligious fund-raisers on the grounds that they owe an accounting of their use of contributions to their members and donors but not to government or the public at large; no one is *compelled* to donate to a religious cause); they should be able to follow the dictates of conscience with respect to military service, Sabbath observance, dietary restrictions, health care, etc., so long as they pose no genuine hazard to the health and safety or the like rights of others.

These are not "special privileges," but the carefully tailored provisions necessary to the effective performance of the survival function of religion. One might wish that these same shieldings might apply to all persons and organizations and activities in a free society, but if they do not, the free exercise clause should at least apply them to religion, and—so long as strict neutrality does not prevail—it generally does.

Response to Dean M. Kelley

It is clear that Kelley and I have a radically different understanding of the meaning and impact of a strict-neutralist interpretation of the religion clauses. For one thing, he does not understand the *development* of the concept since Kurland first proposed it. It is partially as a result of this difference with Kelley that I have begun to call the concept "equal separation." Perhaps a head-to-head response to the concerns raised in Kelley's chapter will lead to other clarifications.

Kelley's first objection is that "strict neutrality (which from now on will be called equal separation) would have the admitted result of largely nullifying the religion clauses of any independent effect." Not so. The religion clauses are a critically important part of the Constitution. In the Bill of Rights they are indeed "the first freedoms." The point of equal separation is *decidedly not* that religious individual's and groups' activities and practices should be brought down to the level of other similar individual's and groups' activities and practices, but that the latter should be elevated to the same level as the former. The role of religious freedom and nonestablishment is to serve as the cornerstone against which the rights of citizens are measured and with which they are brought into line. To phrase it another way, under the equal-separation theory, the rights guaranteed by the religion clauses are independent but not isolated.

Under equal separation the free exercise clause is not redundant; it is of central importance in setting the standard of freedom. The free exercise clause provides protection for religious groups and activities, but that protection must then be extended to other similar groups and individuals.

The difference may be illustrated by the example of conscientious objection to military service. Kelley believes equal separation would do away with conscientious objector status based on religious belief. On the contrary, the Supreme Court has gradually recognized that the right to such status should be expanded to include others, not necessarily religious, who hold equally compelling personal objections to participation in war.

One of Kelley's objections I find particularly puzzling. I argue that religious speech, press (publication), and assembly are fully protected by other sections of the First Amendment and that no additional

protection is necessary. Additional or "double" protection could only mean that speech *not* protected under the speech clause *is* protected by the religious clause. But what is not protected? Libel, pornography, words akin to prohibited action (for example, yelling fire in a crowded theater, fighting words), fraudulent advertising, and certain obnoxious invasions of an individual's privacy. Certainly Kelley is not arguing that people with religious motivations ought to be protected while engaging in such types of speech? Therefore, I am still not clear why this bothers him.[54]

Two other issues may be touched briefly before addressing several specific concerns. First, Kelley uses the press as an example of an activity which might enjoy "special privileges" since it is not harnessed with an establishment clause. In fact, the courts have developed an excellent model of separation here; the press is protected but given no special privileges in constitutional law. Reporters and editors have no *special* rights of access, freedom from libel laws, immunity from testifying before grand juries, and so forth. They have the same rights as other citizens. This works quite well, I believe.

Second, Kelley implies that the motivation for proposing an equal-separation theory is so that religious schools and agencies can "move up to the 'public trough'" along with other private social service providers, or that participation in publicly funded programs is a compensation for loss of other liberties. Nonsense. Religious entities already receive direct and indirect public funding and other aids in amounts the American public would find stunning if it were brought to their attention.[55] Moreover, I find the "trough" image both inaccurate and offensive. To consider the work done with the poor, the handicapped, the homeless, the ill, the addicted, etc., as somehow just a means to get church hands in the public till is an insult. I am sure that upon reflection Kelley will want to change that image. Realistically, I see no end to utilization of religious agency services, no matter what First Amendment theory, if any, the courts adopt. Because of the cultural and political changes outlined in Chapter 1, we can expect an expansion of such usage. The purpose of the equal-separation theory is to provide a fair, equitable, predictable (and understandable) standard for applying the religious clauses in specific cases.

CHURCH AUTONOMY

Dean Kelley has performed an enormously helpful task by outlining a "catalog" of needs and interests of religion he fears would be swept away by the application of equal separation. Addressing each specifically, perhaps the fear can be alleviated, or at least our differences clarified.

A. *The Autonomy of Religious Bodies to Govern Their Own Internal Affairs*

Kelley quotes Douglas Laycock to make the point that autonomy is "an essential element of free exercise." Of course autonomy is essential to religious institutions and it must be protected by the free exercise clause. The equal-separation theory requires only that the same autonomy protect other similar bodies such as charitable, fraternal, and educational organizations. It would also ask, "what are the limits of that autonomy?" While religious and other voluntary groups should have a constitutionally protected right to choose their own leaders, resolve their own disputes, etc., no one seriously argues that they can do so in a shootout with AK-47s or by stuffing ballot boxes. The topic of limitation on religious autonomy is critical and one to which we shall return later.

1. *Church Property*. Neither Kelley nor I have agreed with all court decisions in the settlement of property disputes. Injustices have been done. We are agreed that it is not the business of government, including the courts, to settle theological disputes. Under the equal-separation theory both *Watson v. Jones*, which allowed the highest church authority in any particular denomination (most denominations are either congregational, that is, locally controlled, or hierarchical) to make final determination of ownership, and *Jones v. Wolf*, which required courts to look solely at the secular instruments of property ownership, are acceptable legal doctrines. The "implied consent" doctrine of *Watson v. Jones* is constitutional as long as property disputes between other similar voluntary organizations are decided according to the same standard.

The real force of *Jones v. Wolf* is to require religious organizations to get their legal documents such as property titles, articles of incorporation, etc., in line with their particular structures of authority before disputes occur. This alignment when implemented will go a long way toward lessening the number of church-property disputes which come to the courts. Some may object that government has no right to force such consistency. Unfortunately, it is either the church or some of its members that appeal to the secular courts for a decision. Granted the realities that property ownership in this country is controlled by secular law, and religious people do appeal outside their own organizations to the courts for decisions, requiring clear secular documentation does not appear unreasonable and certainly not unconstitutional.

2. *Church Employment*. This is a troubling area and may be one of those instances where, under the suspect-classification doctrine,

"deference is due" to religious organizations purely and simply because they are religious. However, I am not quite ready to concede that. Let me make an argument for equal separation in this area.

First, all organizations, both governmental and private, have traditionally had the right to hire their policy-making executives and fill their sensitive staff positions based on the particular needs, standards, objectives, and values of the particular entities. Private organizations are allowed further flexibility. In general, affirmative-action requirements arise only when such organizations wish to do business with governments. Private, nonprofit organizations, among which religious groups are counted, are even less restricted. Therefore, those who argue that an equal-separation theory would require Catholics to ordain women, Methodists to ordain non-Methodists, etc., radically misunderstand affirmative-action law. Kelley does not make such an argument, but others have.

Let us suppose for an instant that legislation were proposed requiring certain racial, sexual, and sexual-preference quotas for all organizations, including private voluntary ones. Would it apply equally to churches? The answer, from an equal-separation perspective, is that religious groups ought to be in the forefront of resistance to such intrusive legislation, precisely on religious liberty, that is, constitutional, grounds. This is an instance where the autonomy required for religious liberty would serve as a foundation.[56]

The troubling employment problems come in three other areas: hiring standards for nonpolicy-making employment such as janitorial, maintenance, and clerical positions; in church agencies which do receive government funding for "secular" services; and government requirements for religious organizations which receive only indirect or passive "benefits" such as tax-exempt status.

The Supreme Court has upheld the right of a religious organization to hire its own members exclusively, even for nonsensitive positions.[57] This is not compatible with the equal-separation theory unless the Court extends the same rule to other similar organizations.[58]

For church agencies which contract with governments to perform social services, the same standards apply to all other agencies with similar contracts. Conflicts can most certainly arise, as when the City of New York and the Catholic diocese clashed over ordinances prohibiting discrimination based on sexual preference. The diocese refused to hire homosexuals in its child adoption/placement agency (homosexuality is "sinful" in Catholic moral teaching). Eventually the city and diocese worked out a compromise. Equal-separation theory by no means rules out political resistance to attempted regulation or compromises, but it does rule out privileged positions. If the church agency accepts public funding it must abide by the consequent public regulations. If compromise cannot be reached—a compromise that provides the same regulations for nonreligious groups—equal separation would require that the church agency not be allowed to contract for services. This is a major point with which Kelley agrees.

The same principle follows for employment-related issues when religious organizations do not contract for services but merely maintain a tax-exempt status. Can they be required, for example, to file reports on employment statistics with the Department of Labor? Equal-separation theory would require the same standards of all nonprofit organizations. Church officials might well (and justly) object that such forms are overly complex and time-consuming. One would hope their resistance, joined with that of other nonprofit agencies, would force simplification and limit the proliferation of such forms.

3. *Confidentiality of Internal Communication.* Privacy from excessive government inquiry is an area of growing concern over the internal affairs of organizations, relationships, and individuals in our "information age." Kelley worries that the "priest-penitent" privilege would disappear under the theory of equal separation, while attorney-client, husband-wife, and physician-patient privileges would continue. That kind of conclusion makes me realize that either I have not communicated well with Kelley (my problem) or he has not understood well (his problem). In any event, it is hard to think of a clearer example of where a religious right ought to be included in a broader classification and priest-penitent communication ought to be protected on an equal-separation basis.[59]

B. *Outreach Activities of Religious Bodies*

In Part II of his chapter Kelley presents his argument in outline form. As much as possible I shall respond in similar fashion; we both realize more detailed argument must be pursued in other forums. While he lumps evangelism, conversion, solicitation, and fund-raising together, it is useful to separate them. Kelley acknowledges that proselytizing and preaching are protected under the free speech and press clauses (and were originally protected by these clauses before the court also added a religious liberty component). "Why," he asks, "should it be necessary for religion to take a back seat to speech or press? It did not do so in the minds of those who wrote the First Amendment, why should it in ours?" The answer, of course, is that it should not; religious liberty requires the front seat; it should be fully protected *equally* with other constitutional rights. The words of James Madison's "Memorial and Remonstrance" are instructive: "A just Government . . . will be best supported by protecting every Citizen in the enjoyment of his Religion with the same equal hand which protects his person and his property." Later in the essay he adds, "[T]he equal right of every citizen to the free exercise of his Religion according to the dictates of conscience is held by the same tenure with all our other rights." So what's the problem?

The area of fraud in the name of religion deserves a book-length treatment. No denomination has been immune; human avarice, weakness, and hypocrisy apparently know no borders. "Religious" fraud has always been a profound embarrassment to legitimate religious people and organizations. But should religious liberty be such a precious freedom that government averts its eyes from fund-raising methods, claims, or schemes which, if conducted by nonreligious organizations, would be considered fraudulent? Should this be the last bastion of a caveat emptor ("let the consumer beware") legality? Should the slow, the gullible, the desperate, the lonely, the uneducated, be left unprotected to fend for themselves simply because people selling them things claim to do so in the name of God?

Fraud perpetrated by people under the cover of religion has not only been a religious scandal but something of a legal dilemma for the courts. The first fraud case to reach the Supreme Court, *United States v. Ballard* (1944), presents the problem fairly clearly. Consider the facts:

> There were claims that Guy W. Ballard had attained a supernatural state of immortality; that all the Ballards had been selected as divine messengers through whom the teachings of St. Germain and other "ascended masters" would be communicated to mankind; that the Ballards had the power to conquer disease, death, old age, poverty, and misery; . . . that books, charts, and phonograph records issued by defendants had special salutary qualities which would be transmitted to purchasers; that since a cataclysm was about to engulf the earth, it was wiser to give money to defendants than to invest it in banks, homes, insurance, etc.[60]

Now compare a more recent report:

> A federal jury in Peoria, Illinois has convicted a man and woman of bilking lonely men out of more than $4.5 million in what was described as a sex-fantasy scheme run under the cover of a bogus church. Donald S. Lowry, 59, and Pamela St. Charles, 25, were found guilty of mail fraud, conspiracy, and money-laundering in the scheme, which they carried out under the auspices of the "Church of Love."
>
> Lowry, who founded the Church of Love in 1965, and St. Charles sent older men nude photographs and letters supposedly from "angels" who were said to occupy a paradise called Chon-

da-Za. The men were solicited to donate money to provide for the angels' needs, which included garden seed, winter coats, and sewing machines.

Prosecutors said about 31,000 men had contributed to the church since its founding. Lowry, facing a possible 125 years in prison, used the money to finance a luxurious lifestyle, including a fleet of expensive cars. The jury rejected Lowry and St. Charles' defense—that the fantasy was a harmless diversion that "help keep lonely men occupied."[61]

Every reader can undoubtedly come up with his or her own examples of what appear to be fraud by those claiming to be "religious." How would the equal-separation theory handle such instances? While the rules of law coming out of *U.S. v. Ballard* are not all that clear (the case was eventually thrown out because of the systematic exclusion of women from the jury), one principle seems clear: Juries cannot be asked to assess the truth or falsity of religious *beliefs* or reported mystical experiences, no matter how bizarre or improbable. Such is the gist of Justice Douglas's opinion for the majority. Equal separation would take seriously Justice Jackson's concurring opinion in which he states, "I have no doubt that religious leaders may be convicted of fraud for making false representations on matters other than faith or experience, as for example if one represents that funds are being used to construct a church when in fact they are being used for personal purposes."[62]

In brief, fraud perpetrated by those claiming to be religious persons is no more to be tolerated than fraud by nonreligious persons. But the law does not reach to beliefs or religious experiences. It reaches only to concrete, material, provable facts, such as falsifying documents, raising money for one stated purpose and spending it for another, etc. During its 1989 term the Supreme Court considered a case, *Hernandez v. Commissioner of Internal Revenue*,[63] in which the IRS challenged the use of an "E-Meter" by the Church of Scientology for auditing and training. The IRS claimed donations given in return for auditing and training were payments for services rendered and therefore not deductible charitable expenses. The case apparently turned on the methods of marketing and payment, not on the efficacy of the E-Meter. The Court upheld the IRS' denial of deductible charitable contributions because there was a quid pro quo exchange. The dissenting opinion of Justice O'Connor argued that there was discrimination among religions here, and she appears to have a point. Disturbing as that is, this is a tax dispute, not a fraud case.

After a review of the antics of various TV evangelists one should probably add here that scandal is not synonymous with fraud, nor are lavish and lascivious life-styles necessarily illegal. There do remain enormous expanses of religious activities best left to the judgment of those who provide the financial support for them.

C. *Protecting Personal and/or Unusual Personal Beliefs*

There are a wide variety of religious practices, some mentioned by Kelley, most not, that are considered "non-normative" by most members of society and often in conflict with normative practices. Recent cases have involved conflicts over the preservation of sacred lands, snake handling, use of hallucinatory drugs or plants, severe disciplining of children, and stopping work for brief periods of prayer. Religious individuals have refused an enormous variety of activities such as seeking medical assistance, working under a woman or black supervisor, having one's picture on a driver's license, displaying an auto license with a motto on it, using a Social Security number or paying Social Security tax, cooperating with government in any way, installing or using indoor plumbing or electricity, voting, joining any nonreligious organization, educating their children in a school, etc.

The list is endless and will undoubtedly continue to grow. Such cases defy any attempt to provide a principled solution acceptable to everyone. Nonetheless it is possible to outline an argument from an equal-separation perspective which shows the contours of a possible public policy in this area that protects both the principles of religious liberty and political equality. The first question is whether and under what circumstances religiously motivated actions can be prohibited under an equal-protection doctrine, or people required to do what their religions prohibit them from doing? To put it bluntly, can a government under the First Amendment ever require that religious obligations bend to government regulations?

The answer based on constitutional interpretation, historical precedent, and contemporary practice in the United States is clearly "yes." (Since this is an argument about what the First Amendment permits I will not argue the moral rectitude of such provisions.) Polygamy, cannibalism, human sacrifice, the immolation of spouses, ritualistic prostitution, child marriages, sexual abuse of children, sexual harassment, the killing of blasphemers or heretics, driving beyond the speed limit, and parking in no-parking zones are a few of the many examples of situations in which religious motivation or the requirements of conscience are insufficient to overcome government regulation. Clearly there is a price to be paid, even by religion, for living in a constitutional democracy.

Second, if it is true that religion must sometimes bend, are there any guiding principles on where to draw the line between when religion must bend and government must bend? The simplistic answer is that the Constitution has already drawn that line, but we know from the thousands of cases arising since the founding that it really hasn't. It has only provided the boundaries within which the lines must be drawn. The following list of principles is proposed to provide some guidance. (I do not pretend these are complete; I would hope others will be stimulated to develop them further within the equal-separation framework.)

1. Principles determining when religion must bend to government regulation: from the side of religion
   a) Religious activity must be voluntary. Members cannot be physically held against their will or in situations tantamount to bondage, for example, in inaccessible areas without means to leave if they wish.
   b) Religious activity must not lead to substantial suffering of others unable to make voluntary decisions.
   c) Religious activity must not prohibit or substantially retard the ability of individuals to develop a capacity to make voluntary decisions.
   d) Religious activity must not pose a substantial risk of injury to others who are not voluntary participants.
   e) Religious individuals or groups which seek exemption from general requirements must be willing to provide or participate in viable, comparable alternatives.
2. Principles determining when religion must bend to goverment regulation: from the side of government
   a) Government must provide equal opportunity for religious activity (for example, it cannot single out religious buildings for exclusion from residential areas).
   b) Government must provide equal protection for religious activity (for example, police, fire, traffic control).
   c) When religious activity is limited by government action, the government must provide for viable alternatives (for example, in military and prison environments).
   d) When considering regulations, ordinances, or construction, government must consider the impact on religious liberty along with the impact on other rights. (It may be worth repeating here, since it seems to be a widely misunderstood concept, that under the equal-separation theory religion can be used to *identify* a fundamental right; it cannot be used as a basis for extending a privilege or imposing a burden not equally shared by similar individuals and organizations.)

e) Government cannot impose a significant burden on religious expression or association without a compelling state interest or without having exhausted viable alternative means to meet that interest.

f) If government imposes a significant burden it must provide the means to meet that burden (for example, if it requires that a church be preserved as a historical landmark against the will of the members, it must provide the means to do so).

g) Government must consider what, if any, significant harm will be done by providing exemptions from general laws.

h) Government must consider what, if any, significant advantage will accrue to groups or individuals if they are given exemptions from general laws.

These guidelines may be of some help in drawing lines between when government regulations must bend to religious needs and when religious obligations must bend. A third and critical question from the equal-separation perspective is whether laws or exemptions can then be extended to persons and organizations which are not religious. If the lines are drawn well, in the vast majority of cases this should be no problem. For example, if an adult has the right to refuse medical treatment for religious reasons, why shouldn't other adults have the same right? If a person may refuse to have a picture on a driver's license, why not make that right available to all? (As an alternative option there could be a written description of the person required.) If a person wishes to cover the motto on a license plate for religious reasons, others should be allowed to cover the motto for their own reasons. (However, if a person refuses to display a license plate at all based on religious reasons, this seems to be a case where religious obligation must bend.)

Finally, what happens in cases where generally applicable laws are judged to be necessary and yet conflict directly with a significant religious obligation? An example might be the use of peyote by the Native American church. Can government make an exception based solely on a religious claim and not available to anyone else? In this case the religion-based exception is treated as a suspect classification.

Government must show a compelling interest in the general law (for example, that peyote is more damaging than legal addictive substances such as liquor and tobacco) and religion must show a compelling interest in the use of peyote, that is, it is not just an optional practice such as Catholics' saying the rosary or wearing a medal. Such determinations are then subject to heightened judicial scrutiny. Perhaps one can go further and argue that if an exception is made, government is not then obligated to provide benefits for conditions resulting from the use of peyote, for example, employment benefits for persons fired for use of drugs, or waiving charges for persons subsequently driving under the influence of a hallucinogen.

Both Kelley and I are disturbed by recent court cases in this area as they relate to religious claims of Native Americans and other non-mainstream religious people.[64] An article by Ira Luper, "Where Rights Begin: The Problem of Burdens on the Free Exercise of Religion," provides an excellent alternative approach along equal protection lines.[65]

IS RELIGION SIMILAR TO ANYTHING ELSE?

Kelley raises a number of other issues that will be dealt with in responses to other writers. The concluding paragraphs of his chapter provide a superb and moving account of the uniqueness and secular importance of religion. With this I have no disagreement. Perhaps one reason we remain friends is that we share a profound appreciation of the spiritual and secular value of religion and religious organizations and a commitment to protect religious liberty. We disagree only on the most effective, honest, and fair means for doing so within the context of the Constitution. We agree that religion is of profound societal value. Religion has enormous cultural, social, and political significance. Indeed, one of the fastest growing fields of political science is the study of religion and politics.

In terms of the ultimate meaning and purpose it provides, there are few, if any, associations or belief systems similar to religion. (My slight hedging here is to accommodate differing views about the definition of religion, whether Marxism or humanism is a religion, etc.) Ultimate meaning and purpose are beyond the reach of law and politics.

However, religion and politics overlap in that they deal with such earthly concerns as property, human resources and ambitions, human failings and sufferings. In that overlap lie the other similar individuals, groups, institutions, and activities. To propose an equal-separation theory of the First Amendment is not to deny the independent and valuable, indeed indispensable, role of religion in society. Religious exercise must be protected. Period. Equal separation proposes to protect that independence by requiring equal treatment. Absolute separation, if it were seriously followed, would lead to the marginalization of religion; supportive separation would lead to its submersion. As veterans of the civil rights movement can attest, liberty without equality is only half a dream.

NOTES

1. Philip Kurland, *Religion and the Law* (Chicago: Aldine Pub. Co., 1962), p. 18.

2. Paul Weber, "Neutrality and First Amendment Interpretation," Chapter 1 of this volume.

3. Ibid., p. 10.

4. Ibid.

5. Ibid., p. 11.

6. Ibid.

7. L. Tribe, *American Constitutional Law*, 2d ed. (Mineola, NY: Foundation Press, 1988), p. 1189.

8. Douglas Laycock, "Towards a General Theory of the Religion Clauses: The Case of Church Labor Relations and the Right of Church Autonomy," *Columbia Law Review*, vol. 81 (1981): 1373, 1389.

9. *Kedroff v. St. Nicholas Cathedral*, 344 U.S. 94 (1952) Frankfurter concurrence.

10. *Watson v. Jones*, 13 Wallace 679 (1872).

11. *First Presbyterian Church of Schenectady v. United Presbyterian Church*, 62 N.Y.S. 2d 110 (1984).

12. *Elijah Lovejoy Presbytery v. Jaeggi*, 682 S.W. 2d 465 (1984).

13. *Foss v. Dykstra*, 341 N.W. 2d 220 (1983).

14. *Babcock Memorial Presbyterian Church v. Presbytery of Baltimore*, 464 A. 2d 1008 (1983).

15. *Presbytery of Seattle v. Rohrbaugh*, 485 P. 2d 615 (1971).

16. *Doris Fonken v. Community Church of Kamrar*, 339 N.W. 2d 810 (1983).

17. *Presbyterian Church v. Mary Elizabeth Blue Hull Memorial Presbyterian Church*, 393 U.S. 440 (1969) (two churches), and *Jones v. Wolf, supra*.

18. *Watson v. Jones, supra* and *Presbyterian Church v. Hull Church, supra*.

19. *Kedroff v. St. Nicholas Cathedral, supra*, and *Maryland and Virginia Churches v. Sharpsburg Eldership*, 396 U.S. 367 (1970), (Brennan concurrence).

20. *McClure v. Salvation Army*, 460 F.2d 553 (5th Cir. 1972), *cert.* denied, 409 U.S. 896 (1972).

21. *Equal Employment Opportunities Commission v. Southwestern Baptist Theological Seminary*, 651 F.2d 277 (1981).

22. *National Labor Relations Board v. Catholic Bishop of Chicago*, 440 U.S. 490 (1979).

23. Section 702, Civil Rights Act of 1964 as amended 1972.

24. *Corporation of the Presiding Bishop v. Amos*, 107 S.Ct. 2862 (1987).

25. Vt. Stat. Ann. tit. 12, sec. 1607.

26. *U.S. v. Ballard*, 322 U.S. 78 (1944).

27. Larson v. Valente, 456 U.S. 228 (1982).

28. *Regan v. Taxation with Representation*, 461 U.S. 540 (1983).

29. *McDaniel v. Paty* 435 U.S. 618 (1978).

30. *Holy Spirit Association v. Tax Commission*, 450 N.Y.S. 2d 192 (1982).

31. States in which state regulatory authority was curtailed: *Ohio v. Whisner*, 351 N.E. 2d 750 (1976); *Vermont v. LaBarge*, 134 Vt. 276 (1976); *Kentucky v. Rudasill*, 589 S.W. 2d 877 (1979); *Bangor Baptist Church v. Maine*, 576 F. Supp. 1299 (1983). States in which it was upheld: *Sheridan Road Baptist Church v. Michigan*, 348 N.W. 2d 220 (1984); *Rivinius v. North Dakota*, 328 N.W. 2d 220 (1982); *North Dakota v. Shaver*, 294 N.W. 2d 883 (1980); *Nebraska* ex rel. *Douglas v. Faith Baptist Church*, 301 N.W. 2d 571 (1981).

32. *Cf. Forest Hills Early Learning Center v. Grace Baptist Church*, 56 USLW 2658, (4th Cir. 1988).

33. *Wisconsin v. Yoder*, 406 U.S. 205 (1972).

34. 54 Stat. 885, 889 (1940), emphasis added.

35. 42 U.S.C. Sec. 2000e(j), emphasis added.

36. *Trans World Airlines v. Hardison*, 432 U.S. 63 (1977).

37. *Sherbert v. Verner*, 374 U.S. 398 (1963), *Thomas v. Review Board*, 450 U.S. 707 (1981), *Hobbie v. Florida*, 107 S.Ct. 1046 (1987).

38. Weber, "Neutrality and First Amendment," p. 9.

39. *In re Jenison*, 375 U.S. 14 (1963).

40. *Quaring v. Peterson*, 728 F. 2d 1121 (8th Cir. 1984), aff'd by equally divided court *sub nom. Jensen v. Quaring*, 105 S.Ct. 3492 (1985).

41. *Callahan v. Woods*, 736 F.2d 1269 (9th Cir. 1984).

42. *Bowen v. Roy*, 476 U.S. 693 (1986).

43. 29 U.S.C. Sec. 169, 94 Stat. 3452.

44. *Tooley v. Martin-Marietta Corp.*, 648 F.2d 1239 (9th Circ. 1981); *Nottelson v. Smith Steel Workers*, 643 F.2d 445 (7th Cir. 1981).

45. For example, *People v. Woody*, 394 P.2d 813 (1964); *Whitehorn v. Oklahoma*, 561 P.2d 539 (1977).

46. Quoted in *Wilder v. Sugarman*, 385 F. Supp. 1013 (1974).

47. *Wilder v. Bernstein*, 848 F.2d 1338 (2d. Cir. 1988).

48. *Abington Township v. Schempp*, 374 U.S. 203 (1963), Brennan concurrence.

49. Weber, "Neutrality and First Amendment," pp. 10, 15.

50. J. Milton Yinger, *The Scientific Study of Religion* (New York: Macmillan, 1970), p. 21.

51. Talcott Parsons, Introduction, Max Weber, *Sociology of Religion* (Boston: Beacon Press, 1963), pp. xxvii, xxviii.

52. *Corporation of the Presiding Bishop v. Amos, supra.*

53. That seems to be the thrust of the school-aid cases from *Lemon v. Kurtzman*, 403 U.S. 602 (1971) through *Grand Rapids v. Ball*, 473 U.S. 373 and *Aguilar v. Felton*, 473 U.S. 402 (1985), though the Court has not articulated this rationale very well.

54. Other scholars seem to agree with this viewpoint. See William P. Marshall, "Solving the Free Exercise Dilemma: Free Exercise as Expression," 67 *Minnesota Law Review* 545 (1983); Jesse Choper, "Defining 'Religion' in the First Amendment," 1982 *University of Illinois Law Review* 579 (1982).

55. See Paul J. Weber and Dennis Gilbert, *Private Churches and Public Money* (Westport, CT: Greenwood Press, 1981).

56. This is in no sense to be construed as opposition to affirmative-action efforts. It is only to acknowledge sound public policy and constitutional limits

to such efforts. Even minority groups would presumably pause before supporting a legal requirement that a certain proportion of their ministers and congregations be white male, that a certain proportion of basketball teams be white or
female, etc.

57. *Presiding Bishop v. Amos*, 107 S. Ct. 2862 (1987).

58. It is good to remember that such court decisions have real results for real
people. For example, in the wake of the *Amos* decision a church in Kentucky
required not only that workers in its day-care center be Baptists, but that they
belong to *this* Baptist church. As a result two workers, one a Baptist, the other a
Catholic, were fired. The latter had worked at the day-care center for 15 years. It
is hard to celebrate such "victories" for religious freedom!

59. This may be as good a time as any to acknowledge that in most categories
of law there are gray areas—tough cases, vague lines, exceptions, and lack of
development. That is certainly true with attorney-client, husband-wife, and
priest-penitent privileged-communication cases. For example, should the exception include reporter-source and social worker-client relationships? Is there
information not protected, for example, telling an attorney of a crime you are
about to commit, or the requirement to report child abuse? Unfortunately,
establishing a general principle such as equal separation does not provide a clear
and specific right answer in each hard case; it can only provide the legal
framework within which to resolve such cases.

60. 322 U.S. 78 Petition for Certiori, pp. 4–5, quoted in Philip Kurland, *Religion
and the Law* (Chicago: Aldine Press, 1962).

61. Reported in *Church and State*, February 1989, p. 16.

62. *United States v. Ballard*, 322 U.S. 78 at 92–93 (1944).

63. 57LW4593 (1989).

64. See *Lyng v. Northwest Indian Cemetery Protective Association*, 108 S. Ct. 1319
(1988); *Mozert v. Hawkins County Board of Education*, 827 F.2d 1058 (6th Cir. 1987),
cert. denied, 108 S. Ct. 1029 (1988).

65. Ira C. Luper, "Where Rights Begin: The Problem of Burdens on the Free
Exercise of Religion," 102 *Harvard Law Review* 933 (1989).

3

Neutrality and the Establishment Clause

James M. Dunn

Theory is not my forte. It would be a total waste of my time and yours for me to pretend to offer an evaluation of Paul Weber's strict-neutrality approach. The concept of strict neutrality is not offensive to my separationist sensibilities and is useful in some instances. As a non-lawyer and a lowly layman in the realm of political science, I will not begin to propose a perfectly coherent or self-consistent doctrine regarding neutrality. Being an undisciplined, non-creedal Baptist I'm not expected to fit my religious or political beliefs into a summa theologica, an institutes of religion, or a professor of politics.

Whatever happened to the First Amendment? "Congress shall make no law respecting an establishment of religion or prohibiting the free exercise thereof . . . ?"

The Supreme Court has insisted that it means just what it says: "no law." Now, alas, we are being robbed by reinterpretation.

One conservative think-tanker, Walter Berns, advocates "a program of assistance on a non-discriminatory basis, across the board, to all churches, all religions, all sects."

Justice William H. Rehnquist delivered a veritable tirade in his dissent on the *Jaffree* case, in which the Supreme Court ruled out government-managed moments for silent prayer in Alabama schools. He says, "The evil to be aimed at" by the First Amendment was "the establishment of a national church, and perhaps the preference of one religious sect over another."[1]

Attorney General Edwin Meese laments the Supreme Court's "hostility" to religion. Education Secretary William J. Bennett would establish a vague Judeo-Christian value system for public schools. He does not bother to tell us how he would reconcile the conflicts in his hyphenated, lowest-common-denominator established religion between the Judeo part and the Christian part. True believers all, these people are laboring brilliantly to rewrite history.

Their revised standard version of the First Amendment holds that it simply rules out favoritism among religious groups and prohibits an official state church, but endorses God in general and supports generic religion.

The Supreme Court, history, and common sense consistently prove that the establishment clause embraces much broader restraints on government than these simple prohibitions.

The Rehnquist dissent in *Jaffree* selects snippets of history from the First Congress that supposedly make his point. It may well be that Justice Rehnquist, as Stan Hastey says, "has decided to lend his considerable influence to those who would discard separation of church and state as the standard for proper church-state relations in this country."[2]

At the very least Mr. Rehnquist stops too soon in his history lesson and fails to report how the Senate rejected precisely the nonpreferential aid argument that he and the Religious Right advocate.

The debate reveals the recommended alterations to the First Amendment. The key sentence is *"Congress shall make no law respecting an establishment of religion, or prohibiting the free exercise thereof . . . "*

After the first House of Representatives had hammered out a version of the religious-liberty amendment to be sent to the Senate, third among the proposed amendments at that time, it was time for the Senate to act.

Stokes and Pfeffer in their invaluable *Church and State in the United States* quote from page 70 of the *Journal of the First Session of the Senate.*

On the following day (August 25) the Senate received a communication from the House requesting the concurrence with the amendment adopted. A lively debate soon began. We fortunately have this record of the discussion on September 3:

On motion to amend article third, and to strike out these words "religion, or prohibiting the free exercise thereof," and insert "one religious sect or society in preference to others":

It passed in the negative.

On the motion for reconsideration:

It passed in the affirmative.

On the motion that article the third be stricken out:

It passed in the negative.

On motion to adopt the following, in lieu of the third article: "Congress shall not make any law infringing the rights of conscience, or establishing any religious sect or society":

It passed in the negative.

On motion to amend the third article, to read thus: "Congress shall make no law establishing any particular denomination of religion in preference to another, or prohibiting the free exercise thereof, nor shall the rights of conscience be infringed":

It passed in the negative.

This action was significant in showing that Congress was not satisfied with a proposal which merely prevented an advantage to any one denomination over others as far as Church-State separation was concerned. It wished to go further.[3]

It is strange indeed that with a highly selective reading of history those who would have government promote religion come up with exactly the proposals that were rejected by the first Senate. There were those in that day as in this who wanted simply to prohibit "establishing any particular denomination of religion" and rule out aid to "one religious sect or society in preference to others."

Yet, it seems from the outcome of the 1789 debate that the non-preferential aid advocates lost and the narrow view, that the only real danger was the establishment of a national church, was also defeated.

How then does one respond to the modern counterparts of those who failed to advance toleration over freedom? First, this limited liberty was clearly not intended by the Founders who prevailed. Then, an accommodationist policy toward religion is not possible now even if it had been the intent of the Founders. Finally, such government entanglement with religion is not desirable even if it were possible.

A CIVIL RELIGION WAS NOT INTENDED BY THE FOUNDERS

The Founders were sharply divided. Madison, Jefferson, and George Mason stood against Patrick Henry, who opposed passage of the Virginia Statute for Religious Liberty in 1786. Many observers see it as the most important church-state law in our history. When Patrick Henry blocked passage of the bill Jefferson wrote Madison from France, giving him advice on how to get the religious-freedom bill passed. "What we have to do, I think, is devoutly to pray for his death."[4] That's sharp division. Rehnquist in his *Jaffree* dissent pettily points out that Jefferson was in France when the Bill of Rights was under consideration. Is it possible to imagine the gathering that gave us the First Amendment without the hovering presence of Jefferson? It was Jefferson who gave us the phrase, "a wall of separation between church and state." It's downright silly to act as if those specific words, "separation of church and state," have to be in the Constitution for the concept to be there.

Madison in pleading for Virginia's ratification of the new Constitution said, "There is not a shadow of right in the general government to intermeddle with religion." This view was consistent with his earlier comment on the Statute for Religious Liberty when he wrote Jefferson that the bill had "extinguished forever the ambitious hope of making laws for the human mind."[5] Madison's logic requires a separation of church and state well beyond a flimsy injunction against the establishment of a national church.

Madison's plea is relevant today: "Who does not see that the same authority which can establish Christianity, in exclusion of all other Religions, may establish with the same ease any particular sect of Christians, in exclusion of all other Sects?"

George Washington himself wrote with regard to the treaty with Tripoli: "The Government of the United States of America is not in any sense founded on the Christian Religion." He may have been overstating a bit but the point he wanted to make is clear. The Founders intended some distance between religion and government.

The Founders were divided but the majority favored separation of church and state. It was precisely *for* religious freedom, not against it, that Jefferson wanted to keep the church out of the state's business and vice versa. These moving words of Jefferson encircle the dome of the Jefferson Memorial: "I have sworn on the altar of God eternal vigilance against every form of tyranny over the mind of man." That is the spirit of liberty.

In that spirit the House and Senate compromisers who gave us the First Amendment wisely wanted neutrality on the part of government in regard to religion. Constitutional scholar Douglas Laycock, Fulbright-Jaworski professor of law at the University of Texas, reflecting on the wording, says it well:

> This is the broadest version considered by either house. It speaks generically of "religion," not "*a* religion," "a national religion," or "any particular denomination of religion."
>
> It forbids any law "respecting" establishment of religion—that is, any law that relates to an establishment in any way. In light of the alternatives Congress considered and rejected, it is best understood as requiring the government to be entirely neutral towards religion.[6]

Justice Rehnquist appeals to the Northwest Ordinance of 1787 and the tax-supported religion aimed at the Indians as arguments for the accommodationist views he sees in the Founders. "The actions of the First Congress, which re-enacted the Northwest Ordinance for the governance of the Northwest Territory in 1789, confirm the view that Congress did not mean that the Government should be neutral between religion and irreligion."[7] There is no more shameful chapter in American history than our attempts to merge the military and missionary urges in dealing with the first Americans. Native Americans suffered much from government's attempts to blend force with faith. If anything demonstrates dramatically why the state should stay out of religion, the sordid story of our treatment of the American Indians does exactly that.

IMPARTIAL AID TO ALL RELIGIONS IS NOT POSSIBLE NOW EVEN IF IT HAD BEEN INTENDED

The impartiality required for any sort of juggling between religions, antireligions, and nonreligions is beyond moral capacity. Reinhold Niebuhr's words are relevant: "Man's capacity for justice makes democracy possible, but man's inclination to injustice makes democracy necessary."[8] The objectivity demanded for nonpreferential aid, the above-it-allness, would put one attempting such a task a notch above God. The sort of dispassionate evenhandedness called for is unheard of in either politics *or* religion. Put these lively disciplines together and it is ludicrous to think of an established government policy of balanced support for all religions.

Beyond that theological argument stands the empirical challenge of more than 3,000 religions in the United States all entitled to equal footing. Try describing them, understanding them, identifying with them and their aspirations. Imagine the entanglement of assisting religions fairly.

Support for religion from the state is not possible even if some Founders envisioned it. John Leland, a Colonial Baptist preacher who was one of James Madison's teachers and peers, put it well: "Experience has informed us that the fondness of magistrates to foster Christianity has done it more harm than all the persecutions ever did." If you doubt it, look at the sad plight of Christianity in countries where religion has been cursed with official approval by the state: Sweden, Denmark, England, Spain, Italy. Church-state separation has clearly benefited both church and state. We're better off without government blessing, thank you!

Free churches tend to want to stay free. Persons of conscience of all religious and nonreligious hues insist that it is impossible to attain an idyllic state of governmental fairness with aid and benefits for all religions.

GOVERNMENT-BLESSED RELIGION IS NOT DESIRABLE EVEN IF IT WERE POSSIBLE

History has plenty of horrible examples of government trying to use religion for its ends or the dominant regional religion ruling the roost to the great distortion of justice, persecution of minorities, and religion-spawned hatreds and prejudices. Jews, Baptists, and Quakers have been protesting church-state entanglement from those days to these.

When the state gets into the missionary business, it fouls things up. When government claims to aid all religions, it never fails to play favorites. When government tries to find an agreeable level of religious involvement, it winds up advancing an emasculated, all-purpose god, not the specific Deity of revealed religion.

The merger of a sort of fuzzy Judeo-Christian consensus with patriotic Americanism has produced a civil religion that challenges church-state separation and threatens all freedoms. This quasi-religion depends upon patriotic fervor to be its holy spirit, Adam Smith to be its prophet, and television and movie actors to be its priests and missionaries. It has a bumper sticker for a creed: "America, Love it or Leave it."

Billy Graham recognizes the danger to authentic religious faith posed by this media-fed monster. He says, "To tie the Gospel to any political system, secular program, or society is wrong and will only serve to divert the Gospel. The Gospel transcends the goals and methods of any political system or any society, however good it may be."[9]

Dr. Samuel Johnson insisted that "patriotism is the last refuge of a scoundrel." Maybe the pious patriotism that blends nationalism with religion is actually the first refuge for a set of scoundrels who would gain cheap and easy mob support.

God should never have been expelled from America's classrooms in the first place, President Reagan said. *My* God has perfect attendance records, never absent or even tardy. The god that can be banned from school is the tiny, insignificant god of civil religion.

Robert Linder calls civil religion:

That generalized form of national faith which mixes religious metaphors with nationalistic aspirations; it is the state's use of consensus religious sentiments, concepts and symbols for its own purposes. It transcends specific denominations, mixes piety with patriotism and traditional religion with national life until it is impossible to distinguish between them.[10]

It is a mistake to assume that the free exercise clause is pro-religion and the no-establishment is hostile to religion. The two clauses do contradict each other if pushed to extremes but taken together both religion clauses of the First Amendment provide the bulwark for religious liberty. The separation of church and state historically rooted in the First Amendment is the necessary corollary of religious freedom.

Religious liberty is not a gift of the state. Government has the touch of mud in matters religious. Strict neutrality, not benignity, is the proper role for government in regard to religion. We want freedom, not tolerance. Toleration is a human concession. Freedom is the gift of God. Toleration implies a superior and inferior. Freedom has us all standing before God on equal footing. Toleration is a weasel word. Freedom sings. "It is precisely for freedom that Christ has set you free" (Galatians 5:1).

Government is neutral, not supportive of religion, so citizens are not forced to support religious practices and opinions they oppose; government is not evaluating or supervising religious institutions, so the state is not engendering divisiveness and religious warfare.

Happily, another member of the Supreme Court, Justice Harry A. Blackmun, has clung to the traditional appreciation of Madison's insight. In a speech delivered at the National Archives, Justice Blackmun held that the establishment clause was "designed in part to ensure that the advancement of religion comes only from the voluntary efforts of its proponents and not from support by the State." Blackmun and Baptists historically have shared "Madison's view that both religion and government function best if each remains independent. This means more than institutional separation. It means that the State must not become involved in religious affairs."[11]

I share the agony of those who attempt to apply the religion clauses of the First Amendment. The biblical injunction in Matthew 22, "Render therefore unto Caesar the things which are Caesar's, and unto God the things that are God's," presents a similar problem. We are given no lists of God's things and Caesar's things, nor have 2,000 years of Christian history brought forth consensus on the passage.

Yet we struggle on, attempting to deal with the principle of separation as a dynamic, vital doctrine. We strive to maintain a creative tension, continually reassessing what separation means. "What God hath put asunder let not man join together" has taken on the force of a commandment for those of us who see church-state separation as an essential corollary of religious liberty. Church-state separation is more than a chapter in a con law course for many who identify with a Roger Williams philosophy of church-state relations.

One need not cling to the wall-of-separation terminology to hold fast to the belief in church-state separation. Martin Marty may be right when he insists that all we have today is a "zone" of separation between church and state. As a Texan I plead that if not a wall, we keep at least a strand of barbed wire.

Fortunately, Jefferson and Madison left something more substantial than "clues" that they sought to accomplish more than structural separation. The Virginia Statute for Religious Freedom, the "Memorial and Remonstrance," and Madison's later writings give a distinct line of direction.

That line of direction leads to the description by Justice Hugo Black in *Everson v. Board of Education*. One need not be an absolutist or even subscribe self-consciously to any school of thought on the First Amendment to respond affirmatively to the logic and good sense of Mr. Black's characterization of church-state separation. Those who try to understand the proper relationship of church and state from theological insights appreciate the practical protections for all religion suggested by Hugo Black's words. Those who come to the First Amendment with estimates of the nature of humankind and lessons from history understand the need for a proper distance between these two social institutions. Those who wrestle with a dynamic ethic for a society in flux can see the need for separation of church and state. The relegation of the concept to the "goal" category does not make it useless or irrelevant. Subscribing to the ideal, one is pulled toward it. Accepting the validity of church-state separation, one tests proposed public policies by it.

With apologies to Reinhold Niebuhr one might say: A person's capacity for religious liberty makes the separation of church and state possible. Her or his inclination toward oppression makes it necessary.

One would also comment on the frequently cited quote of a separationist, Justice William O. Douglas. The context of the lonesome quotation is important. Douglas did not advocate nonpreferential aid for religion. He was at the time supporting the adjustment of policies to allow for released time.[12] He later repudiated even that slight accommodation.[13]

When one gives attention to the historical situation that spawned the First Amendment, it is clear that although the Founders left religion to the states, the Virginia pattern prevailed. This demonstrates the dedication of the same persons who gave us the First Amendment to apply the standard of separation at the state level. Also, the acknowledgment that we clearly face a new ball game does not diminish the good case which can be made for rules of fair play, freedom of conscience, and elemental justice, still best served by separation of church and state.

Paul Weber asks good questions, poses prickly problems and challenges. Without responding to all the particulars one can invoke a principle and illustrate it. Yes, the laws should and do apply to religious groups as to other nonprofit organizations. The sordid stories of the entrepreneurs of televised religion offer the illustration. The laws should be enforced against tax evasion, private inurement, fraudulent misrepresentation and solicitation, false advertising, mail fraud, etc. We do not need, however, a new arm of the Internal Revenue Service, already busy and overloaded, with the task of managing religion, beginning with broadcasters. Other governments have a secretary of religion. We do not need one.

The idea of strict neutrality is appealing, but like many things appealing, satisfying, or fattening, it must be taken in small doses. An overdose of strict neutrality could lead to the violation of both the nonestablishment and free exercise clauses. The theory offers a good illustration of how a conceptual construct shatters when shoved into some ordinary situations.

Neutrality should not mean that because we fund public schools with tax dollars we should spend public monies for private and parochial purposes. Kurland would advocate vouchers for church schools and church participation in publicly funded social welfare programs. Strict separation makes more sense to me than strict neutrality.

Neutrality should not mean that because we have prohibited discrimination on the basis of religion in corporate America we should insist that a Mormon church cannot give preference to employing Mormons or a Baptist college cannot favor Baptist professors of religion.

There is an interpretation of strict neutrality that defeats the purposes of both religion clauses. A pattern of nonpreferential aid to all religions as suggested by Mr. Rehnquist in his dissent in the *Jaffree* case stands the "no-establishment" clause on its ear and neuters the traditional understanding of church-state separation. On the free exercise side, the same justice as evidenced in *Hobbie*[14] would throw away the "compelling state interest" test and lower the threshold for government meddling in religion. Mr. Rehnquist would substitute a "rational" basis test as the occasion for government intrusion in religion. What's "rational" for Mr. Rehnquist is often not "rational" to me.

The strict-neutrality notion's greatest weakness lies in that the framers gave us more than an equal-protection clause. Many of us are nervous about any scheme that tends to minimize the first 16 words of the Bill of Rights. The first liberty is religious liberty and the freedom of conscience so indissoluble from it is the basis for freedom of speech and freedom of the press.

The establishment clause prohibits aid to or entanglement with religion. Free exercise protects religious conduct and practices as the speech clause protects freedom of speech.

Mr. Helms with his zeal for court stripping would alter the manner in which the federal courts deal with church-state issues.

Mr. Reagan with a school prayer amendment to the Constitution would amend the First Amendment.

Mr. Rehnquist and others would toss out the metaphor of a wall of separation between church and state.

I think I'll stay with Jefferson and Madison.

Response to James M. Dunn

In larger measure than expected I find myself in agreement with Dunn. He spends a good part of his chapter attacking the jurisprudence of former Attorney General Edwin Meese, Chief Justice Rehnquist, and the accommodationists (whom I call supportive separationists) in general. He is particularly upset because he sees in the conservative accommodationists an attempt to rewrite history and to alter the original meaning of the First Amendment. This is ironic in that Meese and the others have often been characterized as strict constructionists who purport to be faithful to the "original intent" of the Founders.

Dunn, and the strict separationist position he espouses, claim for themselves the mantle of faithful guardians of original intent, at least for the First Amendment. That poses the first problem for strict separationists: there are major difficulties determining what the original intent of the Founders was (especially when measured against their actions), and how that intent can be faithfully applied to twentieth-century controversies. Numerous scholars simply disagree that the Founders intended strict separation in the manner, or with the sternness Dunn seems to advocate, scholars such as Walter Berns,[15] Michael Malbin,[16] Richard John Neuhaus,[17] and Robert Cord[18] to name but a few. I do not argue that these scholars are correct but only that original intent is not so easily determined. It is not enough to quote Madison and Jefferson, because the First Amendment represented a compromise between the Virginia Deists and the New England Calvinists. The compromise was that the national government, that is, Congress, "shall make no laws respecting an establishment of religion," but states could. Indeed, the word "respecting" was carefully chosen, for it meant that Congress could neither establish *nor disestablish* a church. That was a power left to the states.[19]

Later in the chapter, Dunn cites with approval Justice Black's characterization of church-state separation in *Everson v. Board of Education*.[20] What he fails to point out is that in that precise case the Court, through Justice Black, applied the First Amendment to the states, gutting the compromise which lay at the very heart of the amendment. What five Supreme Court justices effectively did was rewrite the amendment so that it now means *neither* Congress nor the states shall make laws—so much for original intent![21]

But granting, for the sake of argument, that the words of Madison and Jefferson do reflect the intent of most of the Founders, how clear is their intent? I have argued elsewhere that Madison was far more interested in the equal treatment of religion along with other rights than later commentators have given him credit for.[22] For example, in the *Memorial and Remonstrance* Madison uses the word "separation" but once and "equal" or "equality" 14 times. I would not conclude from this that Madison was not a separationist. Rather, his vision of separation contained more of an element of equality than strict separationists acknowledge.

What about Jefferson? Surely here was a strict separationist! Robert Cord has pointed out a number of instances in which Jefferson as president made accommodation to religious interests, including an 1803 treaty with the Kaskaskia Indians which provided government money to build a church and pay a priest's salary![23] Treaties are, of course, *sui genis*, but several other writings are equally interesting. After retiring from the presidency, Jefferson devoted much of his attention to establishing the University of Virginia. Consider a section of the regulations he wrote for the university:

> Should the religious sects of this State, or any of them, *according to the invitation held out to them*, establish within, or adjacent to, the precincts of the University, schools for instruction in the religion of their sect, the students of the University will be free, and expected to attend religious worship at the establishment of their respective sects, in the morning, and in time to meet their school in the University at its stated hour.
>
> The students of such religious school, if they attend any school for the University, shall be considered as students of the Univer-

sity, *subject to the same regulations, and entitled to the same rights and privileges* (emphasis added).[24]

Is Jefferson sounding like an equal separationist? Consider a lengthy, thoughtful report Jefferson wrote to the Virginia legislature in his capacity as rector of the university:

> In the same report of the commissioners of 1818 it was stated by them that "in conformity with the principles of the constitution, which places all sects of religion on an equal footing, with the jealousies of the different sects in guarding that equality from encroachment or surprise, and with the sentiments of the legislature in freedom of religion, manifested on former occasions, they had not proposed that any professorship of divinity should be established in the University; that provision, however, was made for giving instruction in the Hebrew, Greek, and Latin languages, the depositories of the originals, and of the earliest and most respected authorities of the faith of every sect, and for courses of ethical lectures, developing those moral obligations in which all sects agree. That, proceeding thus far, without offense to the constitution, they had left, at this point, to every sect to take into their own hands the office of further instruction in the peculiar tenet of each."
>
> It was not, however, to be understood that instruction in religious opinion and duties was meant to be precluded by the public authorities, as indifferent to the interests of society. On the contrary, the relations which exist between man and his Maker, and the duties resulting from those relations, are the most interesting and important to every human being, and the most incumbent on his study and investigation. The want of instruction in the various creeds of religious faith existing among our citizens presents, therefore, a chasm in a general institution of the useful sciences. But it was thought that this want, and the entrustment to each society of instruction in its own doctrine, were evils of less danger than a permission to the public authorities to dictate modes or principles of religious instruction, or than opportunities furnished them by giving countenance or ascendancy to any one sect over another. A remedy, however, has been suggested of promising aspect, which, while it excludes the public authorities from the domain of religious freedom, will give to the sectarian schools of divinity the full benefit the public provisions made for instruction in the other branches of science. These branches are equally necessary to the divine as to the other professional or civil characters, to enable them to fulfill the duties

of their calling with understanding and usefulness. It has, there-fore, been in contemplation, and suggested by some pious in-dividuals, who perceive the advantages of associating other studies with those of religion, to establish their religious schools on the confines of the University, so as to give to their students ready and convenient access and attendance on the scientific lectures of the University, and to maintain, by these means, those destined for the religious professions on as high a standing of science, and of personal weight and respectability, as may be obtained by others from the benefits of the University. Such establishments would offer the further and greater advantage of enabling the students of the University to attend religious exer-cises with the professor of their particular sect, either in the rooms of the building still to be erected, and destined to that purpose under impartial regulations, as proposed in the same report of the commissioners, or in the lecturing room of such professor. To such propositions the Visitors are disposed to lend a willing ear, and would think it their duty to give every encouragement, but assuring to those who might choose such a location for their schools, that the regulations of the University should be so modified and accommodated as to give every facility of access and attendance to their students, with such regulated use also as may be permitted to the other students, of the library which may hereafter be acquired, either by public or private *munifence*. But always understanding that these schools shall be independent of the University and of each other. Such an arrangement would complete the circle of the useful sciences embraced by this institu-tion, and would fill the chasm now existing, on principles which would leave inviolate the constitutional freedom of religion, the most inalienable and sacred of all human rights, over which the people and authorities of this state, individually and publicly, have ever manifested the most watchful jealousy: and could this jealousy be now alarmed, in the opinion of the legislature, by what is here suggested, the idea will be relinquished on any surmise of disapprobation which they might think proper to express.[25]

I would like, finally, to include a letter from Jefferson not often quoted today—for obvious reasons—which expresses some of the complexities, hopes, and biases the great man harbored. I should probably resist pointing out to Dunn the obvious approval Jefferson shows for four sects having alternate use of the courthouse for religious services. Of the courthouse! This is strict separation?

TO DOCTOR THOMAS COOPER
MONTICELLO, November 2, 1822.

DEAR SIR,—Your Favor of October the 18th came to hand yesterday. The atmosphere of our country is unquestionably charged with a threatening cloud of fanaticism, lighter in some parts, denser in others, but too heavy in all. I had no idea, however, that in Pennsylvania, the cradle of toleration and freedom of religion, it could have arisen to the height you describe. This must be owing to the growth of Presbyterianism. The blasphemy and absurdity of the five points of Calvin, and impossibility of defending them, render their advocates impatient of reasoning, irritable, and prone to denunciation. In Boston, however, and its neighborhood, Unitarianism has advanced to so great strength, as now to humble this haughtiest of all religious sects; insomuch, that they condescend to interchange with them and the other sects, the civilities of preaching freely and frequently in each others' meeting-houses. In Rhode Island, on the other hand, no sectarian preachers will permit a Unitarian to pollute his desk. In our Richmond there is much fanaticism, but chiefly among the women. They have their night meetings and praying parties, where attended by their priests and sometimes by a henpecked husband, they pour forth the effusions of their love to Jesus, in terms as amatory and carnal, as their modesty would permit them to use to a mere earthly lover. In our village of Charlottesville, there is a good degree of religion, with a small spice only of fanaticism. *We have four sects, but without either church or meeting-house. The court-house is the common temple, one Sunday in the month to each. Here, Episcopalian and Presbyterian, Methodist and Baptist, meet together, join in hymning their Maker, listen with attention and devotion to each others' preachers, and all mix in society with perfect harmony.* It is not so in the districts where Presbyterianism prevails undividedly. Their ambition and tyranny would tolerate no rival if they had power. Systematical in grasping at an ascendancy over all sects, they aim like the Jesuits, at engrossing the education of the country, are hostile to every institution which they do not direct, and jealous at seeing others begin to attend at all to that object. The diffusion of instruction, to which there is now so growing an attention, will be the remote remedy to this fever of fanaticism; while the more proximate one will be the progress of Unitarianism. That this will, ere long, be the religion of the majority from North to South, I have no doubt.

In our university you know there is no Professorship of Divinity. A handle has been made of this, to disseminate an idea that this is an institution, not merely of no religion, but against all religion. Occasion was taken at the last meeting of the Visitors, to bring forward an idea that might silence this calumny, which weighed on the minds of some honest friends to the institution. *In our annual report to the legislature, after stating the constitutional reasons against a public establishment of any religious instruction, we suggest the expediency of encouraging the different religious sects to establish, each for itself, a professorship, of their own tenets, on the confines of the university, so near as that their students may attend the lectures there, and have the free use of our library, and every other accommodation we can give them; preserving, however, their independence of us and of each other.* This fills the chasm objected to ours, as a defect in an institution professing to give instruction in all useful sciences. I think the invitation will be accepted, by some sects from candid intentions, and by others from jealousy and rivalship. *And by bringing the sects together, and mixing them with the mass of other students, we shall soften their asperities, liberalize and neutralize their prejudices, and make the general religion a religion of peace, reason, and morality* (emphasis added).[26]

Dunn ends his chapter with the sentence, "I think I'll stay with Jefferson and Madison." Me too. But that doesn't begin to solve the problems of church-state relations we face today. Ironically both Edwin Meese and James Dunn claim to represent the "original intent" of the Founders, yet they differ radically. That ought to tell us something.

A further difficulty is that original intent is only one of several approaches to constitutional interpretation. One might wish that constitutional scholars and judges limited themselves to interpreting what the framers wrote and/or intended, but in fact they do not, and never have. Beginning with John Marshall in the 1803 decision, *Marbury v. Madison*, courts have continuously modified and developed the constitutional language in order to apply that language to contemporary problems about which the Founders gave us no clue—the regulation of railroads, labor unions, the environment, telephones, television, airplanes, and computers, to name but a few. That process of interpretation and reinterpretation will continue.

There is substantial literature on the legitimacy of the various approaches, and attempts to justify one or another theory of constitutional interpretation based on a variety of principles or rules.

In teaching constitutional law courses, I classify these approaches as (1) plain meaning of the words (of the Constitution), (2) intent of the Founders, (3) historical development (which means slow, case-by-case growth and change through the courts), (4) adaptation within the "spirit" of the Constitution (such as the development of the right to privacy), and (5) adaptation to meet the felt needs of the time.[27]

To lay readers such scholastic battles may appear esoteric and unrelated to practical political decisions, but they are far from it. Such ideas matter. Judges, scholars, and critics defend and justify their opinions, and in the case of judges, their decisions, in terms of one or another approach to the Constitution. The "original intent" approach is not persuasive or useful to, and thus tends to be ignored by, adherents of other schools of constitutional interpretation. Equal separation is proposed as the principle most compatible with the various schools of constitutional jurisprudence without being tied to any one approach.

Finally, there is an area where Dunn and I are at odds—aid to religiously affiliated organizations. That will be discussed in my responses to Professors Monsma and Marty.

NOTES

1. *Wallace v. Jaffree*, 472 U.S. 38 (1985).
2. Stan Hastey, "Rehnquist Fails in Effort to Rewrite First Amendment," Commentary in Baptist Public Affairs, News Service of the Baptist Joint Committee on Public Affairs, July 22, 1985.
3. Anson Phelps Stokes and Leo Pfeffer, *Church and State in the United States*, revised 1-vol. ed. (New York: Harper & Row, 1964), p. 98.
4. Robert S. Alley, *James Madison on Religious Liberty* (Buffalo, NY: Prometheus Books, 1985), p. 65.
5. Ibid., p. 62.
6. Douglas Laycock, "Founders Wanted Total Neutrality," *USA Today*, August 12, 1985.
7. *Jaffree*, 472 U.S. 38 (1985)
8. Reinhold Niebuhr, *The Children of Light and the Children of Darkness*, 1944, Foreword.
9. Billy Graham, "Why Lausanne?" *Christianity Today*, September 13, 1974, p. 4.
10. Robert D. Linder, "Reagan at Kansas State," *The Reformed Journal*, December 1982.
11. Harry A. Blackmun, "The First Amendment and Its Religious Clauses— Where Are We? Where Are We Going?" speech delivered at the National Archives, Washington, D.C., June 23, 1987.
12. *Zorach v. Clauson*, 343 U.S. 306 (1952).
13. As Douglas matured on the bench he became more of a separationist, not less, to the point of repudiating *Everson v. Board of Education*, 330 U.S. 11 (1947) which upheld bus transportation for parochial school students. (See Douglas, J., concurring, *Engel v. Vitale*, 370 U.S. 421 (1962).)
14. *Hobbie v. Unemployment Appeals Commission of Florida*, 107 S.Ct. 1046 (1987).

15. Walter Berns, *The First Amendment and the Future of American Democracy* (New York: Basic Books, 1976).

16. Michael Malbin, *Religion and Politics: The Intention of the Authors of the First Amendment* (Washington, D.C.: American Enterprise Institute, 1978).

17. Richard John Neuhaus, *The Naked Public Square* (Grand Rapids, MI: William B. Eerdmans, 1984).

18. Robert Cord, *Separation of Church and State* (New York: Lambeth Press, 1982). There is a developing school of thought which includes the scholars just cited and is sometimes referred to as the "Serious Revisionists" or "New Revisionists." This group essentially challenges the legitimacy of all the Supreme Court's decisions which rely on application of the Bill of Rights to the states through the Fourteenth Amendment. They would return forcefully to the view that states may regulate, aid, or even establish a religion if they so choose, and that federal aid to religion is constitutional as long as it is available to all religions on an equal basis.

The latter point is developed by Professor Monsma. The revisionists' rejection of Supreme Court legitimacy for over 50 years is considered so far beyond the scope of mainstream theory that it has not been seriously discussed in this book.

19. See Mark DeWolfe Howe, *The Garden and the Wilderness: Religion and Government in American Constitutional History* (Chicago: University of Chicago Press, 1965).

20. [330 U.S. 1 (1947)].

21. For a thoughtful contemporary discussion of the difficulty of determining and applying original intent, see Ralph Lerner, "Believers and the Founders' Constitution," *This World*, vol. 26, (1989), p. 80.

22. Paul J. Weber, "James Madison and Religious Equality: The Perfect Separation," *Review of Politics*, vol. 44 (April 1982).

23. Robert Cord, *Separation of Church and State*, p. 58 ff.

24. "Regulations," October 4, 1824. In Saul Padover, ed., *The Complete Jefferson* (Freeport, NY: Books for Libraries Press, 1969), pp. 1100–11.

25. "Report of the Visitors of the University of Virginia," ibid., Saul Padover, 957–958.

26. Ibid.

27. For two widely differing evaluations of the various approaches see Gary L. McDowell, *The Constitution and Contemporary Constitutional Theory* (Cumberland, VA: Center for Judicial Studies, 1985), and Lief Carter, *Contemporary Constitutional Decision-Making* (New York: Pergamon Press, 1985).

4

The Neutrality Principle and a Pluralist Concept of Accommodation

Stephen V. Monsma

Commentators on the Constitution often note that the Constitution should not be seen as a static entity, impervious to changing circumstances and values. Instead, in the famous words of John Marshall, the Constitution is a document "intended to endure for ages to come, and consequently, to be adapted to the various crises of human affairs."[1]

Nowhere is this more true than in the difficult, contentious area of the separation of church and state. Let no one underestimate the challenge of breathing life into the theoretical concept of "the separation of church and state." If the rights of believers and nonbelievers, Christians and Jews, Catholics and Protestants, fundamentalists and mainline Protestants, as well as those of the adherents to a wide variety of religious traditions and sects are all to be respected and given their just due, a rigid, wooden church-state theory which is blind to societal and political realities must be avoided.

One attempt to assist in the process of developing an equitable theory of church-state separation is Philip Kurland's strict-neutrality principle which Paul Weber has articulated and expounded in his chapter, "Neutrality and First Amendment Interpretation." In this chapter I react to Weber's presentation, thereby seeking to contribute to ongoing efforts of breathing life into the concept of church-state separation.

I do so first, by describing the nature and depth of the difficult, vexing church-state dilemma American society is facing today. Then I evaluate how both current Supreme Court doctrine and Kurland's neutrality principle as articulated by Weber seek to resolve this dilemma, and then suggest a third approach to resolving the church-state dilemma based on a pluralistic view of society.

THE CHURCH-STATE DILEMMA

The heart of the church-state dilemma lies, first, in the strong American commitment to the separation of church and state. American society generally accepts the proposition that both church and state benefit when neither one supports or interferes with the other. The Jeffersonian metaphor of a wall of separation captures the spirit of the American ideal of church-state separation. But the dilemma emerges from the fact that in real life church and state are not and cannot be totally separate. This section explores the dilemma which arises from American culture's commitment to church-state separation in a real-life world where church and state intersect or overlap in countless ways.

To understand the nature of the dilemma, it is helpful to note several key historical developments which have had a profound effect on the context within which church-state issues are being debated and decided, and which Weber outlined in an earlier article and in his chapter in this volume. These are: the application of the religion clauses of the First Amendment to the 50 states, the rise of an intrusive administrative state, the expansion and diversification of religious organizations, the development of technologies which raise religious-freedom issues, and greater population density, mobility, and diversity.[2]

Although I fully agree with Weber on the accuracy and the continuing significance of all five of these historical developments, I would like to reemphasize and expand upon Weber's second and third developments.

It is hard to overemphasize the significance of the rise of the administrative state, which today educates children, provides welfare services to the poor, regulates relations among the races and sexes, engages in an ongoing armaments race, seeks to defend human rights around the globe, and regulates and even runs family planning, sex education, adoption, and foster-care programs. In all of these examples, the government had little or no involvement a hundred years ago. And this is only the beginning of the list. I say this not to imply any criticism of the rise of such a state. In an urban, highly mobile, highly bureaucratized society, government regulation and programs of this nature are essential.

My point is that the government is now deeply involved—through both regulatory and service programs—in many areas of activity in which churches and other religiously based organizations are also involved, or which touch on issues deeply impregnated with values and beliefs with particularly clear religious relevance. In developing an equitable concept of church-state separation one needs to take this situation into account.

An additional development Weber mentions is "the enormous expansion and growth of religious organizations" and their involvement in running "day-care centers, retirement homes, hospitals, schools at all levels. . . . "[3] This development continues apace. But American Christianity is seeing not only a resurgent and renewed vitality on which many have commented,[4] but also the resurgence of a Christianity concerned with social and political issues. This is true across the various Christian traditions. Witness the Catholic bishops' pastoral letters on war and peace, economic justice, and human life, or Martin Luther King and Jesse Jackson's ringing affirmations for racial equality to which their faith led them. The mainline Protestant denominations, who continue to emphasize social issues, have been joined in the social and political fray by evangelical and fundamentalist Christianity, as symbolized by leaders as disparate as Jerry Falwell and Jim Wallis.

What must be emphasized about this development—apart from its sheer size and pervasiveness—is that these persons see their social and political activism as a necessary, required outgrowth of their religious faith. It is an integral part of it, not something which is optional. It is as much a part of their faith as kneeling to receive the host at communion. The Catholic bishops have, for example, written:

Followers of Christ must avoid a tragic separation between faith and everyday life. They can neither shirk their earthly duties nor, as the Second Vatican Council declared, "immerse themselves in earthly activities as if these latter were utterly foreign to religion, and religion were nothing more than the fulfillment of acts of worship, and the observance of a few moral obligations."[5]

One needs to read only lightly in the writings of the other Christian traditions mentioned above to find the same basic commitment.

The rise of the intrusive administrative state and the rise of a vigorous, socially involved Christianity lie at the heart of today's church-state dilemma. Government in the form of the intrusive administrative state and religion in the form of a vigorous Christianity are both growing and expanding their spheres of involvement and activity. As a result, religion and government intersect at many points. To understand the nature of the church-state dilemma it is helpful to understand these points of intersection. They can be grouped into three categories.

Government and religion intersect, *first*, when government directly performs certain functions or services in settings which lead to societal expectations that some expression of religious faith should be integrated into them. There are three especially important instances of this first category. The first instance occurs when government provides services or has created a setting in which a government program encompasses almost all the waking hours—the entire life—of its participants, such as government-sponsored or run nursing or retirement homes, foster-care homes for children, prisons, and the military service. In these cases the question understandably arises of how the religious needs and aspirations of the persons included in the programs are to be met. Since a governmental agency structures or controls almost the entire life of the participants, if that agency does not meet or provide for their religious aspirations, they will not be met. The answer is usually to provide chaplains (either government-paid or not) and religious exercises with greater or lesser degrees of voluntarism.

Second, there are state occasions of historical or ceremonial importance, such as inaugurations of presidents, celebrations of important historical events, dedications of new government facilities, and the opening of legislative sessions. Again the pervasiveness of religious beliefs in society and the solemnity of these occasions understandably lead to the call for a recognition of the hand of the Almighty. The answer here is the familiar invocation usually given by an invited clergyman or sometimes by a government-paid chaplain.

The final, as well as the clearest and best-known example of this category, is the public school. Prior to the rise of universal public schools, educating the young was largely done by church or community groups which integrated religion into the curriculum. All generations in all societies have sought to pass onto the next generation their most deeply felt values, traditions, and beliefs. Thus one would expect a society's education efforts to include the deeply felt religious beliefs dominant in that society. Yet the religious pluralism and secular concept of the state argue against doing so in the public schools. Here society has developed no clear answers. Explicit references to religiously rooted values, beliefs, and religious rituals have, in legal theory if not always in practice, been read out of the public schools, and alternative, religiously based schools have had to operate virtually without any governmental assistance. What to many persons is the unsatisfactory nature of this answer is stimulating much of the ongoing debate concerning church and state.

A *second* area or category of instances where religion and government intersect is when government and religion-oriented organizations provide similar or parallel services. I am thinking here again of education—as with public and religion-oriented schools—but also of a very wide range of social services, such as food banks, shelters for the homeless, foster care for children who have suffered from abuse or neglect, pregnancy counseling and adoption services, and more. Here questions often arise of whether or not government should either subsidize these services financially or purchase services through these religion-oriented organizations.

Given the American biases in favor of decentralization and the maintenance of limited government, and given the fact that often government can obtain for society more services for less money from private agencies than it can provide itself, there often are pressures for it to do so. But this raises the question of whether and under what conditions government should subsidize or purchase services through religion-oriented organizations. The answer is usually to avoid direct subsidization, but sometimes to purchase services. When this is done, ambiguity exists concerning the extent to which religion-rooted organizations may favor adherents of their own religion and engage in such religious activities as prayer and Bible lessons.

A *third* category of instances in which government and religion intersect is when government deals with public-policy issues directly and immediately related to religious beliefs. Issues such as abortion, gay rights, and pornography quickly come to mind. But nuclear arms policies, capital punishment, human rights abuses overseas, civil rights for racial minorities, and others also fall into this category. What such policy issues have in common is that Christianity gives—or at the very least seems to many Christians to give—clear indications what a moral, or justice-oriented policy would be in these areas. Many serious Christians believe they would be violating their religious beliefs if they would sit idly by while—as they see it—the world plunges ever closer to nuclear war, or basic God-given human rights are violated in South Africa, or the lives of unborn children are snuffed out, or the state protects and sanctions sexual practices contrary to nature and God's will. Attempts are mounted, therefore, to influence governmental policies in directions dictated by one's religious beliefs.

There has been general freedom in this area as long as one observes certain limits on religious references. The *New York Times*, for example, editorially criticized President Reagan in 1984 for linking certain public-policy positions to his religious beliefs, which, it claimed, "should be private piety." Presidents, it went on, should limit themselves to "an ecumenical summons of the spirit."[6] The Supreme Court has stated in an incredible passage that "political division along religious lines was one of the principal evils against which the First Amendment was intended to protect. The potential divisiveness of such conflict is a threat to the normal political process."[7] At the very least, American political culture is ambiguous concerning whether and in what ways religious beliefs can legitimately serve as a basis for persons'—and especially public officials'—public-policy positions and pronouncements.

In summary, American constitutional tradition and political culture alike affirm the separation of church and state, often even embracing the extreme Jeffersonian metaphor of a wall of separation. Yet it is clear that in practice religion and government at many and frequent points intersect. If such intersection is officially accommodated and encouraged to the point that the church-state distinction is lost, church-state separation flounders and society runs the risk of experiencing the evils history teaches can flow from a lack of separation. Yet if efforts are made to strengthen and brick up the wall of separation into an impregnable fortress, religion's freedom to act as a vital, active force in society is curtailed. Then society loses much of the dynamism and energy religion brings to solving tough societal problems, and the administrative state becomes an enemy of religion.[8] The dilemma is all too clear. Theories of church-state separation need to be judged by their ability to resolve this dilemma in an equitable manner.

THE SUPREME COURT AND THE CHURCH-STATE DILEMMA

The key clauses of the Constitution relating to the church-state issue are, of course, the free exercise and establishment clauses of the First Amendment. In interpreting the free exercise clause the Supreme Court has pursued a delicate balancing act which has tried to give due recognition to both the right of religious groups to be free from excessive government regulation and the need for societal order and the protection of deeply held societal values. This balancing effort is seen in *Wisconsin v. Yoder*, in which the Court held that Wisconsin could not force Amish parents to send their children to school beyond the eighth grade:

> To be sure, the power of the parent, even when linked to a free exercise claim, may be subject to limitation . . . if it appears that parental decisions will jeopardize the health or safety of the child, or have a potential for significant social burdens. But in this case, the Amish have introduced persuasive evidence undermining the arguments the State has advanced to support its claims in terms of the welfare of the child and society as a whole.[9]

In striking balances such as this, the Court has at times been criticized for particular decisions, but has faced little criticism for the basic approach of seeking to balance religious freedom with the need for social order and public safety, health, and welfare.

In regard to the establishment clause, however, no such broad agreement exists. The Court's basic approach or principle by which it has sought to interpret the establishment clause has spawned many, often bitter, debates. At the heart of the Supreme Court's approach to interpreting the establishment clause is the very broad, absolutist interpretation Justice Black articulated in 1947:

> The "establishment of religion" clause of the First Amendment means at least this: Neither a state nor the Federal Government can set up a church. Neither can pass laws which aid one religion, *aid all religions*, or prefer one religion over another.[10]

In line with the sweeping language of this decision, the Court has banned prayer and Bible reading in public schools, various forms of financial aid to religiously based schools, joint public-religious school programs, and religious displays on public property.

The crucial problem to which an absolute-separation interpretation leads is that it puts the establishment clause on a collision course with the free exercise clause. If consistently followed, it would put churches and other religious organizations at a disadvantage as compared to parallel or similar groups without a religious basis. Under it a secular club could presumably erect a display on public property calling attention to itself and its activities, but a religious organization could not; public funds could be made available to all nonpublic schools, except religiously based ones. And in fact, literature or camera clubs and young Democratic or young Republican groups are allowed to meet before or after school hours in most public schools, but in two separate cases, lower federal courts have held that student-initiated Bible study and prayer groups could not meet in schools before or after school hours.[11] The Supreme Court, by refusing to review these cases, left them standing.

Especially instructive is a California appeals court ruling in late 1988 which the United States Supreme Court let stand.[12] A California school district, in light of decisions such as those just mentioned, had allowed a student-initiated Bible study group to meet, but only if it met outside the school building on the lawn. This the students had agreed to do. But the students had distributed some fliers, informing other students of their meetings. This the school authorities would not allow. In upholding the school district the state appeals court judge wrote that the establishment clause requires public schools to "limit their [students'] right to air religious doctrine."[13] It is hard to conceive of a clearer violation of the free exercise of religion. Free speech is being censored simply because it is religious speech.

In short, the absolute-separation interpretation of the establishment clause penalizes religiously based groups compared to similar or parallel groups not religiously based. But the free exercise clause was intended to assure that individuals or groups would not suffer disadvantages because of their religious beliefs. As the Court itself said in a free exercise case: "Government may neither compel affirmation of a repugnant belief, nor penalize or discriminate against individuals or groups because they hold religious views. . . . "[14] Yet this is exactly where an absolute-separation interpretation of the establishment clause leads.

Fortunately, the practice of the Supreme Court has been better than its theory. The Court has approved prayers at the start of legislative sessions, governmental aid to religiously based colleges and universities, Sunday-closing laws, a form of tax credits for parents incurring expenses in the education of their children (including children attending religious schools), tax exemptions for churches, and religious symbols in a municipal Christmas display, and has indicated it would approve a religious motto on coins and an acknowledgment of God's help in the pledge of allegiance to the flag.

The Court has done so by dodging and squirming to avoid the full consequences of its own articulated absolute-separation doctrine. At times it has simply ignored its own enunciated doctrine and made an exception to it, as when it approved a paid chaplain in the Nebraska legislature.[15] But most frequently the Court has avoided the full consequences of its absolute-separation doctrine by claiming that the religious aspects in these cases were really not religious at all. For example, in a concurring opinion Justice William J. Brennan proclaimed with a straight face that the motto "In God We Trust" has "ceased to have religious meanings" and that the words "under God" in the pledge of allegiance are not an affirmation of faith but merely recognize "the historical fact that our Nation was believed to have been founded 'under God.'"[16] A creche was allowed in a municipal Christmas scene because it was judged to have "a secular purpose" and could in no way be considered "an endorsement of religion."[17] Sunday-closing laws were held not to "violate the establishment clause because Sunday had become so secularized that laws requiring that it be maintained as a day of rest and relaxation for most workers could no longer be said to serve a truly religious purpose."[18]

There are profound problems with the way the Supreme Court has led the United States as a society and political system in regard to the establishment clause. It has not solved the church-state dilemma in an equitable manner. When the Court follows its absolute-separation doctrine, it runs the danger of offending the free exercise clause by placing religion at a disadvantage. When the Court in practice breaks from its own doctrine, that doctrine still hangs as a constant sword over the heads of religious organizations. There are voices, such as those of former Supreme Court Justice Arthur Goldberg, which have argued for the strict imposition of the absolute-separation doctrine. Thus he has argued that aid to church-related colleges and universities, religious mottos on coins and in the pledge of allegiance, tax exemptions for churches, and more should all be held unconstitutional.[19] As long as the Court clings to its absolute-separation doctrine it encourages such calls which, if acted upon, would violate the free exercise of religion by favoring secularism over religion.

Even more seriously, the price religion must often pay for its admission to the public arena is to deny its heart and soul—to deny the religious character of its actions and commitments and reduce itself to just another secularized aspect of American life. What to the devout Christian is a scene of the holiest and most profound miracles of human history—Almighty God himself stooping to be born of a peasant girl in wretched circumstances, thereby demonstrating the depths of God's love for His children—is permitted on public property only if it reduces itself to the level of reindeer with red bulbs for noses that flash on and off.

Church-related colleges and universities—founded and sometimes today still supported by deeply devout believers—are allowed to receive public aid on the basis that they are not "pervasively sectarian" and that the aid goes only to support their "secular aspects" (which presumably are kept in hermetically sealed compartments).[20] In some instances this secular nature of church-related colleges and universities is accurate; in other instances it is no more than a convenient fiction. In such situations as these religion is forced to deny its very essence and parade in secular garb if it is to pass Supreme Court muster. That is to discriminate against religion.

The Court itself has recognized the tension between its interpretation of the free exercise and establishment clauses: "But this Court repeatedly has recognized that tension inevitably exists between the free exercise and the establishment clauses . . . and that it may often not be possible to promote the former without offending the latter."[21] Commentators receive few challenges when they describe this area as a "tangled body of law" or as "confused."[22]

THE NEUTRALITY PRINCIPLE AND THE CHURCH-STATE DILEMMA

In light of the church-state dilemma described in the previous section Weber has advanced the strict-neutrality principle Philip Kurland originally proposed in 1962. In explaining this principle Weber quotes these words of Kurland in reference to the establishment and free exercise clauses: "... government cannot utilize religion as a standard for action or inaction because these clauses prohibit classification in terms of religion either to confer a benefit or to impose a burden."[23] In short, religion is irrelevant as a classification—either to grant privileges or to impose limitations.

At first glance this principle would seem to resolve the dilemma, and indeed it does offer a marked improvement over current Supreme Court doctrine. The establishment clause would no longer be interpreted to impose burdens on religious groups that are specific to them as religious groups. Any burdens they incur would be those shared by nonreligious groups in similar situations. The California high school Bible study group would be able to pass out fliers advertising its meetings just as any other student group could do. Nor would it be forced to meet out on the lawn if other, secularly based student groups were allowed to use classrooms for their meetings. The religious character of a group would no longer be a liability, and therefore, the establishment clause would seem no longer to be at odds with the free exercise clause.

Upon closer examination, however, the Weber-Kurland principle does not fully escape the horns of the church-state dilemma, especially as it relates to the issue of public cooperation with or assistance to religious groups that are providing certain services which have a secular purpose. In fact, I would argue that in a very important way the strict-neutrality principle has embedded within it a self-contradictory element. Weber at one point says that under the neutrality principle religious groups would not be subjected to "coercion or disability based on religious affiliation, belief or practice ... ,"[24] but later says religious groups must conform to all requirements imposed on similar secular organizations. The problem with this is that requiring religious organizations to conform to all the requirements imposed on similar secular organizations will sometimes coerce them or put them at a disadvantage based on their "religious affiliation, belief or practice."

A goal of the principle is, in Kurland's words, neither "to confer a benefit" nor "to impose a burden" upon religious groups as compared to similar secularly based groups. Thus—as Weber makes clear— religiously based organizations could be treated no differently than similar or parallel secularly based organizations. This means not only that religious organizations would have to "keep the same records and maintain the same standards as other participants," but also conform—in the case of schools—to the same hiring, curriculum and textbook and other such requirements of the secularly based schools.[25]

This presumably would mean that an Orthodox Jewish school which receives governmental aid could be forced to hire Christian teachers, or a fundamentalist Christian school forced to adopt a textbook teaching naturalistic evolution, or a Catholic adoption agency forced to place a child of a Catholic young woman in a non-Catholic family. It is only a slight exaggeration to say that the neutrality principle says to Orthodox Jewish, fundamentalist, and Catholic organizations that they, along with parallel secularly based organizations, may receive governmental aid as long as they cease to be Jewish, fundamentalist, or Catholic!

The neutrality principle thereby results in a situation close to where Supreme Court practice—in distinction from its absolute-separation doctrine—already is. Religious groups can receive governmental aid in support of their secularly beneficial activities or services as long as they agree to deny their religious values and look and act very much like secular groups or organizations. The problem is that although the goal of the neutrality principle is not to subject religious organizations to coercion or disadvantages due to their religious character, subjecting religious and secular groups to the same regulations and requirements will at important points adversely affect the religious organizations' very reason for existing. One is thereby right back to the establishment clause clashing with the free exercise clause.

In his chapter Weber sees the 1988 *Bowen v. Kendrick* decision of the Supreme Court as reflecting the strict-neutrality position. This appears to be the case. This decision upheld the 1981 Adolescent Family Life Act and its provision which made funds available to charitable, nonreligious, and religious groups alike to teach teenagers sexual prudence in an attempt to reduce the incidence of teenage pregnancies. Unfortunately this decision also clearly reveals the fact that the neutrality principle does not resolve the problem of the establishment clause clashing with the free exercise clause. The decision turned in large part on whether or not any public funds—even incidentally— were being used to advance religious doctrines in the process of achieving the secular goal of reducing the number of unwanted pregnancies among teenage girls. One news report on the decision reported that Justice Scalia in oral argument had advocated that "a church-affiliated group could use the money to teach that premarital sex is 'wrong' but not that it is 'sin.'"[26] Here the Court is saying government and religion may act in partnership to deal with a severe social problem as long as religion ceases to be religious. Religion may enlist in the fight against social evils if it checks its sword at the door!

The one way out of this problem Weber's chapter suggests is the use of the "suspect-classification" principle the Court has used in relation to the equal-protection clause. Thus a public aid program to religious schools that would allow these schools to hire only teachers who are adherents of their faith would immediately be suspect of having created an unconstitutional classification. The presumption would be against its constitutionality, yet the possibility of a case being made which would allow it to pass constitutional muster would exist. Weber's articulation of the neutrality principle thus contains a crack which may allow it to escape the self-contradictory feature I have been pointing out.

But to force religion into the suspect-classification category when the First Amendment seeks to elevate it to a position of protection is troubling. Existing Supreme Court precedents in regard to the equal-protection clause indicate that religious groups would be placed in a highly vulnerable position if their ability to protect their particular religious practices and character would be dependent on overcoming the suspect-classification stigma. Elsewhere in this volume Dean Kelley points out a number of protections religious groups may lose should religious classifications be put into the suspect-classification category.

If the free exercise and the establishment clauses are both to be given their due, a way must be found not to disadvantage religiously based organizations or practices vis-à-vis similar secularly based organizations and practices without forcing the religiously based organizations to deny or water down their religious principles. In the following section I suggest the outlines of an approach which I believe may accomplish this. It makes use of some key features of the neutrality principle but makes a couple of major modifications in it in an attempt to escape the dilemma described above.

PLURALISM: AN APPROACH TO THE SEPARATION OF CHURCH AND STATE

It is a truism to say that American society is pluralistic. But many things can be meant by such a claim. I am using pluralism here to refer to the existence of a multiplicity of groups, each of whose members are bound together by common beliefs and interests. I am not primarily thinking of groups such as business corporations or pressure groups which have been purposefully established for the attainment of certain specific, limited goals. Rather, I am thinking primarily—although not exclusively—of groups with an organic or affective nature, that is, groups which are based on a sense of loyalty, shared beliefs, and common backgrounds, and which have emerged naturally instead of by rational planning and calculation. Family, kinship, ethnic, neighborhood, and religious groups come quickly to mind. I suspect many of the problems in relation to the interpretation of church-state separation have their roots in an unconscious underplaying of the significance and role of these groups or structures in the life of the nation.

Thinkers such as Jacques Maritain and Robert MacIver have noted the existence of such groups standing between the individual on the one hand, and the society, community, or nation on the other. Maritain refers to the body politic and then to "a multiplicity of other particular societies which proceed from the free initiative of citizens. . . . Such is the element of pluralism inherent in every truly political society."[27] MacIver uses the term association to refer to "an organization of social beings . . . for the pursuit of some common interest or interests."[28] Both include pluralistic groups such as the family and church among the examples they cite.[29] Similarly, Peter Berger and Richard Neuhaus have argued there are four types of structures or institutions which are especially important in American society: the neighborhood, the family, the church, and voluntary associations.[30]

These groups are not peripheral to society, with the individual and the government occupying center stage. Modern societies do not consist simply of the individual on the one hand and the total society or the state on the other. Instead there are the many organic, affective, subsocietal groups that command their members' feelings of loyalty and commitment. The individual, the intermediate groups or structures, and the government or state are all crucial, essential facets of society. Thus intermediate groups should not be viewed as being in a subservient position to the state, existing only at its sufferance. Instead, as John Coleman has described Maritain's views, they "should be as autonomous as possible because family, economic, cultural, educational, and religious life matter as much as does political life to the very existence and prosperity of the body politic."[31]

The importance of these pluralistic structures or groups for society and government emerges from their functioning—as Berger and Neuhaus point out—as mediating structures "between the individual in his private life and the large institutions of public life."[32] More specifically, they play at least four crucial roles. First, they are crucial both in the socialization process and in giving their members a sense of identity, purpose, and belonging which the huge, impersonal structures of a mass society—including the state—cannot. Second, the groups and structures of a pluralistic society also meet many of the normal, day-to-day physical, emotional, and social needs of individuals, and also provide networks of support and help in times of crisis or special needs, such as unemployment, death, divorce, and other traumas. Third, they often serve a mediating role in the sense that governmental services and regulations are provided through them. Fourth, the identification with and sense of attachment to the various subsocietal groups help form a bulwark against totalitarian claims of the government. When the claims of the two clash, it is far from certain that the government's claims are the ones which will prevail.

In short, if it were not for a pervasive network of effectively operating pluralistic structures, government could not operate. It would not have the underlying web of supportive attitudes it needs to operate in a free and effective manner, and it would quickly be overwhelmed and crushed by the needs not being met elsewhere. Society and effective government would disintegrate.

Religious loyalties and organizations play an especially important role along these lines in the United States. This is the case because religion is vitally important to very wide segments of the American public. Observers such as Tocqueville, D. W. Brogan, and Seymour Martin Lipset have all commented on the importance and profound influence of religion on American society and government.[33] Kenneth Wald more recently has written: "Institutionally, churches are probably the most vital voluntary organizations in a country that puts a premium on 'joining up.'"[34] Whether gauged by church attendance, financial contributions, or reported importance of church in one's life, Americans joining of churches is clearly an indication of deeply felt beliefs.[35]

In summary, when one combines the crucial importance of pluralistic, intermediate groups or structures for a healthy society and government with the large, vital role religion plays in American society, the importance of a doctrine of the separation of church and state which gives churches and other religious groups their proper due is critical. If they are not given their due, if they are not allowed the freedom to act as free, pluralistic structures in society, the health and effectiveness of society and government will be seriously weakened. If they are given more than their due, they themselves may start to improperly limit or absorb the state or other free, pluralistic structures. The proper balance is critical. How to determine and recognize that balance is the key question.

If religious groups are to be encouraged to play the active, constructive, yet limited role in society that pluralistic theory envisages for them, two essential conditions must be met. First, the establishment clause must be interpreted to allow governmental recognition and accommodation of secularly and religiously based organizations alike, as long as they are given without discrimination, and to allow governmental aid in support of activities of religious groups which have a secular goal or purpose (even though religious beliefs and goals are intertwined with the secular goals and purposes). Second, the free exercise clause must be broadly interpreted to allow religious organizations to act freely, also when receiving governmental funds in support of secular programs, as long as there are checks to assure that their actions do not endanger the social order or the health and safety of the community or themselves, and do not misspend public funds, thereby violating the secular goals or purposes for which they received them. In what follows I explicate and defend this basic position.

The first condition comes close to being a restatement of the neutrality principle Weber defends in his chapter. It would allow religious as well as secular organizations to receive governmental recognition, accommodation, and aid without either one or the other being discriminated against. Religion as a category would be irrelevant. Religious and nonreligious groups would receive the same types of accommodation and recognition. Religious groups would no longer be discriminated against. If secular clubs in a high school are allowed to advertise their activities and to use school classrooms for their meetings, religious groups could as well. In the case of governmental aid, the relevant question would be whether or not certain secular goals or purposes are being achieved which society through government has deemed to be beneficial.

Without this first condition being met theoretical and practical problems arise. Theoretically, as seen earlier, religious groups are disadvantaged or discriminated against as compared to secular groups engaged in similar or parallel activities, thereby raising free exercise problems. Practically, a vital means by which pluralism says societal needs can be met is left untapped or, at best, underutilized. What is probably the most vital, dynamic force in American society today is relegated to the sidelines, to the detriment of both religion and society.

The enormous contributions religion-oriented groups could make to meeting severe social problems such as drugs, failing public schools, unwanted pregnancies, unemployment, homelessness, and more are discouraged and depreciated. Under this first condition, however, a central-city Catholic school could receive public funds to help in educating children from disadvantaged backgrounds, a Baptist counseling center could receive public funds to help provide services to unmarried, pregnant young women, a Jewish synagogue could receive public funds to help resettle and teach citizenship skills to recent immigrants, and a Black Muslim center could receive public funds for a creative antidrug effort.

Currently all such services must usually: (1) be provided entirely with private funds, which limit their scope and effectiveness (especially when one considers that the supporters of private associations are already paying taxes to support similar services the administrative state is providing), or (2) be provided entirely by governmental bureaucracies with all the problems attached to public bureaucracies, or (3) be provided by secular organizations which can qualify for public funds, but often lack the community support, sense of values and identity, and long-term commitment which in the United States adheres to religious groups more than any other. I strongly suspect a key reason why the United States is experiencing more severe social problems such as homelessness, drug abuse, and high drop-out rates than other modern, Western nations is its inability to fully tap into and unleash the power and creativity of the most vital force present in American society.

There is a second condition essential to religious groups playing the vital role pluralism envisages for them which must also be met. It is that the free exercise clause must be interpreted broadly enough that religious groups can operate in the political arena *as religious groups*. It is this condition that I find missing—or at least underemphasized—in Weber's and Kurland's propounding of their neutrality principle. The free exercise clause lies at the heart of religious freedom in the United States or any other free society. The strict-neutrality principle is on the right track when it suggests the establishment and free exercise clauses should be read as one, but it creates problems when it concludes this reading should lead to religious and nonreligious groups being subjected to the same standards and requirements.

Richard John Neuhaus points in the correct direction when he argues that the basic, fundamental purpose of the clause(s) is (are) to "avoid any infringement on the free exercise of religions."[36] Freedom of conscience, freedom of religious belief and practice, freedom from governmental compulsion: this is what the First Amendment religious provisions are all about.[37] Thus Neuhaus is correct when he suggests that the sense of the First Amendment is captured if it were to read: "Congress shall make no law respecting an establishment of religion or *otherwise* prohibiting the free exercise thereof."[38] The clear point of the religion clause(s) of the First Amendment is (are) to assure that religion—and nonreligion—can grow, develop, and be practiced without the long hand of the state dictating belief or practice. In the era of the comprehensive administrative state this principle is crucial.

This the neutrality principle seeks to achieve. But as I argued earlier, interpreting the neutrality principle without recognizing the fundamental nature of the free exercise clause defeats its very purpose. The price religious groups would often have to pay to be treated equally and to contribute to meeting societal needs as fully as they are potentially capable of doing is to give up their religious distinctiveness. That is too high a price to ask them to pay.

There are only two bases on which religious groups should be limited, and information and reports should be asked of them only to satisfy these two bases. These two limitations or requirements—while not placing religious organizations at a disadvantage nor requiring them to sacrifice their religious distinctiveness—are sufficient to assure that an inappropriate establishment of religion is not taking place.

The first is to preserve social order and assure the health and safety of the group members and of the public. Religious groups, for example, can appropriately be forced to conform to fire and sanitation requirements to which all other groups, religious and secular, must conform. Similarly, adherents of certain religious groups and their children have been ordered by lower courts to undergo blood transfusions in life-threatening situations in violation of their religious beliefs. Although there are some difficult cases, the right of the state is appropriate and well-established to regulate and even compel certain behavior in the face of an asserted free-exercise claim when the protection of health, safety, and public order is at stake.

Second, government should also be able to require reports and make independent checks in order to assure that any public funds being given are in fact going toward achieving the secular goal or purpose for which they were provided. This would include making certain that funds were not being misspent or siphoned off to pay for programs for which they were never intended. It would also include the right of the government to assure itself that appropriate standards were being met, so that the secular purposes for which the funds were being given were not subverted. For example, in education the secular purpose for which funds might be given a fundamentalist Christian school would be that society has a population with basic knowledge and skills. Thus government would have a right to assure itself that certified teachers were being used and that basic skills in reading and mathematics were being taught.

What government could not do is to look at the ways in which religion is intertwined with the achieving of valuable secular goals, and insist that these secular goals must be achieved in the same way by religiously and secularly based organizations. Religious groups would thereby remain free to pursue their religious values through their hiring, programming, and other practices.

The approach to church-state separation based on the pluralistic view of society proposed here would no doubt pose its own dangers and problems, but it has the potential to unleash a clearly needed, dynamic force, and any dangers or problems it may pose are not inherently insolvable. Given the confusion and contradictions now attending church-state relations—confusion and contradictions not fully resolved by the strict-neutrality principle—I believe it at least is worthy of additional scrutiny and discussion.

Response to Stephen V. Monsma

Monsma articulates a supportive separationist perspective in a very persuasive argument. He makes several points not developed elsewhere. Foremost is the observation that social, economic, and political "involvement" is not an optional "extra" for many religions. It is an integral part of their religious vision and mission, as important as "cult, code and creed" elements are to other faiths. Whether government officials or representatives of other faiths like it or not, religious people for whom good works are an integral part of faith will be actively participating beyond their church doors.

Monsma underlines the reality that the administrative state has moved into areas traditionally dominated by religion, not vice versa. Particularly important are those areas where government now dominates the setting in which religion has functioned, as in hospitals and schools, or where it has always had a special interest, as in prisons, or those areas in which government now offers parallel services. Finally, he repeats the important insight, critical to a supportive separationist, or as he prefers to call it, a pluralist perspective, that mediating structures such as family, neighborhood, school, and church play a large and necessary role in American society and deserve the protection of government.

These are important insights to keep in mind. Monsma and I do have disagreements, however. At one point he objects that "the price religion must often pay for its admission to the public arena is to deny its heart and soul—to deny the religious character of its actions and commitments and reduce itself to just another secularized aspect of American life." As an equal separationist I do not see the reality in that light. As I attempted to highlight in my response to Dean Kelley, religion *can* be used to identify groups and organizations, that is, they do not need to deny who they are in order to participate in the public arena. The point is that such identification cannot then be used to grant privileges to or impose burdens on religion. When Monsma objects to religion being reduced to "just another secularized aspect of American life" he is probably referring to Justice Brennan's viewpoint that Christmas displays, mottos, etc., are constitutional precisely because they have lost their religious significance. That is not a position espoused by equal separation. It is true under this theory that religious liberty extends equal protection to other groups and organizations.

Religion emphatically does not become secularized; it does lose any uniquely privileged position.

Later Monsma points to what he considers a self-contradictory principle in strict neutrality: on the one hand it holds that religious groups cannot be subjected to coercion or disability based on religious affiliation, belief, or practice, but on the other hand it requires religious organizations to conform to all the requirements imposed on similar secular organizations. This will "sometimes coerce them or put them at a disadvantage based on their religious affiliation, belief, or practice." From the perspective of a supportive separationist he has a point. The issue really goes back to a question asked earlier: Must religious organizations pay a price for functioning in a constitutional democracy? My answer, and one that I believe avoids contradiction, is twofold: (1) religion cannot be coerced or disadvantaged beyond what other similar groups are; (2) where the right to free exercise of religion requires limits on government action, government action must also be limited when it affects similar groups.

What Monsma has helped me to see is that I am operating on an assumption not adequately articulated, namely, that religious groups will actively support and press for the range of freedoms they need in the political and legal arenas. That assumption may be based on my previous research into religious interest groups in Washington, D.C. (two of which are ably represented by Dean Kelley and James Dunn, I might add). Such groups tend to be quite articulate and extraordinarily effective in protecting religious liberties. Equal separation simply wants the results they achieve extended to similar groups. One also hopes that similar groups, when they see their own interests at stake, will support the effort to strengthen religious liberty. It must be admitted, however, that there are points at which some religious groups will feel equality is not enough. That is where the theory pinches and possibly where Monsma and I part company.

Finally, the issue of hiring continues to trouble critics of equal separation, particularly hiring for schools. As Stephen Monsma puts it so well, "[strict neutrality] presumably means that an Orthodox Jewish school which receives governmental aid could be forced to hire Christian teachers, or a fundamentalist Christian school forced to adopt a textbook teaching naturalistic evolution, or a Catholic adoption agency forced to place a child of a Catholic young woman in a non-Catholic family." Monsma then concludes that such organizations "may receive governmental aid so long as they cease to be Jewish, fundamentalist, or Catholic!" I vigorously disagree. Even secular, commercial organizations have the right to hire personnel with the appropriate skills, attitudes, experience, and credentials appropriate for a particular company. They cannot discriminate on the basis of race, sex, religion, national origin, age, etc., *unless* that is appropriate for the position, for example, an attendant in a male or female bathroom. Religious discrimination is sometimes appropriate. The question *then* becomes: Can a religion discriminate and still seek public financing for its projects?

While this may be an area in which the equal-separation theory needs further refinement, let me propose several principles that may help clarify the issue: (1) When government provides grants, funds projects, or contracts out work, it has the right to set some minimal conditions, monitor performance, and measure outcomes. (2) Government may not support religious activities; it may support secular activities even if performed by identifiably religious groups. (3) A "secular project" is defined by the government, not by religious groups. That is, sheltering the homeless or staffing soup kitchens may be seen as works of mercy required for salvation by religious groups and serve a secular legislative purpose from a governmental perspective. (4) It is possible to separate, from a government perspective, religious from secular activities. For example, teaching mathematics, physics, chemistry, English, biology, history, and economics are secular activities. Teaching religious truths or conducting religious rituals are not secular activities. (5) Any religious group has a right to reject government funding of its secular projects and the consequent regulations and limitations. (6) Religious schools which wish to obtain funding for teaching their *secular* subjects would indeed need to separate these from their theological subjects; if they believe this cannot be done they should not seek funding. (7) Schools could not, in hiring teachers who are to be paid out of government funds, discriminate in any illegal manner. They could, however, select teachers willing to function in accordance with the educational philosophy of a particular institution.

Perhaps an example might help. A number of years ago I taught at Marquette University, an avowedly Roman Catholic Jesuit university. The Political Science Department consisted of one Lutheran, one actively observant Jew, one atheistic Jew, one Presbyterian, two whose faith, if any, was unknown, two Jesuits, and four Catholic lay persons. (The Sociology Department down the hall included one very active fundamentalist.) When interviewed for the job each was asked if he or she understood that this was a Catholic institution and whether, whatever their personal beliefs, they would agree not to take public stances in opposition to Catholic doctrine. Such selectivity, so long as it is not a subterfuge for illegal discrimination, seems compatible with the equal-separation theory.

On Monsma's final two examples, I believe he is correct that a Christian school could not expect the government to fund teachers or textbooks to teach scientific creationism as opposed to evolution, since the former is not recognized as science. As for Catholic adoptions, one might point out that many, if not all, Catholic agencies already allow adoption by non-Catholic families. An equal-separationist approach could allow agencies to take the wishes of the natural mother into account in making adoptions, as long as it is not *only* religious preference which is given weight.

In his chapter Monsma agrees that there are prices to be paid and limits to be set for any group to function freely in a constitutional democracy. We may not be so far apart as we first thought.

NOTES

1. *McCulloch v. Maryland* 4 Wheaton 316 (1819). I would like to thank the Earhart Foundation of Ann Arbor, Michigan, for a grant which helped fund my preliminary research on pluralism and the separation of church and state and Pepperdine University for reassigned time with which to work on this essay.

2. See Paul J. Weber, "Excessive Entanglement: A Wavering First Amendment Standard," *Review of Politics* 46 (1984), pp. 488–90 and Paul J. Weber, "Neutrality and First Amendment Interpretation" (in this volume).

3. Weber, "Excessive Entanglement," p. 489. Also see his "Neutrality and First Amendment Interpretation."

4. See, for example, Kenneth D. Wald, *Religion and Politics in the United States* (New York: St. Martin's, 1987), chap. 1, and Everett Carll Ladd, "Secular and Religious America," in Richard John Neuhaus, ed., *Unsecular America* (Grand Rapids, MI: Eerdmans, 1986), pp. 14–30. I recognize, of course, that other religious traditions are present in the United States. Judaism remains strong, while Islam, Buddhism, and Hinduism all have their adherents. Nevertheless, Christianity is by far the largest and strongest religious tradition in the United States, and thus most of this chapter speaks in terms of Christianity.

5. National Conference of Catholic Bishops, *Economic Justice for All* (Washington, DC: National Conference of Catholic Bishops, 1986), pp. vi-vii.

6. New York Times, February 3, 1984, p. A28.

7. *Lemon v. Kurtzman* 403 U. S. 602 (1971). See the excellent discussion of this strange claim in Weber, "Excessive Entanglement," pp. 491–96.

8. This point is explained and defended more fully as this chapter progresses.

9. 406 U. S. 205 (1972).

10. *Everson v. Board of Education* 330 U. S. 1 (1947). Emphasis added.

11. *Lubbock Civil Liberties Union v. Lubbock Independent School District*, 669 F.2d 1308 (5th Cir. 1982) and *Brandon v. Guilderland Control School District*, 635 F.2d 971 (2d Cir. 1980).

12. *Perumal v. Saddleback Valley Unified School District*, 88–340.

13. Los Angeles Times, November 1, 1988, p. I-3.

14. *Sherbert v. Verner* 374 U. S. 398 (1963).

15. *Marsh v. Chambers* 463 U. S. 783 (1983).

16. Justice Brennan's concurring opinion in *Abington School District v. Schnepp* 374 U. S. 203 (1963).

17. *Lynch v. Donnelly* 465 U. S. 668 (1984).

18. *McGowan et al. v. Maryland* 366 U. S. 420 (1961).

19. Cited in Richard John Neuhaus, "Religion—From Privilege to Penalty," *The Religion and Society Report* 5 (March 1988), pp. 1–2. Goldberg's remarks originally appeared in *Sh-ma* (September 4, 1987).

20. *Hunt v. McNair* 413 U. S. 734 (1973).

21. *Committee for Public Education and Religious Liberty v. Nyquist* 413 U. S. 756 (1973).

22. A. James Reichley, *Religion in American Public Life* (Washington, DC: Brookings Institution, 1985), p. 117 and Phillip E. Hammond, "The Shifting Meaning of a Wall of Separation: Some Notes on Church, State, and Conscience," *Sociological Analysis* 42 (1981), p. 227.

23. Weber, "Neutrality and First Amendment Interpretation."

24. Ibid.

25. Ibid.

26. Los Angeles Times, July 10, 1988, p. I-23.

27. Jacques Maritain, *Man and the State* (Chicago, IL: University of Chicago Press, 1951), p. 11.

28. Robert MacIver, *On Community, Society, and Power*, Leon Branson, ed. (Chicago, IL: University of Chicago Press, 1970) p. 30.

29. Maritain, *Man and the State*, pp. 150–52 and MacIver, *On Community, Society, and Power*, pp. 56–57.

30. Peter L. Berger and Richard John Neuhaus, *To Empower People* (Washington, DC: American Enterprise Institute, 1977).

31. John A. Coleman, "A Theological Link between Religion, Liberty, and Mediating Structures," in Jay Mechling, ed., *Church, State and Public Policy* (Washington, DC: American Enterprise Institute, 1978), p. 42.

32. Berger and Neuhaus, *To Empower People*, p. 2.

33. See Alexis de Tocqueville, *Democracy in America*, vols. 1 and 2 (New York: Vintage, 1954); D. W. Brogan, *Politics in America* (Garden City, NY: Doubleday, 1954), especially chap. 5; and Seymour Martin Lipset, *The First New Nation* (Garden City, NY: Doubleday, 1967), especially chap. 4.

34. Wald, *Religion and Politics*, p. 7.

35. See ibid., pp. 8–9, and Ladd, "Secular and Religious America "

36. Richard John Neuhaus, "Contending for the Future: Overcoming the Prefferian Inversion," in *The First Amendment Religion Liberty Clauses and American Public Life* [forthcoming], p. 183.

37. This is evident from studies of the debates and events surrounding the adoption of the Bill of Rights. See, for example, the dissenting opinion of now Chief Justice William Rehnquist in *Wallace v. Jaffree*, 472 U. S. 38 (1985) and Michael J. Malbin, *Religion and Politics: The Intentions of the Authors of the First Amendment* (Washington, DC: American Enterprise Institute, 1978).

38. Neuhaus, "Contending for the Future," p. 183.

5

To Favor Neither Religion Nor Nonreligion: Schools in a Pluralist Society

William R. Marty

The schools are a special case in the general problem of interpreting and applying the religion clauses of the First Amendment. But they are an extraordinarily important case, precisely because the schools are an extraordinarily important institution in any society, and perhaps especially in a large, diverse, and free nation. Consider some familiar truths. We do not live in a homogeneous society. We do not all share the same purposes, values, and understandings. And we do not like to have other people's purposes, values, and understandings imposed upon us or upon our children.

Children, after all, do not come into the world theists or atheists; Christians, Jews, or humanists; hedonists or ascetics; relativists or believers in an objective right and wrong. But they *are* shaped in how they view things by the education they receive in their schools. And education is rarely neutral on the great questions. It teaches some things explicitly, others implicitly. The American Civil Liberties Union, its allies, and its opponents are right, then, to be concerned about the interpretation of the establishment and free exercise clauses of the First Amendment. There is little in this republic that is more important in the long run than the education of the next generation. And the Supreme Court's interpretation of the religion clauses affects, in fundamental ways, what can be taught and practiced in the schools.

Let us consider, then, the Court's interpretations of those vital clauses. In what direction have they tended? A decade and a half ago, in 1974, Francis Canavan, writing in the *Journal of Church and State*, assessed the development of the law on church and state, and concluded, a little wryly: "It may be that, in its effort to achieve neutrality, the Court has thrown the resources of the state behind the establishment of what it once, perhaps in a moment of rashness, called the religion of secular humanism."[1] It has come to be regarded as bad form for the religious to use the term "secular humanism," even if citing the Court, to describe a belief system or worldview emptied of religious content and relying on naturalistic and human-centered assumptions. Still, neither the assessment, however wry, nor the language seems inappropriate as we look back. Consider, after all, the strikingly similar assessment, rendered in language that was complacent, if not triumphant, by Leo Pfeffer, in the same journal only three years later. Leo Pfeffer, it may be noted, is now the dean of those who interpret the religion clauses of the First Amendment, and it is likely that in recent decades he has been the most important influence on that interpretation excepting only the justices of the Supreme Court themselves.

Consider, then, Pfeffer's 1977 assessment, entitled: "Issues that Divide: The Triumph of Secular Humanism."[2] The title captures the theme. In the article Pfeffer speaks of "the strong, if somewhat indefinable, spirit of secular humanism which permeates American cultural and political life."[3] He speaks as well of "organizations, such as the American Civil Liberties Union, which reflect the secular humanist spirit of American society."[4] (Pfeffer's observation that the A.C.L.U. represents the spirit of secular humanism is authoritative in view of his prominent position in the organization, and it will hardly surprise the alert observer, but his observation *is* interesting in light of the enormous influence that organization has had in shaping the Court's understanding of the religion clauses in such a way that it has helped produce Richard John Neuhaus's "naked public square.")[5]

Pfeffer's argument is that under the impact of the Court's rulings, church-related institutions have had to "desectarianize themselves at least to some extent," and that "the now rapid movement towards secularization is certain to continue."[6] Pfeffer argues, in fact, that the influence of secular humanism is already so great that church leaders can no longer count on the support of their laity. He cites as examples divorce and contraception among Catholics. The laity, he notes, have abandoned the Catholic church's official teaching, and Pfeffer observes that: "Here, as in so many other instances, secular humanism has won out, and Catholics have accepted the outcome."[7] Pfeffer concludes, "American secular humanism is manifesting its potency in *altering long-held doctrine and practice* and narrowing the differences that divide Protestants, Catholics, and Jews" (emphasis added).[8]

Canavan, three years earlier, had claimed that *in seeking neutrality,* the Court might have *inadvertently* created an establishment of what *it* had called the religion of secular humanism. Pfeffer, the most prominent and influential representative of that worldview, claimed something more. He claimed that under the impact of court decisions, the churches were being forced, to some extent, to give up their differences, and that even more strikingly, secular humanism had become so powerful that increasingly the various religions cannot make their teachings prevail against it *even among their own members*.

If Pfeffer is correct, and his examples make the assertion plausible, the religious are losing in the contest with a rival worldview even among those who profess religion and attend religious services. That is a striking claim, and it would seem that the religious might attend to it with some anxiety. After all, if Pfeffer is correct, religion is becoming a hollow shell, its *content* increasingly filled, regulated, or controlled by the beliefs and understandings of the nonreligious. And if that is the case, the religious have less and less reason to take heart from the polls that show that most Americans remain religious.

If secular humanism governs the content of belief and the practice of the faithful, the battle the religious have been waging for the human soul is well on its way to being lost. And this brings us back to the schools, one of the most important means of passing understandings from one generation to the next. Pfeffer spoke on this subject with supreme confidence. In conflicts over public and church schools, he pronounced, "it is not Protestantism, Catholicism, or Judaism which will emerge the victor, but secular humanism, a cultural force which in many respects is stronger in the United States than any of the major religious groups *or any alliance among them*" (emphasis added).[9]

Francis Canavan and Leo Pfeffer, writing a little more than a decade ago, viewed the state of the law from different vantage points—the one religious, the other not. But even then they reached similar conclusions about the state and the direction of the law. Were they right? Do we confront, now, not an establishment of religion in the schools, but an establishment of nonreligion, of secularism, of—to use Pfeffer's terminology—secular humanism? Let us consider both the logic and the evidence of the case.

Francis Canavan, in his 1974 article, noted that the Supreme Court "simply assumes that secular education is neutral education."[10] And secular education *is* neutral education—as between religions. It favors neither Protestantism, Catholicism, nor Judaism, for example. But a secular education is not a neutral education as between religion and nonreligion, and that is one of the great divides or issues of truth and culture in modernity. Far from being neutral, what is taught in a secularized public school is an "implicit denigration of religion." As

Michael W. McConnell puts it in "Neutrality Under the Religion Clauses":

> If the public school day and all its teaching is strictly secular, the child is likely to learn the lesson that religion is irrelevant to the significant things of this world, or at least that the spiritual realm is radically separate and distinct from the temporal. However unintended, these are lessons about religion. They are not "neutral." Studious silence on a subject that parents may say touches all of life is an eloquent refutation.[11]

Do the public schools either deliberately or inadvertently favor nonreligion over religion? The evidence is now conclusive and widely admitted. Consider some of that evidence. In 1984, Paul Vitz, a professor of psychology at New York University, conducted a survey of 60 social studies textbooks for the Department of Education. He concluded that the books "'disenfranchised' students from traditional religious backgrounds."

In May 1986, two additional studies were released. The first, a study of 32 history texts conducted by People for the American Way, a liberal group, concluded that "religion is simply not treated as a significant element in American life." While most texts mention religion until the Civil War, religion "virtually disappears" after that. The second study, conducted by Americans United for the Separation of Church and State, "found a similar lack of religion in its look at 30 history texts."[12] Robert Marquand notes that the "religious or moral dimensions of leaders like Dr. Martin Luther King Jr. and Mohandas Gandhi" have been removed from the texts and that one book described the Pilgrims as "people who take long trips."[13]

Whether the studies are done by liberals or conservatives, secularists or religionists, they reveal the same thing: Religion is neither treated seriously nor taken seriously in the history and social studies texts of our public schools. (Allen E. Bergin notes, in addition, that an " . . . examination of 30 introductory psychology texts turned up no references to the possible reality of spiritual factors.")[14] Intentionally or unintentionally, texts in these important fields convey a thoroughly secular worldview.

In ethics and moral education, the same is true. In an essay on teaching values in the schools, Robert Marquand reports that experts say "the values that are taught in public schools are filtered through two general modes of contemporary thought: cultural relativity and values neutrality." One of the important techniques for instilling the values-neutral approach is the "values clarification" approach. Marquand reports that the ethic of values clarification is said by many to have become "the establishment ethic in education schools and associations."[15] (One might note the critiques of the assumptions and impacts of these value-relativism approaches in Bergin, Kilpatrick, and Vitz.)[16]

As for science, as Langdon Gilkey notes, it does not get to ultimate questions, it does not go back to beginnings, it *presupposes* naturalistic explanations. That does not mean that God does not exist. Science does not and cannot get to that question, according to Gilkey.[17] But it does mean that, taken by itself, its impact is secular.

Wherever we look—in history, social studies, reading texts,[18] psychology, values education, the sciences both natural and social— the thrust in the public schools is to treat religion not at all, or as irrelevant, or as superstition. On the whole, silence reigns. Whenever a text or a course rises to the coherence of having a worldview—and intelligent organization of many materials requires a worldview—it must be, and is, a secular worldview. Either incoherence or a secular worldview (in the language of Canavan and Pfeffer, secular humanism) reigns. The impact is thoroughly secular, and thoroughly inimical to a theistic worldview.

John Weiss, a history professor at Cornell, gives us some hint of the impact. In recent seminars, he reports that "only three of 50 students understood a reference to the Sermon on the Mount, and only eight of 75 knew about the book of Job."[19] (These students had received, it may be added, not only a thoroughly biased education, but also a thoroughly bad education that cut them off from many of the great books and much of the thought, art, and achievement of their heritage.) Perhaps, after all, Justice Potter Stewart's dissent from *Schempp* has been proved correct. Banishing religion from the conduct of public institutions does not represent neutrality between religion and secularism. Instead, "conduct of public institutions without any acknowledgment of religion *is* secularism."[20]

A generation ago the liberal's liberal on the Court, Justice William O. Douglas, wrote that "we are a religious people whose institutions presuppose a Supreme Being."[21] Responding to the litigation and guidance of such organizations as the A.C.L.U., the courts have come a long way. Douglas now seems quaint, though it is the courts and the law that have changed, not the American people, who remain, by comparative measures, quite religious.[22]

Today religion, far from being presupposed, does seem to have been driven from the field. Secularism, the belief system of a small but strikingly influential minority, is the reigning and entrenched worldview. Its adherents do seem to press on unceasingly in their efforts to drive religion farther and farther from the public square, untiringly vigilant in searching for remaining contaminations of religion in our public life. In the case of the public schools, they have largely prevailed.[23] It would appear, then, that Canavan and Pfeffer judged correctly "which way we wended." As the broadly supported "Williamsburg Charter" of June 25, 1988, puts it: "constitutional jurisprudence has tended, in the view of many, to move toward the *de facto* semi-establishment of a wholly secular understanding of the origin, nature and destiny of humankind and of the American nation."[24]

The religious can now escape this enforced secularism only by paying twice, once in taxes for the secularizing public schools, again in tuition for private schools. Joseph Sobran draws the appropriate parallel:

> Let us spell out the analogy of this culture to an established church. When the state has an official religion, it may, as in England, tolerate others. But the established church is paid for out of public monies taken compulsorily, as all taxes are, from all citizens. You have to pay for it whether you belong or not. If you want another church in keeping with your own beliefs, you pay for it out of the money the state has left you.
>
> That is how our educational system now works: you pay for the schools from which religion is banned whether your children attend them or not, whether you agree with them or not, whether you think them good influences or not.[25]

The parallel tells. We have, in practice, established secularism as our public worldview.

What should be done? The Court has never said that nonreligion should be favored over religion. Yet in practice nonreligion is now favored. A balance should be restored. Secularists, and their religious allies, were right, of course. Religion should not have been forced upon the nonreligious, as in the past it was. But the counterpart of that is true as well. A secular worldview should not now be forced upon the religious. But it is, and that violates the exact same principles of justice and respect for the rights of others to which the secular appealed in seeking the ousting of religion from the schools.

How can both the religious and the nonreligious be treated fairly? Only by taking the constitutional rights of *both* seriously; only by providing an education to each that does not do violence to their deepest convictions by *imposing* the other's worldview upon them. There are two fundamentally different ways to attempt this. The first method, favored by many, is to restore religion to the public schools and to the texts used in those schools. Religion is to be restored, however, not as the teaching or recognition of something that is true, as it was treated in the last century and much of this one, but as something seen from the outside, if possible, objectively. The intent is to treat the subject of religion neutrally, fairly, objectively, so that religion will neither be imposed on the nonreligious, nor nonreligion upon the religious. The whole range of subjects is to be taught in such a way that no one or group is favored and no one or group is hurt.

The best explication of this approach so far available is, perhaps, that in "Religion in the Public School Curriculum: Questions and Answers."[26] The position it puts forward has been endorsed by a broad range of groups including the American Association of School Administrators, the American Federation of Teachers, the National Education Association, the Americans United Research Foundation, the National Conference of Christians and Jews, the National Council of Churches of Christ in the U.S.A., the National Association of Evangelicals, and the Baptist Joint Committee on Public Affairs.

The constitutional foundation for this method of restoring religion to the schools is given by Associate Justice Tom Clark of the U.S. Supreme Court in his opinion for the Court in *Abington v. Schempp*. As cited in this document:

> [I]t might well be said that one's education is not complete without a study of comparative religion or the history of religion and its relationship to the advancement of civilization. It certainly may be said that the Bible is worthy of study for its literary and historic qualities. Nothing we have said here indicates that such study of the Bible or of religion, when presented objectively as part of a secular program of education, may not be effected consistently with the First Amendment.

In general, the approach is that "religion is *academic*, not *devotional*"; the school may *educate* about all religions, but not *promote* or *denigrate* any religion. Religion, treated in this matter, may appear in the curriculum "[w]herever it naturally arises." "Religion may also be taught about in special courses or units." The examples of special courses cited are "world religions, the Bible as literature, and the religious literature of the West and of the East." With regard to values: "Teaching about religion is not the same as teaching values. The former is objective, academic study; the latter involves the teaching of particular ethical viewpoints or standards of behavior." When teaching values, "teachers may not invoke religious authority."[27]

This approach, Justice Clark's approach, assumes that in a society involved, according to some, in a cultural war between the religious and the nonreligious, genuinely neutral and objective observers can be found to judge what to put into our texts and curriculums. One wonders. Will the same people under whom religion has been so thoroughly removed from the texts now be able to return religion without either promoting or denigrating it? Paul Vitz—whose pioneering study, after being roundly criticized, was vindicated by people of the most varied views who looked into the question of whether religion had been excluded from the public schools—does not think so.

"It is simply not possible," Vitz says, "to force a system to teach facts, much less perspectives or values, opposed by most of the system's leadership."[28] And the leadership of American education is, he thinks, hostile to religion and secular in its orientations. Vitz points to the enormous influence on American education and American schools of education of John Dewey's consciously humanistic and secular philosophy. He points, as well, to the heavy influence upon educational philosophy by Carl Rogers and B. F. Skinner, both humanists hostile to religion, and both enormously influential in counseling and learning theories. Moral education, too, has been thoroughly secularized under the impact of Lawrence Kohlberg and the values clarification theorists, Raths and Simon, all well-known humanists.[29] Of equal importance is the professional organization that dominates public education, the National Education Association. "There can be little doubt that the NEA has a secular and liberal political philosophy and that it has increasingly come to control education."[30]

The leadership of American education is secular and liberal, according to Vitz. One effect of this is that religion has been effectively removed from school texts. Another is that conservatism and traditional values have been equally excluded. The exclusion of the second, conservatism and traditional values, indicates that the exclusion of the first, religion, was not merely a result of worries about separation of church and state or the fear of controversy, as is often assumed, but is also a result of ideological screening.

Inasmuch as a leadership of one worldview and set of values cannot be forced to effectively and fairly present those of another, Justice Clark's remedy, dependent as it is on an absolutely fair and objective treatment of opposing worldviews, will not succeed. That is the kernel of Vitz's argument. To assess it, one wants to know whether conservatism and traditional values have indeed been excluded from the texts in the same manner as religion, for that would indicate an ideological screening of the texts—censorship—and it would give a very poor prospect for the success of Justice Clark's remedy, since the same people who excluded views they opposed will remain in control. Unfortunately, Vitz documents his case pretty thoroughly. To get some sense of the type of thing he found, let us look, in some detail, at one example.

A common feature of textbooks is the allocation of space to biographical sketches of people considered, in some way, exemplary. Some 30 people were allocated such special and positive treatment in the range of social study texts reviewed from grades one to six, covering the post-World War II period, in the Vitz study. Of the 30, 14 are Democrats, 3 are Republicans, and 11 are not classified according to party. On the face of it, that is a little skewed in a nation roughly balanced between Democrats and Republicans. But that understates the bias in two ways: First, the 11 not identified by party are all liberal or leftist in orientation. (The 11—some given more than one sketch—are: Rachel Carson, ecology movement—twice; Vine DeLoria, American Indian rights movement; Delores Huerta, United Farm Workers; Maggie Kuhn, Gray Panthers/Feminism; Martin Luther King, Jr., civil rights leader—three times; Thurgood Marshall, Supreme Court Justice; and Margaret Mead, anthropologist—twice.) Second, the 3 Republicans, all women, are not, as a group, strikingly conservative.[31]

Paul Vitz sums up the bias revealed by the selection of this particular group of people as role models:

> The characteristics of those noted . . . make clear the implicit political agenda of these books. It is even hard to find any Republican role models—the exceptions being Milicent Fenwick, a liberal, pro-abortion, pro-ERA congresswoman; Nancy Kassebaum, a moderate Republican; and Clare Booth Luce, a conservative Republican and an ambassador who was active thirty years ago. A reader would think there are no male Republicans in the country, much less any active conservatives, male or female, of any political stripe during the last twenty years. . . . In short, there is a clear political character of a partisan, liberal bent to these social studies texts.[32]

It *is* instructive to look at the numbers. If we divide by partisan affiliation, a grave disproportion reveals itself: There are 14 Democrats to just 3 Republicans—hardly an accurate representation of the nation. But if we look a little more closely, the disproportion, already grave, explodes. If we divide those chosen as positive models for our children into liberals or people of the left, on the one hand, and conservatives or people of the right, on the other, we find that those on the liberal or left side of the spectrum outnumber those on the conservative or right by *28 to 1* (if Nancy Kassebaum, a "moderate" Republican, is counted as neither). If Kassebaum is treated as a conservative, which does not capture the whole of her voting record, then the ratio of left to right is not 28 to 1, but is halved, to *only* 14 to 1. The silence about conservatives does begin to look like the silence about religion. Conservatism, too, is apparently taboo in our texts. Moreover, given the total absence of *any* male conservative role models, one must suspect that the saving grace of the 3 Republicans was not that they were Republicans or conservatives—only one was clearly that—but that all three were successful, talented women. Of the 30, how many were conservative males? *None.* Of the 30, how many were clearly conservative? *One.* It is difficult, if not impossible, to see this as anything other than conscious or unconscious ideological screening.

Vitz notes that three themes reliably emerge from these texts: minority rights, feminism, and ecological and environmental issues.[33] There is nothing exceptional in that. What is exceptional is that "there are no conservative positions identified or supported in any way in any of these books. For example, there is simply no mention of the anti-ERA movement, the pro-life movement, or opposition to affirmative action, or the tax revolt. The idea that government might be too big, too controlling, is never mentioned."[34] If Vitz is correct, and he was vindicated in his claims about the censorship of religion, then more than religion has been censored from these texts, and the worldview that wields the hand of the censor is clear—it is secular, humanist, and liberal or leftist.

One should add that Paul Vitz, who has catalogued a systematic bias in these books, is not simply a man of the right. Some of those who have doubted his exposure of the pervasive secularism and liberalism of these texts have assumed he is. But in his writings he has attacked the materialism and consumerism of this society and its careerism. He has attacked capitalism as well. These are certainly not themes welcomed by much of the right. But he has also noted that these are features of both the left and right, and he has condemned them both. In *Psychology as Religion: The Cult of Self-worship*, he called for a Christian rather than a leftist or rightist response to our society's problems. And he added that " . . . the usual ideologies of both capitalism and communism are essentially secular, and in their modern forms both are anti-Christian."[35] When Vitz notes a bias against business, as he does, or conservatism, it is not because he is a great admirer of modern capitalism or because he is a typical conservative.

The conclusions derived from the exhaustive study of the texts directed by Vitz are sobering.

These studies make it abundantly clear that public school textbooks commonly exclude the history, heritage, beliefs, and values of millions of Americans. Those who believe in the traditional family are not represented. Those who believe in free enterprise are not represented. Those whose politics are conservative are almost unrepresented. Above all, those who are committed to their religious tradition—at the very least as an important part of the historical record—are not represented.[36]

This censorship of values and positions

makes only the liberal, secular positions familiar and plausible. As a result, the millions of Americans who hold conservative, traditional, and religious positions are made to appear irrelevant, strange, on the fringe, old-fashioned, reactionary. For these countless Americans it is now surely clear that the textbooks used in the public schools threaten the continued existence of their positions.[37]

Vitz, vindicated once, now argues that, in view of the secular and humanistic leadership we now have in education, and its record in screening the texts, the attempt to force religion back into the public schools would result in changes that are merely "superficial—mere tokenism."[38] But if he is correct, he could be too optimistic.

As this is being written, the news is reported that California is going to insist upon the return of religion to its texts. The California superintendent of schools, interviewed on National Public Radio, was asked for examples of what would be inserted. Searching his mind, he came up with three things: the wars of religion in which, he added, millions died; the call for the murder of the author of *The Satanic Verses*; and the movement to religious freedom.[39] All are appropriate, but it is suggestive that two of the things that sprang immediately to mind cast religion in a very poor light, while the third represents virtually the only thing that those who have screened our present texts have felt it necessary to cover concerning religion in America. One is reminded of the dismal conclusion reached by a church historian, Robert Bryan, after surveying the 20 history books approved by the Montgomery County, Maryland, school system:

There is remarkable consensus to the effect that, after 1700, Christianity has no historical presence in America. . . . *These textbooks are written to propound the thesis that America was settled for the sake of religious freedom, and that religious freedom means the absence of religion.* . . . Once the [early Eastern seaboard] settlement has been effected, and the population has escaped the trammels of religion, religion need not be mentioned again. There are exceptions to this general rule, but they are so sporadic as to be incapable of conveying anything like the true importance of religion in America [emphasis in original].⁴⁰

Perhaps, after all, in view of what Vitz and Bryan have discovered, silence about religion would be better than what will be passed through the screen Vitz describes. Passing through such a screen, it is hardly likely that the religion that is returned to the texts will give much comfort to the religious. At the least, like Edmund Burke, one wants to wait to see what is done before one risks congratulations.

A notable, and nonreligious, student of philosophy and culture, Allan Bloom, author of *The Closing of the American Mind*, translator of Plato and Rousseau, and an important commentator on those authors and Shakespeare, among others, gives other grounds for doubt about the adequacy of Justice Clark's approach. The typical modern analysis of texts, he explains, including precisely the comparative religion and Bible as literature approaches mentioned by Justice Clark, fails to take seriously the possible truth of those texts. As Bloom puts it:

One can most clearly see [this] in the case of the Bible. To include it in the humanities is already a blasphemy, a denial of its own claims. There it is almost inevitably treated in one of two ways: It is subjected to modern "scientific" analysis, called the Higher Criticism, where it is dismantled, to show how "sacred" books are put together, and that they are not what they claim to be. It is useful as a mosaic in which one finds the footprints of many dead civilizations. Or else the Bible is used in courses in comparative religion as one expression of the need for the "sacred" and as a contribution to the very modern, very scientific study of the structure of "myths."⁴¹

"Here," he says, "one sees the traces of the Enlightenment's political project, which wanted precisely to render the Bible, and other old books, undangerous."⁴² The "Bible as literature," Bloom notes, does not take the Bible seriously. As he says: "The best that can be done, it appears, is to teach 'The Bible as Literature,' as opposed to 'as Revelation,' which it claims to be. In this way it can be read . . . as we read, for example, *Pride and Prejudice*."⁴³ But the Bible as a compilation of old stories and interesting literary devices is quite different than the Bible as God's revelation to humankind, which is what it claims to be.

Bloom finishes his critique by speaking of the modern critical apparatus ordinarily used in the secular study of the Bible and the modern study of philosophy and literature:

I do not deny that at least some professors love the works they study and teach. But there is a furious effort to make them up-to-date, largely by treating them as the matter formed by some contemporary theory—cultural, historical, economic or psychological. The efforts to read books as their writers intended them to be read has been made into a crime, ever since "the intentional fallacy" was instituted. There are endless debates about methods—among Freudian criticism, Marxist criticism, New Criticism, Structuralism and Deconstructionism, and many other, all of which have in common the premise that what Plato or Dante [or the Bible] had to say about reality is unimportant.[44]

The ordinary substance of the modes of returning religion to the schools favored by Justice Clark is summarized by Bloom as follows: "... comparative religion or comparative literature, i.e., either... indifference or ... a flabby ecumenism compounded out of the lowest common denominator of a variety of old and incompatible crea-tions."[45]

Bloom's critique suggests that the very modes of reintroducing religion into the schools suggested by Justice Clark fail of neutrality. They approach religion from the outside, as the secular do, and fail to take seriously the truth-claims of religion, reducing it to one among many myths, or to mere literature, or to matters of merely historical interest.

Bloom's analysis poses a question to the religious. Would the religious be wise to accept Justice Clark's apparent understanding that it would be sufficient to restore religion to the public schools via the modes of comparative religion and the Bible as literature? Would not one be hard-pressed to find many who think that the effect of a *secular* teaching of comparative religion, as the major mode of studying religion, is to increase students' faith, or to bring them to faith, or even to retain their faith? Would one find many who think that courses in the Bible taught strictly as literature will incline students to take very seriously the possibility that the Bible is revelation from God?

Comparative religion and the Bible as literature, Bloom suggests, would not be very useful to parents who wish their children to gain or retain a faith; indeed, these are favorite modes of the nonreligious in dealing with religion, as religion is approached from the outside, without the necessity of taking very seriously the truth-claims of religion. Such approaches are, in the view of some, quite conducive to an erosion of religion, if not themselves already ordinarily associated with skepticism.

Still, these approaches would get religion back in the schools. In-deed, they might offer a surplus of riches. The Christian majority and the Jewish minority, to take two examples, would find those two faiths returned, to be joined by Islam, Hinduism, Jainism, Confucianism, Buddhism, Shintoism, pantheism, perhaps Greek and Roman religions, or the religions of human sacrifice, and who knows what else? The principal beliefs of each would be taught (competently and sympathetically?) and all summed together as the various religious possibilities. And then students will go on to other classes, where principal aspects of a nonreligious worldview will be taught as truth or science. The religious, if serious about their children's religious upbringing, would be well-advised, if Bloom's analysis is correct, to gather up their resources and send their children to private religious schools. The nonreligious, on the other hand, would have little to fear in Justice Clark's approach.

Justice Clark's approach assumes that in a pluralistic society of fiercely competing worldviews, including the religious and the non-religious, a *secular* education can be provided in the public schools that will be equally fair to all. There is another approach, fundamentally different, which would allow those who believe in Justice Clark's approach to have it for their children, and those who do not believe in that approach to have an education for their children from *within* their own worldview (as the children of humanists *now* have an education from *within their worldview* in the public schools, and as they will continue to under Justice Clark's approach, unlike the religious, who now have an education from within a *secular* worldview, and will continue to do so under Justice Clark's proposal). There is little genuine neutrality in Justice Clark's approach. Let us consider an alternative.

The alternative to a presumably objective treatment of religion in a secular setting is a pluralist educational structure. Such a structure assumes that this society is serious about liberty and diversity, and that if it is serious, it will allow the secular and nonreligious to have a *genuinely* secular education by those who share their naturalistic and humanistic worldview, and the religious to have a *genuinely* religious education by those who share their religion or worldview. It would also allow, of course, those who believe in an entirely objective educa-tion to choose what *they* thought that was. In this view, the pluralist view, the alternatives are a system that purports to be, but cannot be, genuinely neutral between clashing worldviews, and a system that recognizes this nation's commitment to liberty and pluralism by al-lowing parents to have for their children the type of education they, the parents, prefer.

There are various ways of accomplishing a pluralist education. Consider three. One is to honor parents' rights and provide a voucher system so that parents of whatever income can choose the type of education they prefer for their children. This respects the rights of parents, not of whatever group or persuasion happens to control the public schools at the moment. (Those who have enough money already have this option. This approach makes that option, and that freedom, available to all, which is why vouchers are preferable to the more easily obtainable tax credits, which would not give true freedom of choice to the poor or more financially pinched.)

Utilizing vouchers, and allowing parents the power to choose their children's education, parallels, on the elementary and secondary level, what we do already on the college level, where we allow students to use veterans' benefits and other grants and loans "at any accredited institution of higher learning, including religious schools and even seminaries."[46] Indeed, the federal government now provides such educational aid even to minors in the cases of congressional and Supreme Court pages and other congressional employees—again, to be used in either secular or religious schools.[47] Vouchers would respect the freedom of conscience of all, religious and nonreligious, to pursue the education they think appropriate.

There are indications, it may be noted, that many people would prefer this system. Richard Neuhaus reports that:

A Gallup/Phi Delta Kappa Poll indicates that a majority (56%) of American parents prefers voluntary and church-related schools to government schools. Forty-nine percent of parents whose children currently attend government schools say they would send their children to voluntary schools if they had tuition assistance. A recent state-wide poll in Louisiana followed national trends indicating growing support for educational vouchers. *Almost six out of ten favored vouchers, with women more in favor than men, blacks more than whites, low income parents more than the wealthier, those with the most recent experience in the schools more than older people, and those with school-aged children more than those without.*[48]

A few years earlier, another Gallup poll reported that "a majority of respondents in communities where there were already nonpublic schools said that they would prefer to send their children to nonpublic schools." As Paul Weber and Dennis Gilbert summarized the data: "Citizens apparently are not happy with their public schools, and if they could afford it they would make use of alternatives—with sectarian and nonsectarian being chosen in almost equal numbers."[49]

Liberty and pluralism do appeal, and there is nothing in the choices indicated that should frighten either humanists or the religious—as long as they do not wish to *compel* their particular view for everyone else. (And if *that* is their desire, neither the Constitution nor natural justice should impel the nation to accede to their wishes.)

Another method of providing genuine freedom of choice would be a tracking system in public schools. Just as we often track according to type of education sought, now we would track as well, for those who wanted it, according to worldviews. The religious could take one of a number of religious tracks, the nonreligious one of a number of nonreligious tracks. Parents, not others, would determine what type of education their children would receive, and the government would be taken out of the business of taking sides, advertently or inadvertently, between nonreligion and religion.

A third method would allow released time in public schools for systematic presentation of the competing worldviews by those who believe in them to those who wish to receive their presentations. This is less disruptive of our present educational structure, but it would also be less satisfactory to many because it would merely supplement a regular course of instruction that may be systematically oriented toward a different worldview. It would not offer the opportunity to have a whole education built around a coherent worldview.

Any of these methods, though especially the first, would do much to redress the balance and achieve what, in theory, the Court intended all along—to be at least neutral as between religion and nonreligion. None of the Supreme Court decisions has held that it is acceptable to favor nonreligion over religion. Only the practice has done so. Wisdom, and a wise Court, would have the practice conform to the principle.

Still, there are theoretical objections to a genuinely pluralist educational structure. Two demand attention. The first is that such a pluralism would be divisive. There are two replies to that charge. First, this nation is dedicated to liberty. Neither the nation's principles nor its Constitution forbids divisions or requires uniformity of belief or goals. Indeed, the nation cannot be committed to both liberty and to an entire lack of division at the same time. And this century has shown the price paid by nations that seek a coerced uniformity.

More than that, the objection that it would be divisive to allow the religious to have a genuinely religious education is an admission that we gain "non-divisiveness" now by imposing a de facto secularism on all except those who can pay to get out. If divisiveness is the problem, then perhaps we should be thorough, and not allow any of the religious to escape, force all of them into the public schools and admit that what we have in mind *is*, as some religious have charged, to favor nonreligion over religion. Or, since the religious are, after all, a majority, perhaps the logic of nondivisiveness is to compel a religious education upon all. Should we wish either alternative? Do we really want uniformity even at the cost of liberty and constitutional rights? (One can be certain that the A.C.L.U. would not accept the need to avoid divisiveness as an argument for suppressing the rights of anyone possessing a secular worldview. And the A.C.L.U. would be right. But that principle must protect the religious as well.)

A second objection to genuine pluralism in the schools is that we cannot have it because it is forbidden by the Constitution, by the "wall of separation" between church and state. Let us consider that. Let us examine first what the Constitution says, second the understandings and practices of the Founders and the founding generation, third what the justices profess to be doing, and finally what the judges have established that they can do if they wish.

Article VI of the Constitution states that " . . . no religious test shall ever be required as a qualification to any office or public trust under the United States." This is the only mention of religion in the original text of the Constitution. The First Amendment begins: "Congress shall make no law respecting an establishment of religion, or prohibiting the free exercise thereof. . . . " This constitutes what the Constitution has to say about religion. The "wall of separation" phrase is not in the Constitution.

There is heated debate about what the Founders meant. Let us look at what they clearly did *not* mean. First, they clearly did not mean to limit the states. The amendment begins: "Congress shall make no law. . . . " Originally the amendment was a limit on the national government, not on state governments. Indeed, the states clearly could establish a religion, and five of the thirteen still did under the Constitution, and no one thought the First Amendment prevented that. (The five were South Carolina until 1790, under the Constitution but not under the First Amendment ratified in 1791; Maryland until 1810; Connecticut until 1818; New Hampshire until 1819; and Massachusetts until 1833.)[50] States continued, as well, to hold that Christianity was part of the common law well into the nineteenth century, and not only in states with an established religion.[51]

Second, most of the Founders clearly did not intend to establish secularism, or express hostility to religion, or establish a "wall of separation" between the national government and religion. If they did intend those things, they found peculiar ways of expressing their intentions. Walter B. Mead notes, for example, that almost immediately after Congress had passed to the states the proposed Bill of Rights, "they passed a resolution for the observance of a day of public thanksgiving and prayer . . . [for] the many signal favors of Almighty

God." They followed that by creating and paying chaplaincies to serve the Army and both houses of Congress. "And soon religious affirmations were printed on the nation's currency."[52] These, we must admit, are strange ways of establishing secularism or creating a "wall of separation" between church and state.

Even stranger, if the intention was to express hostility to religion, establish secularism, or create a "wall of separation" between church and state, was another action of the same Congress that debated the religion clauses and passed the Bill of Rights on to the states for ratification. As Reichley notes: "... the same first Congress that passed the First Amendment also readopted, with Madison's approval, the Northwest Ordinance of 1787, the third article of which reads: '*Religion, morality, and knowledge, being necessary to good government and the happiness of mankind, schools and the means of learning shall forever be encouraged*' (emphasis added)."[53] This ordinance, one of the great statutes in American history, established a commitment to public education and set forth its purposes. It establishes that the Founders did not intend to establish secularism or to drive religion from the public schools. To the contrary, they helped set up the public schools in part to "promote religious and moral education."

The Northwest Ordinance, repassed by the First Congress, has particular significance for our purposes because it was an act by the national government, to which the First Amendment specifically limited itself, and it specifically dealt with public education, the arena of the current controversy. But it is also true that the *states* were primarily responsible for public education, and they quite generally mixed religious teaching and the public schools.

John W. Whitehead notes that a survey of the record will show that "public schools considered one of their major tasks to be the development of character through the teaching of religion." He cites as examples the *New England Primer*, which "opened with certain religious admonitions followed by the Lord's Prayer, the Apostles' Creed, the Ten Commandments, and the names of the books of the Bible," and the McGuffey *Eclectic Readers*, which stressed "'religion, morality, and knowledge' in that order." Published in 1836, McGuffey's readers sold more than 120 million copies by 1920, which "put them in a class with only the Bible and *Webster's Dictionary*."[54] Through most of this nation's history, it was not thought that the Constitution required us to drive religion from public schools.

Walter Mead notes that "it was not until well into the twentieth century that the Supreme Court began to read into the due process clause of the Fourteenth Amendment a doctrine of strict neutrality on matters of religion at the state level of government, even though there is no evidence of such intention in the thinking of the post-Civil War drafters and ratifiers of that Amendment."[55] There is, however, evidence that it was *not* the intention of that generation to use the Fourteenth Amendment to incorporate the First Amendment religion clauses' restrictions on the national government and apply them to the states and state schools. As Reichley notes: "In 1876 when the Grant administration tried to secure passage of a constitutional amendment that would have prohibited state aid to church-related schools, no one is recorded as having suggested that such aid might already be unconstitutional."[56] That was to await the middle of the next century. (The Grant amendment was aimed at aid to Catholic schools, not at the generalized Protestantism then prevalent in the public schools.) Indeed, even the logic is odd. Justice Potter Stewart thought so. He thought it ironic "that a constitutional provision evidently designed to leave the States free to go their own way should now have become a restriction upon their autonomy."[57]

The founding generation did not intend to establish secularism or drive religion from the schools or the public square. Neither did their successors until the very recent past. Nothing in our history requires us to interpret the Constitution in such a way that it systematically favors secularism over religion, as much of recent constitutional interpretation has in practice. But even in the string of cases which has had the effect of establishing secularism, there are statements by the justices that they do not intend to establish secularism or favor nonreligion over religion. Thus Justice Tom Clark, speaking for the Court, said in *Schempp* that "the State may not establish a 'religion of secularism' in the sense of affirmatively opposing or showing hostility to religion, thus 'preferring those who believe in no religion over those who do believe.'"[58] In practice that is in fact exactly what the Court has done. But the principle is right, and acknowledged, and the time is right to begin applying the principle of refusing to prefer either religion or nonreligion.

Professor Canavan wondered, years ago, whether the Court had not inadvertently established secular humanism while aiming for neutrality. It was not, in view of subsequent practice, an idle question. But if the aim of the Court was neutrality, it is not too late to find adequate ways to reach that goal. The theory of constitutional law involved can be left to others. Paul Weber and Dennis Gilbert have argued, for example, that the Constitution requires "fiscal neutrality," and that parochial schools should be neither advantaged nor penalized in determining eligibility for state aid.[59] That is one approach. There are others.

The Supreme Court itself has seemed to seek some interpretation of the law more neutral than in the past as between the religious and the secular. In 1983 in *Mueller v. Allen* the Court held that Minnesota could allow state taxpayers to claim tax deductions for tuition, textbooks, and transportation at *either* public or private schools. Reichley notes that in practice more than 90 percent of those qualifying had their children in religious schools. But Justice William Rehnquist, writing for the majority (five to four), "held that because the deductions were available to the parents of students in both public and private schools, the Minnesota law could not be considered a support for religion."[60]

There is more than one way to reach the goal, but the goal of a genuine neutrality in the schools between the religious and the non-religious is a requirement of fundamental fairness and equal protection, or equal liberty. It should not be beyond either a jurisprudence of original intent or a jurisprudence of a "growing Constitution" to arrive at a more reasonable and historically justified solution than we now have. An establishment of "secular humanism," to use the term used by both Canavan and Pfeffer, was not the purpose of the First Amendment and violates deep standards of justice and fairness. This nation should find a way to end that establishment, just as it ended the earlier semi-establishment of a generalized Protestantism, and for the same good reasons. The Court should protect the rights of *both* the religious and the secular. It fails that standard today.

A final word: A great many of the religious supported ending the semi-official establishment of religion that forced religion upon the nonreligious. They gave that support because it was right. The measure of humanist integrity today will be an equal willingness to support the ending of the present semi-official establishment of secular and humanist education in favor of a genuine pluralism. Failure to support disestablishment would indicate that what humanists found objectionable in the imposition of religion was not the imposition of an orthodoxy, but merely the imposition of an orthodoxy not their own. Humanists of principle can be counted on to pass this test.

ACKNOWLEDGMENT

This chapter draws upon a paper, "To Favor Neither Religion nor Non-Religion: A Problem in Pluralism," presented at the eleventh Illinois Political Studies Conference in Charleston, Illinois, April 15–17, 1987. It was refocused and greatly revised during professional development assignment time provided by Memphis State University, support which I greatly appreciated.

Response to William R. Marty

Religions and schools: No topic elicits more feeling and less willingness to compromise than this one. Small wonder, since no institution beyond the family takes as much of our children's time or exerts a more formative influence on their intellectual, social, and cultural growth. Parents are required by law in every state to send their children to school through eight grades and/or until they reach some age, usually 16. Governments will pay for that schooling in public schools from which religion in recent years has been carefully and consciously excluded. If parents choose, they may elect to send their children to private, even religious schools totally at their own expense. Such schools must teach an array of secular subjects mandated by the states. Meanwhile parents must, along with all other taxpayers, continue to support public schools, which schools, many parents believe, actively promote a competing worldview sometimes called secular humanism.

Is such "double taxation" and the coercive enticement of a free education devoid of religion (for those who choose public schools), a fair and just arrangement? Marty says no, there is a major injustice inherent in the current public school structure. Others, including Dean Kelley and James Dunn, disagree. Keeping religion out of the public schools neither advances nor burdens religion; it simply keeps it separate and dependent on its own resources. Nor does such separation create a vacuum filled by a secular humanist worldview. Who is right?

Marty spells out as well as anyone I have read the conservative Christian lament about the public schools. His is a pessimistic assessment which documents the "nonreligious" and liberal biases in public school texts. All things considered, however, I am not persuaded. A recent poll indicated that 94 percent of Americans believe in God; 77 percent believe in an afterlife.[61] Presumably that 94 percent includes the vast majority of schoolteachers. To believe that they consciously or unwittingly teach something contrary to their own beliefs stretches credulity. As for the liberal bias in texts, perhaps so. But if that is the case they have been an astounding failure. Not only have we elected conservative presidents five out of the last six times, but opinion polls show a steady movement to the right. And unless Marty's students at Memphis State are markedly different from mine at the University of Louisville, they are as conservative now as students were liberal in 1968, and definitely more religious!

A great deal of research remains to be done on the impact an equal-separation theory of the religious clauses would have on the schools, but I see the impact as developing along the following lines.

PUBLIC SCHOOLS

Unlike Marty I am optimistic about public schools on one count precisely because equal separation seems to be gaining popularity. Religious voluntary groups are now treated on the same level as other voluntary groups, and the recent effort by conservative, liberal, and various church groups to support teaching *about* religion will soon begin to bring the study of religion back from exile to end the distortion of history, literature, and social studies that exile caused.

Marty rejects the compromise because (1) religion cannot be taught with complete objectivity, and (2) the essential core of any religion— that it tells *the truth*—is absent. As an equal separationist, here I would emphasize the separation aspect. It is emphatically *not* the business of government to teach the true religion in the public schools. (I shudder to think what would be taught in the name of truth! Which truths of which religion would be taught? Since I disagree with several tenets of my own faith community, I would not want even the official version of my own religion taught in the public schools!) Apparently Marty agrees, for he offers no resolution except to abandon the public schools. Equal separation requires no such step.[62]

Before leaving the public school question, there is one aspect which is profoundly disturbing, and perhaps to which equal separation can make a contribution, that is, the utter failure of schools in poverty-stricken areas to provide the skills, ambition, and discipline for students to succeed. Perhaps we ask too much of them, but study after study shows that parochial schools *in the same areas* perform far better on less resources with fewer dropouts, fewer expulsions, and substantially more graduates attending colleges.[63] Surely there is a lesson to be learned here. The nation needs to develop a funding system that encourages imaginative, innovative—or traditional, for that matter— approaches to teaching the poor, the retarded, the handicapped, those children coming out of chaotic homes and those immersed in the drug culture. Ignorance and deprivation are not enough. In the major cities integration has failed. "Today's public education system is a failed monopoly—bureaucratic, rigid and in unsteady control of a dissatisfied captive market," says David T. Kearns, the chairman of the Xerox Corporation.[64] Perhaps the time has come for vision, challenge, and experimentation, whether by business groups, fraternal service organizations, or religious groups. Could tax-supported private schools provide a window of opportunity? We now turn to that consideration.

PRIVATE SCHOOLS

Marty poses the question about public funding of private education in a provocative and controversial context: If this society is serious about liberty and diversity, he claims, "it will allow the secular and nonreligious to have a genuinely secular education ... and the religious to have a genuinely religious education. ... " This pluralist schema could be funded in one of three ways: vouchers, which are essentially checks, given to parents of school-age children, that can only be cashed at the school of their choice; a religious tracking system in the public schools, and released-time programs. One might add a fourth, tax credits for school-related expenditures. Marty prefers the voucher system as giving the greatest amount of freedom over tax credits because vouchers show more promise for equity for the lower economic strata.

What about vouchers? Under the equal separation theory vouchers would be constitutional, as are tax credits. Parents could "cash" their vouchers at any school of their choice, like supermarkets, filling stations, and medieval universities; schools thrive, survive, or fold based on their ability to attract and retain students. This is nothing new; many scholars believe vouchers are constitutional under current standards.

But are vouchers necessary or required under an equal-separation theory? Are they sound policy? One can certainly acknowledge and sympathize with Marty's concern for liberty and diversity, but these must be balanced with other values—equality, integration, and fiscal responsibility for starters. Opponents of vouchers fear (1) a skimming of potential leaders, not only the wealthy, but the educationally interested, the capable, the ambitious, and the disciplined, from the "unchosen" public schools, leaving only the truly disadvantaged and troubled; (2) the creation of privileged, protected enclaves afraid to mingle, (3) the creation of religiously and ethically isolated islands, a balkanized educational system, (4) the loss of input into the broader educational system from religious and moral leaders, (5) the enormous potential cost of such a system. The truth is that private schools save taxpayers billions of dollars annually; public schools could not support the additional influx of students if religious schools were suddenly to close, at least not without monstrous tax increases. The same financial burden would develop if a voucher system were created, and (6) there remains a deep-seated revulsion on the part of some against tax funds going to Catholic schools, even if it travels indirectly through the parents. In brief, a full-blown voucher system might create more problems than it solves.

Nevertheless, there are appealing aspects to the voucher concept. Giving parents and children more choices and greater control improves educational achievement. Alliances of business and education can achieve positive results. Religious schools do a better job of educating poor children than public schools. Even public enterprises do better when faced with competition.[65] These values are in addition to the liberty and diversity of which Marty writes.

What is clear is that vouchers are not a means to receive tax funds without government control; states will regulate and monitor closely those schools certified to "cash" vouchers. Such schools could expect to be required to accept a proportional share of the handicapped and economically disadvantaged, to teach a required curriculum, etc. However, for those groups willing to accept the challenge of teaching the poor and disadvantaged, whether religious or not, perhaps a voucher plan available to parents at the low end of the economic spectrum is worthy of further research and experimentation.

NOTES

1. Francis Canavan, S.J., "The Impact of Recent Supreme Court Decisions on Religion in the United States," *Journal of Church and State* 16 (Spring 1974):236.

2. Leo Pfeffer, "Issues That Divide: The Triumph of Secular Humanism," *Journal of Church and State* 19 (Spring 1977):203–216.

3. Ibid., p. 207.

4. Ibid., p. 209.

5. See Richard John Neuhaus, *The Naked Public Square: Religion and Democracy in America* (Grand Rapids, MI: Wm. Eerdmans, 1984).

6. Pfeffer, "Issues That Divide," p. 211.

7. Ibid., p. 213.

8. Ibid., p. 216.

9. Ibid., p. 211.

10. Canavan, "Impact of Recent Supreme Court Decisions," p. 224.

11. Michael W. McConnell, "Neutrality Under the Religion Clauses," *Northwestern University Law Review* 81 (Fall 1986):162.

12. Robert Marquand, "Textbooks Fail to Give Religion Credit for Its Impact on American History, Reports Say," *The Christian Science Monitor*, June 2, 1986, pp. 3–4.

13. Robert Marquand, "Right from Wrong: Finding a Way to Teach Values in the Schools," *Commercial Appeal* (Memphis), April 5, 1987, p. E.1.

14. Allen E. Bergin, "Psychotherapy and Religious Values," *Journal of Consulting and Clinical Psychology* 48, 1 (1980): 98.

15. Marquand, "Right from Wrong," p. E.1.

16. For criticisms of the values relativism approaches, see Bergin, "Psychotherapy and Religious Values"; Paul C. Vitz, *Psychology as Religion: The Cult of Self-Worship* (Grand Rapids, MI: Wm. Eerdmans, 1977); and William Kirk Kilpatrick, *Psychological Seduction: The Failure of Modern Psychology* (New York: Thomas Nelson, 1983) and *The Emperor's New Clothes: The Naked Truth About the New Psychology* (Westchester, IL: Crossway, 1985).

17. Langdon Gilkey, "Creationism: The Roots of the Conflict," *Christianity and Crisis*, April 26, 1982, p. 111.

18. Paul C. Vitz, *Censorship: Evidence of Bias in Our Children's Textbooks* (Ann Arbor, MI: Servant Books, 1986), pp. 3 and 61–76.

19. Marquand, "Right from Wrong," p. E.1.

20. Cited in A. James Reichley, *Religion in American Public Life* (Washington, D.C.: The Brookings Institution, 1985), p. 165.

21. Cited in Richard John Neuhaus, *The Naked Public Square: Religion and Democracy in America* (Grand Rapids, MI: Wm. Eerdmans, 1984), p. 80.

22. "By all the indices of public opinion surveys, most Americans regard religion as either 'very important' (56 percent in 1984 according to Gallup) or 'fairly important' (30 percent) in their personal lives. More than 90 percent of Americans indicate some kind of religious attachment, all but about 2 percent within the Judeo-Christian tradition." Reichley, *Religion in American Public Life*, p. 360. See Kenneth D. Wald's interesting discussion of just how exceptional American religious vitality is in his chapter, "A Secular Society?" in his book, *Religion and Politics in the United States* (New York: St. Martins, 1987), pp. 1–21.

23. Secularists are joined, of course, by many of the religious, who pursue a very strict separation of church and state for a number of reasons, including the desire to be fair to the nonreligious and the desire to avoid contamination of religion by the use of it or regulation of it by government. Secularists in the A.C.L.U. are thus joined often by Baptists, among others. Governments appear less and less ready to allow religious institutions control over their own internal affairs, however, whether or not tax monies go to those institutions in any significant amount.

24. "The Williamsburg Charter: A National Celebration and Reaffirmation of the First Amendment Religious Liberty Clauses," *This World* 24 (Winter 1989):46–47.

25. Joseph Sobran, *Single Issues: Essays on the Crucial Social Questions*, 3rd ed. (New York: Human Life Press, 1983), p. 117.

26. "Religion in the Public School Curriculum: Questions and Answers," Baptist Joint Committee on Public Affairs, 200 Maryland Ave., N.E., Washington, D.C. 20002.

27. Ibid.

28. Vitz, *Censorship*, p. 83.

29. Ibid., p. 86.

30. Ibid., p. 88.

31. Ibid., p. 40.

32. Ibid., pp. 39 and 41.

33. Ibid., p. 41.

34. Ibid.

35. Vitz, *Psychology as Religion*, p. 111.

36. Vitz, *Censorship*, p. 77.

37. Ibid., pp. 77–78.

38. Ibid., p. 83.

39. National Public Radio morning broadcast, March 7, 1989.

40. Cited in Vitz, *Censorship*, p. 59.

41. Allan Bloom, *The Closing of the American Mind* (New York: Simon and Schuster, 1987), p. 374. Bloom's comments concern the techniques of analysis. They do not refer to the school controversy.

42. Ibid., p. 374.

43. Ibid., pp. 374–75.

44. Ibid., p. 375.

45. Ibid., p. 308.

46. Michael W. McConnell, "Political and Religious Disestablishment," *Brigham Young University Law Review* (1986):425.

47. Paul J. Weber and Dennis A. Gilbert, *Private Churches and Public Money: Church-Government Fiscal Relations* (Westport, CT: Greenwood Press, 1981), p. 172.

48. *The Religion and Society Report* 4 (May 1987):8.

49. Weber and Gilbert, *Private Churches and Public Money*, p. 167. Weber and Gilbert deal with concerns that such aid would increase segregation, amount to a tax break for the wealthy, and harm public schools. They conclude that it would do none of these, but they do observe that "there is something profoundly disturbing in the realization that public school students would flee to private schools at considerable added expense if given even a modest incentive," p. 169.

50. Reichley, *Religion in American Public Life*, p. 111.

51. John W. Whitehead, *The Freedom of Religious Expression in the Public High Schools* (Westchester, IL: Crossway Books, 1983), pp. 5–6.

52. Walter B. Meade, *United States Constitution: Personalities, Principles, and Issues* (Columbia, SC: University of South Carolina Press, 1987), p. 207.

53. Ibid.

54. Whitehead, *Freedom of Religious Expression*, pp. 5–6.

55. Meade, *United States Constitution*, p. 207.

56. Reichley, *Religion in American Public Life*, p. 119–120.

57. Cited in George Anastaplo, "The Religion Clauses of the First Amendment," *Memphis State University Law Review* 11 (1980–81):183–84.

58. Whitehead, *Freedom of Religious Expression*, p. 16.

59. Weber and Gilbert, *Private Churches and Public Money*, pp. 165–180 and 185–190.

60. Reichley, *Religion in American Public Life*, p. 163.

61. *Newsweek* poll, March 27, 1989, p. 53; 58 percent believe there is a hell and 6 percent think they have a good or excellent chance of getting there.

62. Marty does not raise the issue, but it should be mentioned that common prayer in public schools is not compatible with equal separation. Private prayers and moments of silence are compatible.

63. For a fascinating analysis, see John E. Chubb and Terry M. Moe, "Politics, Markets and the Organization of Schools," *American Political Science Review*, vol. 82, no. 4, (December 1988). Also, James S. Coleman and Thomas Hoffer, *Public and Private High Schools* (New York: Basic Books, 1987).

64. As quoted in the *New York Times*, Monday, July 11, 1988, p. 13.

65. See in support of these statements, "Public Services Found Better if Private Agencies Compete," *New York Times*, April 26, 1988, p. 1; "Giving Parents a Choice," *Newsweek*, September 19, 1988, p. 77; "A Blueprint for Better Schools," *U.S. News and World Report*, January 18, 1988, p. 60.

6

Thomas Jefferson's "Wall": Absolute or Serpentine?

Robert M. Healey

In his chapter advocating the doctrine of "strict neutrality" as the constitutional foundation for interpreting the religion clauses of the First Amendment, Paul Weber states that in the American consciousness "separation of church and state" apparently sums up the meaning of the First Amendment precisely because the phrase is broad enough to embrace a wide variety of beliefs and practices. He notes that "separation" is really a *generic* term having at least five distinct meanings, and that the resulting ability of groups espousing conflicting political agendas to "wrap themselves in the mantle of the Constitution" often leads to confusion. For this reason it may be instructive here to review the Supreme Court's past use of the doctrine of "separation," and the influence of the "wall" metaphor in which that doctrine is often couched. That is the purpose of the following essay, which, except for its final six paragraphs, originally appeared in *Journal of Church and State* 30 (Autumn 1988): 441–462.

"Averse to receive addresses, yet unable to prevent them, I have generally endeavored to turn them to some account, by making them the occasion, by way of answer, of sowing useful truths and principles among the people, which might germinate and become rooted among their political tenets. The Baptist address, now enclosed, admits to a condemnation of the alliance of Church and State, under the authority of the Constitution. . . . "[1] So wrote President Thomas Jefferson on 1 January 1802 concerning a request by the Danbury Baptist Association in Connecticut to designate a day of fasting in connection with the nation's past ordeals[2] and his reply with its eye-catching metaphor, "a wall of separation between church and state."[3]

This phrase, which appears nowhere else in Jefferson's writings, became one of his permanent contributions to our political lexicon, a rallying cry for many Americans who perceive threats to their religious freedom. It found its way into our judicial lexicon as well, initially appearing in the literature of the Supreme Court in 1879 in *Reynolds v. United States*.[4] It is commonly believed that Chief Justice Morrison Waite in *Reynolds v. United States* declared for the Court that the metaphor itself "may be accepted almost as an authoritative declaration of the scope and effect of the amendment"; however, Waite was referring to something much more substantial than a figure of speech.[5]

In *Reynolds* the Court unanimously upheld the authority of Congress to prohibit bigamy in territory under its jurisdiction against a challenge under the free exercise clause of the First Amendment. The Court's opinion pointed out that since religion is not defined in the Constitution, one must go to the history of the times when the First Amendment was adopted to ascertain its meaning and the religious freedom that has been guaranteed. Having briefly described the attempts made by some colonies and states before the adoption of the Constitution to legislate concerning religion, and the controversy in Virginia which led to the enacting of Jefferson's Statute for Establishing Religious Freedom, Waite commented, "In the preamble of this Act . . . religious freedom is defined; and after a recital 'that to suffer the civil magistrate to intrude his powers into the field of opinion, and to restrain the profession or propagation of principles on supposition of their ill tendency, is a dangerous fallacy which at once destroys all religious liberty,' it is declared 'that it is time enough for the rightful purposes of civil government for its officers to interfere when principles break out into overt acts against peace and good order.' In these two sentences is found the true distinction between what properly belongs to the church and what to the State."

Waite next related Jefferson's personal disappointment at the absence of an express declaration guaranteeing religious freedom in the proposed Constitution of the United States, and the successful efforts of the First Congress to adopt such an amendment. The Chief Justice continued:

Mr. Jefferson afterwards, in reply to an address to him by a committee of the Danbury Baptist Association . . . took occasion to say: "Believing with you that religion is a matter which lies solely between man and his God, that he owes account to none other for his faith or his worship, that the legislative powers of government reach actions only, and not opinions,—I contemplate with sovereign reverence that act of the whole American people which declared that their legislature should 'make no law respecting an establishment of religion, or prohibiting the free exercise thereof,' thus building a wall of separation between church and State. Adhering to this expression of the supreme will of the nation on behalf of the rights of conscience, I shall see with sincere satisfaction the progress of those sentiments which tend to restore to man all his natural rights, convinced he has no natural right in opposition to his social duties."

The Chief Justice was thus referring to the entire paragraph when he next stated: "Coming as this does from an acknowledged leader of the advocates of the measure, it may be accepted almost as an authoritative declaration of the scope and effect of the amendment thus secured." And in the following sentence the Chief Justice laid down the standard by which *Reynolds* had been decided: "Congress was deprived of all legislative power over mere opinion, but was left free to reach actions which were in violation of social duties or subversive of good order."[6] Waite's quotations both make the same point: the distinction between what properly belongs to the church and to the state lies in the difference between principles and acts. The legislative powers of government reach actions, not opinions. Waite did not mention the "wall" metaphor. Although it was part of the quoted paragraph, other Jeffersonian sentences supplied the standards for deciding the case.

The metaphor was not to be invoked in a Supreme Court judicial opinion concerning free exercise for another 68 years. The same is true of establishment cases. Until *Everson v. Board of Education* in 1947[7] the attitude reflected in Supreme Court decisions could be consistently typified by the sentence "This is a religious people" or one of its variants, which has been traced back to Chief Justice Joseph Story's reference to Pennsylvania as a "Christian country" in *Vidal v. Girard's Executors*.[8] In 1892, Justice David Josiah Brewer applied the concept to the whole United States with the words: "No purpose of action against religion can be imputed to any legislation, State or Nation, because this is a religious people. This is historically true." In defense of this contention Brewer cited the commissions of early explorers, colonial charters and constitutions, the federal Constitution, the religion clauses of the First Amendment, and various court opinions. Then, after a cursory glance at American life as expressed by its laws, business, customs, and society, Brewer concluded: "These and many other matters which might be noticed, add a volume of unofficial declarations to the mass of organic utterances that this is a Christian nation."[9]

The judicial stresses and strains to which the concept of a "Christian nation" might be subject surfaced in 1931 in *United States v. Macintosh*, in which the Court denied American citizenship to theologian D. C. Macintosh. Delivering the opinion of the Court, Justice George Sutherland explained:

> When he [Macintosh] speaks of putting his allegiance to the will of God above his allegiance to the government . . . he means to make *his own interpretation* of the will of God the decisive test which will conclude the government and stay its hand. We are a Christian people, according to one another the equal right of religious freedom, and acknowledging with reverence the duty of obedience to the will of God. But, also, we are a nation with a duty to survive; a nation whose Constitution contemplates war as well as peace; whose government must go forward on the assumption, and safely can proceed on no other, that unqualified allegiance to the nation and submission and obedience to the laws of the land, as well those made for war as those made for peace, are not inconsistent with the will of God.[10]

The question of exemption on grounds of conscience from generally applicable laws of the land was to provide the opportunity for Jefferson's metaphor to "germinate and become rooted" in the decision process of our highest bench.

As a formula to be invoked in Supreme Court opinions, the phrase "separation of church and state" (but not Jefferson's metaphor) made its debut in *West Virginia v. Barnette*. Dissenting from the ruling that struck down a compulsory flag salute for Jehovah's Witnesses' children attending public school, Justice Felix Frankfurter argued that a religion-based exemption from a generally applicable law amounts to official establishment of the faith of those exempted, in contradiction to "separation of church and state."

> The essence of the religious freedom guaranteed by our Constitution is therefore this: no religion shall either receive the state's support or incur its hostility. Religion is outside the sphere of political government. This does not mean that all matters on which religious organizations or beliefs may pronounce are outside the sphere of government. Were this so, instead of the separation of church and state, there would be subordination of the state on any matter deemed within the sovereignty of religious conscience. Much that is the concern of temporal authority affects the spiritual interests of men. But it is not enough to strike down a nondiscriminatory law that it may hurt or offend some dissident view. . . . That claims are pressed on behalf of sincere religious convictions does not itself establish their constitutional validity.

... Otherwise the doctrine of separation of church and state, so cardinal in the history of this nation and for the liberty of our people, would mean not the disestablishment of a state church but the establishment of all churches and of all religious groups.[11]

Frankfurter cited no sources for these comments, and he alone of the justices writing in *Barnette* invoked the doctrine of separation of church and state. Matters would be different four years later. What had germinated in *Barnette* would come to full flower in *Everson v. Board of Education*.

In *Everson* the Supreme Court extended the First Amendment establishment clause to the states under the Fourteenth Amendment. In the opinion of the Court, Justice Hugo Black wrote a definition of the establishment clause.

The "establishment of religion" clause of the First Amendment means at least this: Neither a state nor the Federal Government can set up a church. Neither can pass laws which aid one religion, aid all religions, or prefer one religion over another. Neither can force nor influence a person to go to or to remain away from church against his will or force him to profess a belief or disbelief in any religion. No person can be punished for entertaining or professing religious beliefs or disbeliefs, for church attendance or non-attendance. No tax in any amount, large or small, can be levied to support any religious activities or institutions, whatever they may be called, or whatever form they may adopt to teach or practice religion. Neither a state nor the Federal Government can, openly or secretly, participate in the affairs of any religious organizations or groups and *vice versa*. In the words of Jefferson, the clause against establishment of religion by law was intended to erect "a wall of separation between church and state."

Here Black cited *Reynolds* (the only Supreme Court decision used to validate Jefferson's metaphor) and in conclusion reemphasized his point: "The First Amendment has erected a wall between church and state. That wall must be kept high and impregnable. We could not approve the slightest breach."[12]

Felix Frankfurter was no longer alone. The justices unanimously approved his "cardinal" doctrine—only to find themselves split, five to four, on the decision whether tax-defrayed bus transportation for children attending sectarian schools is a constitutional safety measure or unconstitutional support for a religious activity or institution. With reference to the "wall of separation," Justice Black declared, "New Jersey has not breached it here." To which Justice Robert Jackson replied, "The undertones of the [Court's] opinion, advocating complete and uncompromising separation of Church from State, seem utterly discordant with its conclusion yielding support to their commingling in educational matters."[13] Justice Wiley Rutledge, writing for all four dissenters, objected: "The Amendment forbids any appropriation, large or small, from public funds to aid or support any and all religious exercises. . . . The Constitution requires, not comprehensive identification of state with religion, but complete separation."[14]

This unanimous commitment to Black's *Everson* definition of the meaning of the establishment clause was undiluted a year later in *McCollum v. Board of Education*, in which all four *Everson* dissenters joined with all but one of the *Everson* majority to rule that the released-time religious education program as administered in the Champaign, Illinois, public school system violated the establishment clause. In his opinion of the Court, Justice Black both repeated verbatim his *Everson* definition and quoted *Everson's* dissenting opinions.[15] However, elsewhere symptoms were appearing that the unanimity even on theory eventually might crumble.

Justice Frankfurter's concurring opinion was from start to finish an exposition and defense of the doctrine of separation.[16] Frankfurter saw separation of church and state as the great, voluntarily affirmed American historical tradition, particularly with reference both to public and nonpublic education. On the one hand, "By 1875 the separation of public education from Church entanglements, of the State from the teaching of religion, was firmly established in the consciousness of the nation."[17] On the other hand, "The major efforts of religious inculcation were a recognition of the principle of Separation by the establishment of church schools privately supported."[18] According to Frankfurter, that separation was absolute:

> Separation is a requirement to abstain from fusing functions of Government and of religious sects, not merely to treat them all equally. . . . Separation means separation, not something less. Jefferson's metaphor in describing the relation between Church and State speaks of a "wall of separation," not of a fine line easily overstepped. . . . "The great American principle of eternal separation" . . . is one of the vital reliances of our Constitutional system for assuring unities among our people stronger than our diversities. It is the Court's duty to enforce this principle in its full integrity.
>
> We renew our conviction that "we have staked the very existence of our country on the faith that complete separation between the state and religion is best for the state and best for religion."[19]

Despite this clarion commitment, Frankfurter's opinion also reveals problems. For one, Frankfurter admitted that precise application is not easy. "This case, in the light of the *Everson* decision, demonstrates anew that the mere formulation of a relevant Constitutional principle is the beginning of the solution of a problem, not its answer. This is so because the meaning of a spacious conception like that of the separation of Church from State is unfolded as appeal is made to the principle from case to case.... Agreement, in the abstract, that the First Amendment was designed to erect 'a wall of separation between church and state,' does not preclude a clash of views as to what the wall separates.... Accommodation of legislative freedom cannot be achieved by a mere phrase."[20] Further on Frankfurter commented that "we are dealing not with a full-blown principle, nor one having the definiteness of a surveyor's metes and bounds."[21] In other words, the method of applying this constitutional "test" is neither self-evident nor clear. Furthermore, although Frankfurter not only called separation "absolute" but twice deliberately termed it "eternal," he conceded at one point that separation is not necessary to a free society with the remark, "A totally different situation elsewhere, as illustrated for instance by the English provisions for religious education in State-maintained schools, only serves to illustrate that free societies are not cast in one mould.... Different institutions evolve from different historical circumstances."[22]

Justice Robert Jackson also doubted severely the capacity of the Court in all cases to separate the sacred from secular in our culture, especially in education. He argued:

The task of separating the secular from the religious in education is one of magnitude, intricacy and delicacy.... It is idle to pretend that this task is one for which we can find in the Constitution one word to help us as judges to decide where the secular ends and the sectarian begins in education. Nor can we find guidance in any other legal source. It is a matter on which we can find no law but our own prepossessions. If with no surer legal guidance we are to take up and decide every variation of this controversy ... we are likely to make the legal 'wall of separation between church and state' as winding as the famous serpentine wall designed by Mr. Jefferson for the University he founded."[23]

One member of the *Everson* majority, Justice Stanley Reed, became the single dissenter in *McCollum*. Reed maintained that from the opinions of his fellow justices he could not tell just what in the Champaign weekday religious education plan they had ruled unconstitutional, that the Court apparently intended to declare the plan to be "an establishment of religion," but that "the phrase 'an establishment of religion' may have been intended by Congress to be aimed only at a state church." Passing years, he admitted, had brought about a broader meaning, but nothing as broad as *McCollum*.[24] Reed read history quite differently from Frankfurter. He held that "the incidental advantages that religious bodies, with other groups similarly situated, obtained as a by-product of organized society" had previously passed the test of constitutionality.[25] "This is an instance where, for me, the history of past practices is determinative of the meaning of a constitutional clause, not a decorous introduction to the study of its text."[26]

Reed had approved Black's definition of the establishment clause in *Everson*. He reaffirmed it now but challenged the interpretation that otherwise swept the field in *McCollum*. Insisting that the Champaign released-time religious education course was in no way contrary to the Court's position in *Everson*, Reed argued,

> It seems clear to me that the "aid" referred to by the Court in the *Everson* case could not have been those incidental advantages that religious bodies, with other groups similarly situated, obtain as a by-product of organized society. This explains the well-known fact that all churches receive "aid" from government in the form of freedom from taxation. The *Everson* decision itself justified the transportation of children to church schools by New Jersey for safety reasons. . . . While obviously in these instances the respective churches, in a certain sense, were aided, this Court has never held that such "aid" was in violation of the First or Fourteenth Amendment.[27]

Reed went on to construe the phrase "wall of separation between church and state" in light of Jefferson's proposal as rector of the University of Virginia that students be permitted to attend denominational schools established on the university confines. In Reed's estimate, "Thus, the 'wall of separation between church and state' that Mr. Jefferson built at the University which he founded did not exclude religious education from that school. The difference between the generality of his statements on the separation of church and state and the specificity of his conclusions on education are considerable. A rule of law should not be drawn from a figure of speech."[28]

The Court was going to shift in Justice Reed's direction. In *Zorach v. Clauson* the Supreme Court sustained a New York released-time religious education program which, unlike the system struck down in *McCollum*, was held off the public school premises. In the opinion of the Court, Justice William O. Douglas rejected the claim that the New

York program violated either the free exercise or the establishment clauses through coercion. As for the doctrine of separation of church and state, he declared, "There cannot be the slightest doubt that the First Amendment reflects the philosophy that Church and State should be separated. And so far as interference with the 'free exercise' of religion and an 'establishment' of religion are concerned, the separation must be complete and unequivocal. The First Amendment within the scope of its coverage permits no exception; the prohibition is absolute." But Douglas immediately qualified this strong and apparently uncompromising language by announcing that the First Amendment "does not say that in every and all respects there shall be a separation of Church and State. Rather it studiously defines the manner, the specific ways, in which there shall be no concert or union or dependency one on the other."

After listing eight traditional American practices and customs that would have to be abandoned in a climate of alienation caused by pressing separation of church and state too far, Douglas gave three examples of ways in which public schools commonly excused pupils temporarily from class attendance for religious reasons. He concluded, "The teacher in other words cooperates in a religious program to the extent of making it possible for her students to participate in it."[29]

Douglas's justification of this common public school practice was reminiscent of the "this is a religious people" tradition of Justice Brewer.[30] According to Douglas:

We are a religious people whose institutions presuppose a Supreme Being. We guarantee the freedom to worship as one chooses. We make room for as wide a variety of beliefs and creeds as the spiritual needs of man deem necessary. We sponsor an attitude on the part of government that shows no partiality to any one group and that lets each flourish according to the zeal of its adherents and the appeal of its dogma. When the state encourages religious instruction or cooperates with religious authorities by adjusting the schedule of public events to sectarian needs, it follows the best of our traditions. For it then respects the religious nature of our people and accommodates the public service to their spiritual needs.... The government must be neutral when it comes to competition between sects. It may not thrust any sect on any person. It may not make a religious observance compulsory. It may not coerce anyone to attend church, to observe a religious holiday, or to take religious instruction. But it can close its doors or suspend its operations as to those who want to repair to their religious sanctuary for worship or instruction.

In summary, Douglas declared: "We follow the *McCollum* case. But we cannot expand it to cover the present released-time program unless separation of Church and State means that public institutions can make no adjustments of their schedules to accommodate the religious needs of the people. We cannot read into the Bill of Rights such a philosophy of hostility to religion."[31]

It was now Justice Black's turn to dissent, in company with Justices Frankfurter and Jackson, who could discern no significant distinction between the *McCollum* and *Zorach* programs. They held that, contrary to the opinion of the Court, the *Zorach* program did rely on coercion. Black cited *McCollum*, maintaining that both then and in *Zorach* the state afforded "sectarian groups an invaluable aid in that it helps to provide pupils for their religious classes through the use of the State's compulsory public school machinery. *This* is no separation of Church and State." Aware that the *McCollum* decision had provoked widespread criticism and controversy, Black declared: "In dissenting today, I mean to do more than give routine approval to our *McCollum* decision. I mean also to reaffirm my faith in the fundamental philosophy expressed in *McCollum* and *Everson*." To the contention that the *Zorach* decision was justified because Americans are a religious people, Black replied, "It was precisely because Eighteenth Century Americans were a religious people divided into many fighting sects that we were given the constitutional mandate to keep Church and State completely separate. . . . Now as then, it is only by wholly isolating the state from the religious sphere and compelling it to be completely neutral, that the freedom of each and every denomination and of all nonbelievers can be maintained."[32]

Justice Frankfurter in dissent obviously felt deserted by the majority of his brethren but managed to keep a stiff upper lip. "The result in the *McCollum* case . . . was based on principles that received unanimous acceptance by this Court, barring only a single vote. I agree with Mr. Justice Black that those principles are disregarded in reaching the result in this case. Happily they are not disavowed by the Court. From this I draw the hope that in future variations of the problem which are bound to come here, these principles may again be honored in the observance."[33] Justice Jackson also felt that principles once almost unanimously endorsed were now being disregarded, nor could he in closing resist firing off two bitter parting shots: "The wall which the Court was professing to erect between Church and State has become even more warped and twisted than I expected. Today's judgment will be more interesting to students of psychology and of the judicial processes than to students of constitutional law."[34]

These acid comments were really symptoms that the "wall" was in trouble. The earlier spell cast by the metaphor had broken. Douglas's brief description of the requirements of the First Amendment exposed the limitations of the doctrine as a test. One could apply it consistently only by ignoring the fact that throughout much of American life, especially in education, it is almost impossible to separate the religious from the secular.

Nevertheless, the doctrine continued to play a role in later cases. Justice Black, for instance, never retreated from his original stand. His opinion of the Court in *Torcaso v. Watkins* repeated his *Everson* definition (complete with Jefferson's metaphor), recalled the justices' near unanimity on principle in *Everson* and *McCollum*, and quoted Frankfurter on separation between the state and religion in *McCollum*.[35] Similarly, in the opinion of the Court for *Engel v. Vitale*, Black held that "the State's use of the Regents' prayer in its public school system breaches the constitutional wall of separation between Church and State," and quoted passages by Roger Williams, "one of the earliest exponents of the doctrine of separation of church and state."[36] Justice Frankfurter, concurring on sustaining Sunday-closing laws in *McGowan v. Maryland*, reiterated. "The not rigidly precise but revealing phrase 'separation of church and state' . . . is not a self-defining concept"; and "agreement in the abstract that the First Amendment was designed to erect 'a wall of separation between church and state' does not preclude a clash of views as to what the wall separates."[37]

By contrast, one observes growing wrath in Justice Potter Stewart concerning the "wall." His dissent in *Engel v. Vitale* included, "Moreover, I think that the Court's task, in this as in all other areas of constitutional adjudication, is not responsibly aided by the uncritical invocation of metaphors like the 'wall of separation,' a phrase nowhere to be found in the Constitution."[38] Dissenting again in *Abington v. Schempp*, he protested, "The First Amendment declares that 'Congress shall make no law respecting an establishment of religion, or prohibiting the free exercise thereof. . . . ' It is, I think, a fallacious oversimplification to regard these two provisions as establishing a single constitutional standard of 'separation of church and state' which can be mechanically applied in every case to delineate the required boundaries between government and religion. . . . The two relevant clauses of the First Amendment cannot accurately be reflected in a sterile metaphor which by its very nature may distort rather than illumine the problems involved in a particular case."

Stewart decried "the ritualistic invocation of the nonconstitutional phrase," but his objections, like those of Justice Reed in *McCollum*, did not win the day.[39] The Supreme Court, like many another conservative institution, has great difficulty abandoning or repudiating whatever it has resoundingly affirmed. If such a need arises, a preferred procedure is to honor the *whole* tradition publicly, simultaneously deemphasize or lighten the stress on aspects grown troublesome, and fashion a new approach that avoids direct denial. This was Justice Tom Clark's method when explaining the invalidation of public school Bible-reading ceremonies in the Court opinion of *Schempp*.

In a summary of the Court's record from 1940 to 1964, Clark included complimentary references to Black's *Everson* definition (but omitting Jefferson's "wall"), Rutledge's *Everson* dissenting opinion, Frankfurter's concurrence in *McCollum*, and Douglas' qualified reaffirmation in *Zorach*.[40] To Clark these were part of a larger, wider ranging case record indicating that "the establishment clause has been directly considered by this Court eight times in the past score of years and, with only one Justice dissenting on the point, it has consistently held that the clause withdrew all legislative power respecting religious belief or the expression thereof."

Clark characterized the Court's tradition, however, not as separation but as "wholesome neutrality." He then fashioned a two-part test (developed into a three-part test in *Lemon v. Kurtzman*) for challenged legislation. "To withstand the strictures of the establishment clause there must be a secular legislative purpose and a primary effect that neither advances nor inhibits religion."[41] Measured against this standard, the *Schempp* rituals were struck down by the Court because, "They are religious exercises, required by the States in violation of the command of the First Amendment that the Government maintain a strict neutrality, neither aiding nor opposing religion."[42] Clark's Court opinion made no further reference to separation of church and state or the "wall."

Chief Justice Warren Burger caused the Court to increase the distance between itself and the "wall" by calling for a flexibility of First Amendment construction that nearly repudiated the doctrine of separation. This became evident in *Walz v. Tax Commission*. Delivering the opinion of the Court's upholding the constitutionality of tax exemptions for churches, Burger commented, "The establishment and free exercise clauses of the First Amendment are not the most precisely drawn portions of the Constitution. The sweep of the absolute prohibitions in the Religion clauses may have been calculated; but the purpose was to state an objective, not to write a statute. . . . The Court has struggled to find a neutral course between the two Religion clauses, both of which are cast in absolute terms, and either of which, if expanded to a logical extreme, would tend to clash with the other." Noting that "the course of constitutional neutrality in this area cannot be an absolutely straight line," Burger moved on to state:

The general principle deducible from the First Amendment and all that has been said by the Court is this: that we will not tolerate

either governmentally established religion or government interference with religion. Short of those expressly prescribed
governmental acts there is room for play in the joints productive
of a benevolent neutrality which will permit religious exercise to
exist without sponsorship and without interference. Each value
judgment under the Religion clauses must therefore turn on
whether particular acts in question are intended to establish or
interfere with religious beliefs and practices or have the effect of
doing so.

In his effort to put distance between the Court and the "wall" of strict
separation, Burger made liberal use of strict separationists themselves. To justify the rights of churches and adherents of particular
faiths to take strong stands on political, legal, and constitutional
matters he declared, "No perfect or absolute separation is possible;
the very existence of the Religion clauses is an involvement of sorts."
He also declared, "The hazards of placing too much weight on a few
words or phrases of the Court is abundantly illustrated within the
pages of the Court's opinion in Everson," citing Justice Black's construing the First Amendment in absolute separationist terms while
simultaneously upholding public bus transportation for sectarian
school pupils.[43] Responding to Justice Douglas's current dissent,[44]
Burger quoted Douglas's previous words, "The First Amendment,
however, does not say in every and all respects there shall be a
separation of Church and State" and "We are a religious people whose
institutions presuppose a Supreme Being."[45] Insisting, then, that
"there is no genuine nexus between tax exemption and establishment of
religion," Burger stated that the tax exemption "restricts the fiscal relation between church and state, and tends to complement and reinforce
the desired separation insulating each from the other. Separation in this
context cannot mean absence of all contact; the complexities of modern
life inevitably produce some contact and the fire and police protection
received by houses of religious worship are no more than incidental
benefits accorded all persons or institutions within a State's boundaries,
along with many other exempt organizations."[46]
    In 1971, in *Lemon v. Kurtzman* the Court, applying the three-part test,
struck down two state programs supplementing teachers' salaries and
purchasing some secular services of nonpublic schools. Again delivering the opinion of the Court, Chief Justice Burger tried to increase the
distance between the majority of the Court and Jefferson's metaphor
with the comment, "Judicial caveats against entanglement must recognize that the line of separation, far from being a 'wall,' is a blurred,
indistinct, and variable barrier depending on all the circumstances of
a particular relationship."[47] Little evidence appeared of resistance or

counterattack by any associate justice in defense of the "wall." Two years later in *Committee for Public Education and Religious Liberty v. Nyquist*, when the Court struck down three financial-aid programs for nonpublic elementary and secondary schools, Justice Lewis Powell, in the Court opinion, declared, "This Nation's history has not been one of entirely sanitized separation between Church and State. It has never been thought either possible or desirable to enforce a regime of total separation."[48] It should be noted, however, that he discussed the doctrine more favorably later in a footnote.

From 1973 to 1982, Burger's view of the "wall" as a "blurred, indistinct, and variable barrier" continued dominant in the Court.[49] Serious discussion of the doctrine revived with the case of *Valley Forge Christian College v. Americans United for Separation of Church and State*, in which the Court ruled that a taxpayers' organization dedicated to separation of church and state had no standing to challenge the constitutionality of a no-cost transfer of surplus U.S. property to a religious institution.[50] Vigorously dissenting, Justice William J. Brennan reviewed *Everson* at length to show that in 1947 the Court had agreed unanimously that the establishment clause definitely restricts the power to tax[51] "to support religion, religious establishments, or establishments having a religious foundation whatever their form or special religious function."[52] Likewise dissenting, Justice John Paul Stevens stated that "we must recognize that our principle of judicial scrutiny of legislative acts which raise important constitutional questions requires that the issue here presented—the separation of state and church—which the Founding Fathers regarded as fundamental to our constitutional system—should be subjected to judicial testing."[53]

The judicial scrutiny Stevens wanted came later that year for Massachusetts' zoning regulations for liquor licenses. In *Larkin v. Grendel's Den* the Court struck down a statute that effectively granted churches veto power over applications to sell liquor within a 500-foot radius of their buildings. Speaking for the Court, Chief Justice Burger discussed the "wall" metaphor somewhat more favorably than he had previously. "Jefferson's idea of a 'wall' . . . was a useful figurative illustration to emphasize the concept of separateness. Some limited and incidental entanglement between church and state authority is inevitable in a complex modern society . . . but the concept of a 'wall' of separation is a useful signpost. Here that 'wall' is substantially breached by vesting discretionary governmental powers in religious bodies."[54] That said, Burger applied the three-part test to the statute under challenge, despite Justice Rehnquist's dissenting protest that "the Court rings in the metaphor of the 'wall between church and state,' and the 'three-part test' . . . to justify its result."[55] Meanwhile, one week later in *Mueller and Noyes v. Allen*, the Court upheld a state statute providing tax deductions for both public and private school expenses despite Justice Thurgood Marshall's objection against ignoring restrictions which "guarantee the separation between secular and religious educational functions and . . . ensure that State financial aid supports only the former."[56]

For Burger, the usefulness of the "wall" of separation did not bar prayer led by government-paid chaplains in U.S. legislatures. In his Court opinion for *Marsh v. Chambers*, he defended the practice's constitutionality as a comparatively trouble-free historic American custom.[57] This elicited from Justice Brennan a dissent containing an extended, documented explanation of the establishment clause that spelled out four of its major purposes and then categorically harmonized all the decisions, opinions, and Court-approved practices that might seem at first to violate the clause or those purposes. This was Brennan's schema of judicial rationale on separation and neutrality. Having quoted Black's *Everson* dictum containing Jefferson's metaphor, Brennan declared:

The principles of "separation" and "neutrality" implicit in the establishment clause serve many purposes. Four of these are particularly relevant here.

The first . . . is to guarantee the individual right to conscience . . . not only . . . when the government engages in direct or indirect coercion . . . [but] also . . . when the government requires individuals to support the practices of a faith with which they do not agree. . . .

The second purpose of separation and neutrality is to keep the state from interfering in the essential autonomy of religious life, either by taking upon itself the decision of religious issues or by unduly involving itself in the supervision of religious institutions or individuals.

The third purpose of separation and neutrality is to prevent the trivialization and degradation of religion by too close an attachment to the organs of government. . . .

Finally, the principles of separation and neutrality help assure that essentially religious issues, precisely because of their importance and sensitivity, not become the occasion for battle in the political arena . . . that no American should at any point feel alienated from his government because that government has declared or acted upon some "official" or "authorized" point of view on the matter of religion. The imperatives of separation and neutrality are not limited to the relationship of government to religious institutions or denominations, but extend as well to the relationship of government to religious beliefs and practices.[58]

In Brennan's view, legislative prayer clearly violated all these principles of neutrality and separation embedded within the establishment clause.

Brennan then turned to the common counter-argument that "neutrality" and "separation" did not exhaust the full meaning of the establishment clause as it had developed in the Court's cases, stating,

> It is indeed true that there are certain tensions inherent in the First Amendment itself, or inherent in the role of religion and religious belief in any free society, that have shaped the doctrine of the establishment clause, and required us to deviate from an absolute adherence to separation and neutrality. . . . Because the Court occasionally suggests that some of these considerations might apply here, it becomes important that I briefly identify the most prominent of them and explain why they do not in fact have any relevance to legislative prayer.
>
> (1) A number of our cases have recognized that religious institutions and religious practices may, in certain contexts, receive the benefit of government programs and policies generally available, on the basis of some secular criterion, to a wide class of similarly situated nonreligious beneficiaries. . . .
>
> (2) Conversely, our cases have recognized that religion can encompass a broad, if not total, spectrum of concerns, overlapping considerably with the range of secular concerns, and that not every governmental act which coincides with or conflicts with a particular religious belief is for that reason an establishment of religion. . . .
>
> (3) We have also recognized that government cannot, without adopting a decidedly *anti*-religious point of view, be forbidden to recognize the religious beliefs and practices of the American people as an aspect of our history and culture. . . .
>
> (4) Our cases have recognized that the purposes of the establishment clause can sometimes conflict. For example . . . we upheld tax exemptions for religious institutions in part because subjecting those institutions to taxation might foster serious administrative entanglement. . . .
>
> (5) Finally, our cases recognize that, in one important respect, the Constitution is *not* neutral on the subject of religion: Under the free exercise clause, religiously motivated claims of conscience may give rise to constitutional rights that other strongly held beliefs do not. . . . Moreover, even when the government is not compelled to do so by the free exercise clause, it may to some extent act to facilitate the opportunities of individuals to practice their religion.[59]

For each of the exceptions, Brennan gave reasons why legislative prayer could not be included in that category. The passage as a whole constituted a brief systematic statement on the judicial meaning of the "wall of separation." Brennan concluded, "The argument is made occasionally that a strict separation of religion and state robs the Nation of its spiritual identity. I believe quite the contrary. It may be true that individuals cannot be 'neutral' on the question of religion. But the judgment of the establishment clause is that neutrality by the organs of *government* on questions of religion is both possible and imperative. . . . If the Court had struck down legislative prayer today, it would likely have stimulated a furious reaction. But it would also, I am convinced, have invigorated both the 'spirit of religion' and the 'spirit of freedom.'"[60]

The passage, however, did not win the case nor did it provide unanimous decisions for subsequent cases. For instance, *Lynch v. Donnelly* upheld as constitutional a city-provided nativity scene for the municipal Christmas display. Writing the opinion of the Court, Chief Justice Burger maintained that "the concept of a 'wall' of separation is a useful figure of speech *probably* deriving from the views of Thomas Jefferson,"[61] but not an accurate description of the practical aspects of the relationship that in fact exists. The Constitution, he argued, affirmatively mandates accommodation, not merely tolerance, of all religions, and forbids hostility toward any.[62] Furthermore, stated Burger, when construing the establishment clause "we have repeatedly emphasized our unwillingness to be confined to any single test or criterion in this sensitive area."[63] The Court was satisfied that the tax-supported nativity scene passed all three parts of the *Lemon* test.[64] On the other hand, Justice Brennan, dissenting, was fully persuaded that the nativity scene *failed* all three parts of the *Lemon* test.[65] Once again, on the basis of prior decisions, Brennan attempted to delimit the narrow channels that government acknowledgment of religion must follow to satisfy the establishment clause.

First, although the government may not be compelled to do so by the free exercise clause, it may consistently with the establishment clause, act to accommodate to some extent the opportunities of individuals to practice their religion. . . .

Second . . . while a particular governmental practice may have derived from religious motivations and retain certain religious connotations, it is nonetheless permissible for the government to pursue the practice when it is continued today solely for secular reasons. . . .

Finally . . . government cannot be completely prohibited from recognizing in its public actions the religious beliefs and practices of the American people as an aspect of our national history and culture.

To Brennan, however, the nativity scene fit none of those categories. "By insisting that such a distinctively sectarian message is merely an unobjectionable part of our 'religious heritage' . . . the Court takes a long step back to the days when Justice Brewer could arrogantly declare for the Court that 'this is a Christian nation.'"[66]

In 1985 Associate Justice William Rehnquist (now Chief Justice), dissenting in *Wallace v. Jaffree* from the Court's decision striking down an Alabama statute authorizing a daily period of silence in public schools for meditation or voluntary prayer, launched an extended attack upon the metaphor of the wall. In his opening salvo he declared, "It is impossible to build sound constitutional doctrine upon a mistaken understanding of constitutional history, but unfortunately the establishment clause has been expressly freighted with Jefferson's misleading metaphor for nearly forty years." Rehnquist went on to argue,

> Thomas Jefferson was of course in France at the time the constitutional amendments known as the Bill of Rights were passed by Congress and ratified by the states. His letter to the Danbury Baptist Association was a short note of courtesy, written fourteen years after the amendments were passed by Congress. He would seem to any detached observer to be a less than ideal source of contemporary history as to the meaning of the Religion clause of the First Amendment.

Further on in his opinion, however, Rehnquist attempted to bolster his own establishment clause construction by citing both "Jefferson's treaty with the Kaskaskia Indians, which provided annual cash support for the Tribe's Roman Catholic priest and church," and Jefferson's signing into law a congressional trust endowment of up to 12,000 acres of land "for the Society of United Bretheren [sic] for propagating the Gospel among the Heathen." For these and other reasons Rehnquist insisted, "There is simply no historical foundation for the proposition that the Framers intended to build the 'wall of separation' that was constitutionalized in *Everson*."[67]

Rehnquist's performance here left much to be desired. Inconsistently, he attempted to discredit Jefferson as an authority on the meaning of the First Amendment but later nullified that effort by citing two of Jefferson's actions that seemed useful for his own interpretation. In doing the latter he ignored (and as a Supreme Court justice was in no position to share) Jefferson's complex theory of how the three independent but coordinate branches of the federal government were to determine constitutionality. Nor did Rehnquist point out that his quotation from the Kaskaskia treaty was really an independent nation's stipulation of the use to be made on its own land, of its compensation, or that the trust endowment was congressional confirmation of a commitment made before the inauguration of the Constitution.

Rehnquist compounded the inconsistency further by citing false history, for, contrary to his contention, Jefferson actually was in the United States throughout the ratification process: his boat sighted land on 13 November 1789, a week before the first state, New Jersey, voted to ratify the Bill of Rights on 20 November. Nor was Rehnquist right to dismiss the Danbury Baptist letter as "a short note of courtesy," for (as the opening paragraph of this article demonstrates) Jefferson deliberately used the letter to inculcate a political lesson condemning "the alliance of Church and State."[68]

Willing to concede that the wall idea might have served as a useful analytical concept had it led the Court to "unified" and "principled" results in establishment clause cases, Rehnquist protested,

> The opposite, unfortunately, has been true; in the 38 years since *Everson* our establishment clause cases have been neither principled nor unified. Our recent opinions, many of them hopelessly divided pluralities, have with embarrassing candor conceded that the "wall of separation" is merely a "blurred, indistinct, and variable barrier," which "is not wholly accurate" and can only be "dimly perceived." . . . Whether due to its lack of historical support or its practical unworkability, the *Everson* "wall" has proven all but useless as a guide to sound constitutional adjudication. . . . But the greatest injury of the "wall" notion is its mischievous diversion of judges from the actual intentions of the drafters of the Bill of Rights. . . . The "wall of separation between church and state" is a metaphor based on bad history, a metaphor which has proved useless as a guide to judging. It should be frankly and explicitly abandoned.[69]

Rehnquist then dismissed the *Lemon* three-part test as the Court's recent attempt "to add some mortar to *Everson's* wall. . . . The *Lemon* test has no more grounding in the history of the First Amendment than does the 'wall' theory on which it rests. The three-part test represents a determined effort to craft a workable rule from a historically faulty doctrine; but the rule can be only as sound as the doctrine it attempts to service. The three-part test has simply not provided adequate standards for deciding establishment clause cases."[70] Characterizing the Court opinion in *Wallace* as just a continuation of "the sisyphean task of trying to patch together the 'blurred, indistinct, and variable barrier' described in *Lemon*," Rehnquist stated, "We have done much straining since 1947, but still we admit that we can only 'dimly perceive' the *Everson* wall. . . . Our perception has been clouded not by the Constitution but by the mists of an unnecessary metaphor."[71]

Showing little inclination to accept Justice Rehnquist's radical proposal for judicial lobotomy, the following year (1985) in *Grand Rapids School District v. Ball* the Court struck down programs in which classes for nonpublic school students were financed by the public school system and taught by public school employees on nonpublic school premises. Speaking for the Court, Justice Brennan did not mention separation of church and state directly, but under the "effects" part of the three-part test he found the programs flawed in that they might "provide a crucial symbolic link between government and religion." This concern for symbolic "union," "concert," "connection," or "dependency" was repeatedly expressed and finally summarized in the sentence: "This effect—the symbolic union of government and religion in one sectarian enterprise—is an impermissible effect under the establishment clause."[72] Justice Rehnquist dissented with the comment, "In Grand Rapids the Court relies heavily on the principles of *Everson* and *McCollum* . . . but declines to discuss the faulty 'wall' premise upon which those cases rest."[73]

The same day, in *Aguilar v. Felton*, the Court struck down local government use of federal funds to pay salaries of public employees who teach in parochial schools. Brennan's Court opinion, while granting that "separation in this context cannot mean the absence of all contact," nevertheless maintained that the system under review "would inevitably lead to an unconstitutional administrative entanglement between church and state."[74] Dissenting, Chief Justice Burger repeated his words from his former dissent in *Wallace v. Jaffree*, namely, "Our responsibility is not to apply tidy formulas by rote; our duty is to determine whether the statute or practice is a step toward establishing a state religion."[75]

In summary, the metaphor "wall of separation between church and state" used by Jefferson in his reply to the Danbury Baptists caught the attention subsequently of large numbers of Americans concerned for religious freedom, although Jefferson himself apparently never repeated the phrase. The figure of speech found its way incidentally into Supreme Court literature in 1879 when Chief Justice Waite quoted Jefferson's letter in *Reynolds v. United States*. However, the Court's First Amendment rulings and opinions until the mid-1940s really reflect Justice Brewer's comment in *Holy Trinity v. United States*, "We are a Christian nation."

Initially activated as a major factor in Supreme Court reasoning by Justice Frankfurter in *West Virginia v. Barnette*, the doctrine of separation of church and state (and the "wall" metaphor) was first adopted and unanimously approved as a test for constitutionality in 1947 in *Everson v. Board of Education*. Then, and one year later in *McCollum v. Board of Education*, it motivated both the majority rulings and the dissents, thus demonstrating that the justices can agree on a principle while disagreeing on its application.

Sensing that the "wall" principle of strict separation lacked the precision needed to promote religious freedom in all First Amendment cases, the Court majority in *Zorach v. Clauson* returned in part to prior tradition with the words, "We are a religious people." Nevertheless, the principle of separation continued to play a role in later cases such as *Engel v. Vitale* and *Abington v. Schempp*. For *Schempp*, however, Justice Clark attempted to harmonize conflicting precedents by characterizing the Court tradition as "wholesome neutrality" and fashioning a test for challenged legislation that eventually evolved in *Lemon v. Kurtzman* into the three-part test of purpose, effect, and entanglement. Meanwhile, in *Walz v. Tax Commission*, Chief Justice Burger called for a flexibility of interpretation of the doctrine of separation that amounted to putting some distance between the Court and the "wall." Burger's view of the wall as a "blurred, indistinct, and variable barrier" became and continued dominant in the Court for about nine years.

Although the concept of separation was never absent, the Court varied from case to case on how strict that separation should be. Eventually, in *Marsh v. Chambers* and again in *Lynch v. Donnelly*, Justice Brennan worked out a rational exposition of the principle of separation of church and state implicit in the establishment clause, and accounted for exceptions that made the "wall" in his view indeed variable, but by no means blurred or indistinct. His work brought no unity to the Court, nor did the three-part test. *Lynch v. Donnelly* gave us the spectacle of both Burger and Brennan applying the test to the same municipally sponsored nativity scene only to reach directly opposite conclusions.

Fifteen months later in *Wallace v. Jaffree*, Justice Rehnquist mounted an attack on the metaphor of the "wall": first, by attempting (with less than complete historical accuracy) to discredit Jefferson's authority to construe the First Amendment; second, by faulting the metaphor for repeatedly dividing the Court. The Court has not responded favorably to his radical proposal that the metaphor be frankly and explicitly abandoned. The "wall of separation" remains. Chief Justice Burger conceded its usefulness, although he did not always use it. Justice Brennan described contexts in which separation and neutrality do not mean the absence of all contact. And Justice Rehnquist has accused his judicial colleagues of not discussing "the faulty 'wall' premise" (his words) despite two major attempts by Justice Brennan to explain in principle where it applies, and where it does not. Subsequent cases have added little to the development of the doctrine of separation.

This chapter was written before the Supreme Court decided *Bowen v. Kendrick*.[76] Weber holds that among the advantages to be derived from acceptance of the principle of "strict neutrality" by the Supreme Court would be more consistently decided cases. He also maintains, "Whether the Courts will accept a neutrality principle, depends in large measure on whether it is understood, analyzed, critiqued, developed, and ultimately accepted or rejected by the intellectual community that deals with church-state issues." But he does concede, "Unfortunately, the use of a strict-neutrality principle will not do away with lawsuits. . . . " I certainly agree.

Several reasons make me dubious about the capacity of this (or any other) single principle to provide us with a commonly accepted interpretation of the religion clause of the First Amendment, as well as consistency (and predictability) in Supreme Court decisions.

First, "neutrality" may be as *generic* a term as "separation." Its previous use in Court opinions does not promise future unanimity. Justice Clark resorted to the term "wholesome neutrality" in an effort to resolve the conflicting interpretations of "separation" that had divided the Court for 24 years. He then offered a two-part test (the prototype of the *Lemon* three-part test) which he characterized as "strict neutrality."[77] But, as we have seen, the new term and accompanying test provided no more unity of thought or decision than had the "wall of separation." Subsequently, Justice Brennan composed a *schema* in which he explicitly equated "strict separation of religion and state" with "neutrality by the organs of government."[78] Whether his definitions agree or disagree with those of Clark is unclear. We should note, however, that elsewhere the term "neutrality" has been used in a way that deliberately avoids specific definition. Chief Justice Burger, criticizing strict separation, argued that "constitutional neutrality" cannot be a straight line and that "benevolent neutrality" requires "play in the joints."[79]

The history of the Court supports Weber's belief that the neutrality principle would not undermine the *Lemon* three-prong test; apparently Justice Clark devised the prototype of the test as the practical expression of the principle. But the test itself raises problems. It seems at first sight to be specific. But is it any less *generic* than either principle: separation or neutrality? If so, how do we account for Justices

Burger and Brennan applying the test only to disagree at every point on the constitutionality of a municipally sponsored nativity scene in *Lynch v. Donnelly?*[80]

Furthermore, changing perceptions (some would call them inconsistencies) lead to changing uses that individual occupants of the bench devise for both principle and test. An outstanding example is furnished by Chief Justice Rehnquist. As we have seen, his dissenting opinion in *Wallace* (1985) was largely a long and heated condemnation of both the doctrine of separation and the three-part test.[81] That condemnation did not prevent him in *Bowen v. Kendrick* (1988) from mounting a lengthy argument that the Adolescent Family Life Act on its face satisfied the establishment clause precisely because it passed the three-part test. Nor did previous expressions of hostility to the "wall of separation" prevent him from quoting with approval the Senate Committee report's conclusion, " . . . provisions for the involvement of religious organizations [in the AFLA] do not violate the *constitutional separation between church and state.*"[82]

Is it possible that no single principle can adequately interpret the religion clause of the First Amendment? Its phrases prohibit laws that infringe upon two cherished values that may often concur but may equally often conflict. Weber tempers the simplicity of his principle of "strict neutrality" with the exceptions of "a significant personal interest or social unit," and "a suspect classification." Is that in itself a sign that, no matter how much we reason over principle, cases will arise that do not lend themselves to consistency with previous decisions but only to new compromise?

NOTES

This article originally appeared in *Journal of Church and State* 30, 3 (Autumn 1988): 441–62. I am grateful to Dr. Weber for including my essay in this book and for his invitation to participate in the dialogue he endeavors to stimulate.

1. To Levi Lincoln, January 1, 1802, in *Writings of Thomas Jefferson*, ed. Paul L. Ford, 10 vols. (New York: G.P. Putnam and Sons, 1892–99), vol. 8, p. 129.

2. Nathan Schachner, *Thomas Jefferson: A Biography*, 2 vols. (New York, Appleton-Century-Crofts, 1951), vol. 2, p. 701. *In God We Trust: The Religious Beliefs and Ideas of the American Founding Fathers*, Norman Cousins, ed. (New York: Harper, 1958), p. 134.

3. To the Danbury Baptist Association, January 1, 1802, *Writings of Thomas Jefferson*, Andrew A. Lipscomb and Albert E. Bergh, eds., 20 vols. (Washington, D.C.: Issued under the auspices of the Thomas Jefferson Memorial Association, 1903–1904), vol. 16, pp. 281–82.

4. *Reynolds v. United States*, 98 U.S. 145 (1879).

5. Ibid., 164; Martha W. McCarthy, "Religion and the Public Schools," *Harvard Educational Review* 55 (August 1985): 281; Thayer S. Warshaw, *Religion, Education, and the Supreme Court* (Nashville: Abingdon, 1979), p. 17.

6. *Reynolds*, 163–64.

7. *Everson v. Board of Education*, 330 U.S. 1 (1947).

8. *Vidal v. Girard's Executors*, 2 Howard 127 (1844), 198–99.

9. *Church of the Holy Trinity v. United States*, 143 U.S. 457 (1892), 465–70.

10. *United States v. Macintosh*, 283 U.S. 605 (1931), 625. Emphasis in text.

11. *West Virginia Board of Education v. Barnette*, 319 U.S. 624 (1943), 654–55.

12. *Everson v. Board of Education*, 330 U.S. 1 (1947), 15–16, 18.

13. Ibid., 19.

14. Ibid., 52–53, 59–60.

15. *McCollum v. Board of Education*, 333 U.S. 203 (1948), 210–11, nn. 6–7.

16. Ibid., 212–32.

17. Ibid., 217.

18. Ibid., 221.

19. Ibid., 227, 231–32. See *Everson*, 59.

20. *McCollum*, 212–13.

21. Ibid., 218.

22. Ibid., 215–16.

23. Ibid., 237–38.

24. Ibid., 238–44.

25. Ibid., 249. Reed cited *Everson, Cochran v. Louisiana State Board of Education*, 281 U.S. 370, and *Bradfield v. Roberts*, 175 U.S. 291, in his support.

26. *McCollum*, 255–56.

27. Ibid., 248–50.

28. Ibid., 245–47. Reed's notes (nn. 8–13) include portions of Jefferson's letter to the Danbury Baptists, and his letter of November 2, 1822, to Thomas Cooper concerning the "Schools-on-the-Confines" proposal.

29. *Zorach v. Clauson*, 343 U.S. 306 (1952), 312–13.

30. *Holy Trinity* at 465–71.

31. *Zorach* at 313–15.

32. Ibid., 316–19. Emphasis in text.

33. Ibid., 322–23.

34. Ibid., 325.

35. *Torcaso v. Watkins*, 367 U.S. 488 (1961), 492–94. See *Everson*, 15–16, and *McCollum*, 232.

36. *Engel v. Vitale*, 370 U.S. 421 (1962), 425 and 434 n. 20.

37. *McGowan v. Maryland*, 366 U.S. 420 (1961), 460–62. See *McCollum* at 213.

38. *Engel* at 445–46.

39. *Abington School District v. Schempp*, 374 U.S. 203 (1963), 308–9, 314. (Hereafter *Schempp*.) See *McCollum*, 247.

40. *Schempp*, 216–20.

41. Ibid., 222.

42. Ibid., 225.

43. *Walz v. Tax Commission*, 397 U.S. 664 (1970), 668–70.

44. Ibid., 700.

45. Ibid., 669, 672. *Zorach*, 306, 313–14. Emphasis supplied by Burger.

46. *Walz*, 675–76.

47. *Lemon v. Kurtzman*, 403 U.S. 602 (1971), 614.

48. *Committee for Public Education & Religious Liberty v. Nyquist*, 413 U.S. 756 (1973), 760, 770–71 n. 28.

49. For sporadic references to the doctrine of separation or the "wall" see: *Wolman v. Walter*, 433 U.S. 229 (1977) 236, 257, and 266; *McDaniel v. Paty*, 435 U.S. 618 (1978), 623–25, 629 n. 9, 637–38, and 645; *Widmar v. Vincent*, 454 U.S. 263 (1981), 276, and 289.

50. *Valley Forge Christian College v. Americans United for Separation of Church and State*, 454 U.S. 464 (1982).

51. Ibid., 500–4.

52. Ibid., 501; *Everson* at 44 (Justice Rutledge dissenting).

53. Ibid., 514–15.

54. *Larkin v. Grendel's Den*, 459 U.S. 116 (1982), 122–23.

55. Ibid., 129.

56. *Mueller and Noyes v. Allen*, 463 U.S. 388 (1983), 407.

57. *Marsh v. Chambers*, 463 U.S. 783 (1983), 784–95.

58. Ibid., 802–6.

59. Ibid., 809–12.

60. Ibid., 821–22.

61. *Lynch v. Donnelly*, 465 U.S. 668 (1984), 673. Emphasis added.

62. Ibid., 677.

63. Ibid., 679.

64. Ibid., 685.

65. Ibid., 698–704.

66. Ibid., 715–17.

67. *Wallace v. Jaffree*, 105 S. Ct. 2479 (1985), 2509, 2514–15 n. 5, 2516.

68. See Rehnquist's citations anent Jefferson: 7 Stat. 79, and ch. 46, 1 Stat. 490 (ibid., 2514–15 n. 5). For Jefferson the president on constitutional construction see Dumas Malone, *Jefferson and His Time*, Vol. 4 of *Jefferson the President: First Term, 1801–1805* (Boston: Little, Brown and Company, 1970), pp. xviii-xix, 155–56. Malone cites the following letters by Jefferson: to Abigail Adams, 22 July and 11 September 1804; to George Hay, 2 June 1807; and to W. H. Torrance, 11 June 1815. See also my *Jefferson on Religion in Public Education* (New Haven: Yale University Press, 1962), pp. 73–94, 130–40.

69. *Wallace v. Jaffree*, 105 S. Ct. 2479 at 2516–17 (1985).

70. Ibid., 2517–18.

71. Ibid., 2519–20.

72. *Grand Rapids School District v. Ball*, 87 L.Ed. 2d 267 (1985), 278, 281–83.

73. Ibid., 288.

74. *Aguilar v. Felton*, 87 L.Ed. 2d 290 (1985), 298, 300.

75. Ibid., 304; *Wallace v. Jaffree*, 86 L.Ed. 2d 29 (1985).

76. *Bowen v. Kendrick*, 108 S. Ct. 2562; 1988 U.S. LEXIS 3027; 101 L. Ed. 2d. 520; 56 U.S.L.W. 4.

77. *Schempp*, 222, 225.
78. *Marsh*, 821–822.
79. *Walz*, 668–690.
80. *Lynch*, 685, 698–704.
81. *Wallace*, 2518.
82. *Bowen v. Kendrick*, 108 S. Ct. 2562 (1988). Emphasis added.

7

Concluding Reflections

Paul J. Weber

In concluding, it may be useful to look for the common values shared by all the authors, to address specific problems not adequately pursued in the individual chapters, and to make a final assessment of the possibility of developing a commonly acceptable theory of the First Amendment religion clauses. Robert Healey provides an excellent starting point. He performs two valuable services: tracing the historical development of the Supreme Court's use of "separation" language, and raising an issue not addressed by other authors—that the term "strict neutrality" might easily suffer the same fate as the term "separation," being so generic that it has several different specific meanings. Is Healey correct in holding that the underlying problem is not language or theory, but fundamentally different values at war in American culture, and subsequently in the courts? If so, of course, the search for a commonly acceptable principle is quixotic and we should resign ourselves to an annual parade of bruising, divisive battles.

Before surrendering to such a gloomy prospect, however, we may wish to explore what common facts and values the authors in this book share. First must surely be a recognition of the deeply rooted and broadly spread existence of religion in America. We know now that the fond hopes of secularists from Jefferson to Pfeffer were illusory. Religion will not fade away; it is here to stay, and believers will insist on having their say in the public square. By the same token there appears to be a consensus among the authors (although certainly not unanimous agreement among all church-state scholars or citizens) that while most believers want to influence what happens in the public square, they have no desire to take it over. From these propositions I would conclude that if a consensus can be reached on what the religion clauses require, it will not include those who aspire to establish a

Christian nation, or those who aspire to a nation without religious influence. Therefore, there is no serious hope that we can avoid all future conflict. Religion, whatever form it takes, has and will continue to have real enemies. Conversely, some religions need, look for, and if necessary, create enemies. A consensus among the majority of citizens, however, could lessen the range and quantity of conflict.

Second, I believe each of the authors sees the robust reemergence of religion in the 1980s in a wild bouquet of forms as a sign of cultural vitality and a source of hope. Religious dynamism adds particular kinds of values to the political agenda, values such as justice, equality, honesty, communal responsibility, and individual human freedom. Religiously motivated groups and individuals propose potential, often conflicting solutions to human problems at all levels of government and force public debate on issues which many in and out of government would prefer to ignore. Such input is important, perhaps even critical for the continued health of a democratic society. The challenge now, I hope we all agree, is to expand the protective cover of religious liberty without planting the lethal seeds of establishment or fertilizing the toxic weeds of social conflict between competing faiths.

Third, there appears to be agreement that the current state of church-state jurisprudence is unsatisfactory. For better or worse this jurisprudence has been configured by Supreme Court decisions. No one has pointed out the problem with the Court's rulings better than Justice Scalia. As he writes sardonically in one dissent,

> We have said essentially the following: Government may not act with the purpose of advancing religion, except when forced to do so by the free exercise clause (which is now and then); or when eliminating existing governmental hostility to religion (which exists sometimes); or even when merely accommodating governmentally uninhibited religious practices except that at some point (it is unclear where) intentional accommodation results in the fostering of religion, which is of course unconstitutional.[1]

Finally, there appears to be agreement that the freedom to exercise one's religion is an independent, substantive right under the Constitution and that this religious liberty can justly be called "the first freedom." There also appears to be agreement that at times government must adapt to, or acquiesce to meet the needs of religious exercise and that at times the exercises a religion wishes to pursue must be adapted or even prohibited in order to meet the needs of public policy. Even religious liberty has its limits.

We disagree on what constitutes establishment, on where, and especially on how to draw the lines between what is permitted/required of government and what is permitted/required of religion. The disagreement, to put it succinctly, is how best to protect the widest, most just, area of religious liberty. Specifically the disagreement is over whether strict neutrality/equal separation is a constitutional theory which lays a foundation for drawing lines properly and provides the necessary protection for religious liberty and nonestablishment.

Despite a common agreement that current church-state law is inadequate for the legal problems arising in our times, there has been progress toward a neutralist norm, as Professor Healey so clearly shows. The seeds were planted in Justice Reed's lone dissent in *McCollum v. Board of Education*; they were nurtured through Justices Stewart, Clark, Burger, and even Brennan through a dissent in *March v. Chambers*, in which he felt constrained to talk about separation *and* neutrality.

Unfortunately, the term "neutrality" has now become so generic that in responding to the various critics I realized it was necessary to shift terminology and begin to use the term "equal separation." For example, Laurence Tribe distinguishes the major formulations of neutrality as (a) strict neutrality, (b) political neutrality, (c) denominational neutrality, and (d) free exercise neutrality.[2] The equal separation principle proposed here is a combination of Tribe's political neutrality and free exercise neutrality. It is considered an improvement on the original strict-neutrality principle and subsumes Tribe's denominational neutrality. Political neutrality "requires that religious organizations enjoy, on the same basis as nonreligious organizations, the general benefits of the political community, such as the ability to own property and make contracts. . . . Political neutrality embraces both voluntarism, in forbidding actions that would create artificial disincentives for forming religious organizations, and pluralism, in placing religious organizations on the same plane as their nonreligious counterparts."[3]

Free exercise neutrality, on the other hand, requires that government "may (and sometimes must) accommodate religious practices."[4] What equal separation provides beyond the Tribe formulation, is an equal protection/suspect classification type analysis to determine the limits of such accommodation.[5]

One of the most difficult, intractable problems in constitutional law, and certainly in this area, is determining exactly what religion is. At one level this appears to be a problem for equal separation. If religious organizations and activities are to be treated equally with similar organizations and activities, ought we not at least state what the "religion" is which is to be compared? Indeed, a recent law review article argues that *defining* religion is critical to protecting religious liberty.[6]

Stanley Ingber provides an excellent overview of the definitional problem and a history of the attempts to provide a legal definition. Essentially, his argument is that religion is unique for legal purposes and that much of the confusion in the law is due to a refusal to recognize the difference between religion and ideology. Providing such a definition won't help end the confusion. The distinction he proposes is the following:

> Religion acknowledges the existence of a sacred or transcendent reality from which basic human obligations emanate. These obligations are not matters of human debate, evaluation or judgment. They therefore precede those responsibilities created by human-fashioned state institutions, and deserve consideration under the free exercise clause. Ideologies, however, are themselves products of human judgment and consequently do not take precedence over the resulting judgments of a democratic political process. Adherents of an ideology may merely participate in the debate over human goals, protected only by speech, press, assembly, and association rights, in the hope of influencing others and molding state policy to their ideological principles.[7]

Any claim for protection under the free exercise clause, according to this distinction, must come from petitioners who believe in the existence of a transcendent or sacred reality. Any claim to be free of establishment clause constraints requires that there be no acknowledgment of a transcendent reality. (Ingber does refine this by putting "irreligion" under the ban of the establishment clause, but "nonreligion" outside the ban.) This "solution" would, of course, be quite the opposite of an equal separation approach and therefore merits some attention.

First, Ingber is in the odd—and I would argue, ultimately untenable—position of asserting that some individuals who claim to, and sincerely believe themselves to be acting out of religious motives aren't, and others who claim not to be religious are, in spite of themselves, religious! In brief, a legal definition of religion, imposed by legislatures or courts, would only coincidentally conform to whatever theologians, believers, or nonbelievers consider to be religion. That strains credulity.

Second, Ingber acknowledges that the basis of individual conscience can be either religious or ideological. If I understand him correctly, only actions based on the former are protected by the free exercise clause.[8] Assuming two equally intelligent and sincere conscientious objectors, one who believes all war is immoral because God so dictates, and the other who believes all war is immoral because it is destructive of the earth's inhabitants, should one be exempt from the draft and the other not? One allowed to do alternate service and the other sent to prison? Such an outcome would be constitutional under Ingber's approach.

Third, a number of scholars have raised the intriguing question of whether any legal definition of religion is necessarily a violation of the establishment clause. Jesse Choper concludes that "[A]ny definition of religion for constitutional purposes that excludes certain beliefs (or groups) that are reasonably perceived or characterized as being religious by those who hold them (or belong to them) may be fairly viewed as judicial preference of some 'religions' over others."[9] This is exactly what Ingber's distinction between religion and ideology does.

Finally, and ignoring objections many theologians would have to his statements describing religion, I am puzzled that Ingber finds his distinction between religion and ideology so significant, since the legal problem is not beliefs and their sources, but actions. We are still left with the problem that not all actions based on religious belief or compunction can be constitutionally protected, and not all government action objected to on religious grounds can be prohibited. The proposed line to be drawn between religion and ideology is neither proper nor adequate.[10] That is, the distinction does not protect religious liberty in as broad a range as is desirable nor does it provide that equal protection which is at the heart of the strict-separation/equal-protection theory.

The equal-separation approach to definition is: (1) begin with the assumption that if there are no distinct legal advantages or disadvantages to a religious classification, self-definition is acceptable, that is, courts need not enter that theological thicket; (2) a free exercise right is an independent right protected under the Constitution, but one which requires that nonreligious claimants in similar situations be equally protected; or (3) if a claim is to *unique* protection or exemption, a suspect-classification type analysis is triggered—which means heightened judicial scrutiny of existing or proposed government regulation or action, and a requirement of a higher level of justification by the government (the "compelling state interest" test) for limiting the action of an individual or proceeding with its own action.

This takes us to a final issue and one which underlies the debate in this book. It is clear that Kelley, Dunn, Monsma, and Marty are all distrustful of government. That distrust—call it fear if you will—is shared by the author, and indeed was the premise upon which the Constitution itself was based. Our own history and recent experience proves over and over that government officials are not to be unduly trusted. They, like professors and clerics, are only human. The authors differ on how best to protect religious liberty and prevent establishment, granted this distrust.

The argument made in the initial chapter was that granted contemporary conditions—the First Amendment is now applied to the states, we have an expansive administrative government and a wild array of dynamic, expansive religions, we live in a technological age of mass communication, and we have a mobile, hyperpluralist population—strict neutrality/equal separation provides the most usable, fair, and credible interpretation of the First Amendment religion clauses.

Having said that, it remains true that there is no magic formula to settle all disputes between religion and the law, no legal pill to ease the pain of perceived injustice and religious oppression, and certainly no perfect theory to bind judges or legislators. Theories are only guideposts. They function as such only as long as they are perceived as leading to the type of nation citizens wish to establish, and only as long as there is a vigilant, vigorous citizenry to keep their officials on the straight and narrow. The only certain defense of religious liberty and nonestablishment is the vigilance and political action of citizens dedicated to these values, enough of whom also accept the same guideposts. It is our hope that the dialogues in this book point out the promise and the problems of equal separation.

NOTES

1. *Edwards v. Aguillard*, 107 S.Ct. 2573, 2605 (1987) (Scalia, J., dissenting).

2. Laurence H. Tribe, *American Constitutional Law*, 2nd. ed. (Mineola, NY: The Foundation Press, 1988), p. 1188.

3. Ibid., p. 1189.

4. *Hobbie v. Unemployment Appeals Comm'n*, 107 S.Ct. 1046, 1051 (1987).

5. Tribe very thoughtfully addresses the issue of limits on government's accommodation, that is, free exercise neutrality, by proposing three factors which define some—but not all—of the boundaries: evenhandedness, reduction of regulatory entanglement, and the source of the burden to be lifted. If the burden is government imposed, accommodation is permissible; if it is privately imposed, accommodation is not permissible. See Ira C. Luper, "Where Rights Begin: The Problem of Burdens on the Free Exercise of Religion," 102 *Harvard Law Review* 933 (1989).

6. Stanley Ingber, "Religion or Ideology: A Needed Clarification of the Religion Clauses," 41 *Stanford Law Review* 233 (1989).

7. Ibid., p. 332–333.

8. Ibid., p. 251–252.

9. Jesse Choper, "Defining 'Religion' in the First Amendment," 1982 *University of Illinois Law Review* 579 at 580 (1982).

10. I do not mean to infer that Ingber is not aware of these objections; he discusses them at some length. His article provides a number of superb insights especially in relation to secular humanism in the public schools. Nonetheless, to this author the evidence presented does not persuasively support the central argument.

Bibliography

BOOKS

Abraham, Henry J. *Freedom and the Court: Civil Rights and Liberties in the United States.* 4th ed. New York: Oxford University Press, 1982.

Ahlstrom, Sidney E. *A Religious History of the American People.* New Haven, CT: Yale University Press, 1973.

Alley, Robert S., ed. *James Madison on Religious Liberty.* Buffalo, New York: Prometheus Books, 1985.

Amstutz, Mark. *Christian Ethics and U.S. Foreign Policy.* Grand Rapids, MI: Zondervan Books, 1987.

Antieau, Chester James. *Commentaries on the Constitution of the United States.* Buffalo, New York: Law Book Publishers, 1960.

Antieau, Chester James, Arthur T. Downey, and Edward C. Roberts. *Freedom from Federal Establishment: Formation and History of the First Amendment Religion Clauses.* Milwaukee, WI: Bruce, 1964.

Antieau, Chester James, Phillip Mark Carroll, and Thomas Carroll Burke. *Religion Under the State Constitutions.* Brooklyn, New York: Central Book Company, 1965.

Arnold, O. Carroll. *Religious Freedom on Trial.* Valley Forge, PA: Judson Press, 1978.

Arrowood, Charles Flinn, ed. *Thomas Jefferson and Education in a Republic.* New York: McGraw-Hill Book Co., 1930.

Bainton, Roland H. *The Travail of Religious Liberty.* New York: Harper and Brothers, 1951.

Beaver, R. Pierce. *Church, State, and the American Indians: Two and a Half Centuries of Partnership in Missions between Protestant Churches and Government.* St. Louis: Concordia Publishing House, 1966.

Bellah, Robert N. *The Broken Covenant: American Civil Religion in Time of Trial.* New York: Seabury Press, 1975.

Berns, Walter. *The First Amendment and the Future of Democracy.* New York: Basic Books, 1976.

Beth, Loren P. *The American Theory of Church and State.* Gainesville, FL: University of Florida Press, 1958.

Blau, Joseph L., ed. *Cornerstones of Religious Freedom in America.* Boston: Beacon Press, 1949.

Boyd, Julian P., ed. *The Papers of Thomas Jefferson.* 21 vols. to date. Princeton, NJ: Princeton University Press, 1950.

Bradley, Gerald V. *Church-State Relationships in America.* New York: Greenwood Press, 1987.

Brady, Joseph H. *Confusion Twice Confounded: The First Amendment and the Supreme Court.* South Orange, NJ: Seton Hall University Press, 1954.

Brant, Irving. *The Bill of Rights: Its Origin and Meaning.* Indianapolis, IN: The Bobbs-Merrill Company, 1965.

————. *James Madison: The Father of the Constitution, 1787–1800.* Indianapolis, IN: The Bobbs-Merrill Company, 1950.

————. *James Madison.* 6 vols. Indianapolis, IN: The Bobbs-Merrill Company, 1941–61.

Buckley, Thomas E., S.J. *Church and State in Revolutionary Virginia, 1776–1787.* Charlottesville, VA: University Press of Virginia, 1977.

Butts, R. Freeman. *The American Tradition in Religion and Education.* Boston: Beacon Press, 1950.

Buzzard, Lynn R., and Samuel Ericsson. *The Battle for Religious Liberty.* Elgin, IL: David C. Cook, 1982.

Carter, Lief. *Contemporary Constitutional Decision Making.* New York: Pergamon Press, 1985.

Cherry, Conrad, ed. *God's New Israel: Religious Interpretations of American Destiny.* Englewood Cliffs, NJ: Prentice-Hall, 1971.

Cohn, Edmond, ed. *Supreme Court and Supreme Law.* Bloomington, IN: Indiana University Press, 1954.

Conant, James B. *Thomas Jefferson and the Development of American Public Education.* Berkeley, CA: University of California Press, 1962.

Constanzo, Joseph F. *This Nation Under God.* New York: Herder and Herder, 1964.

Cord, Robert L. *Separation of Church and State: Historical Fact and Current Fiction.* New York: Lambeth Press, 1982.

Corwin, Edward S. *The "Higher Law" Background of American Constitutional Law.* Ithaca, New York: Cornell University Press, 1955.

————. *A Constitution of Powers in a Secular State.* Charlottesville, VA: Michie Company, 1951.

Cousins, Norman, ed. *"In God We Trust": The Religious Beliefs and Ideas of the American Founding Fathers.* New York: Harper and Brothers, 1958.

Curry, James E. *Public Regulation of the Religious Use of Land.* Charlottesville, VA: Michie Company, 1964.

Curry, Thomas J. *The First Freedoms: Church and State in America to the Passage of the First Amendment.* New York: Oxford University Press, 1986.

Driesbach, Daniel L. *Real Threat and Mere Shadow: Religious Liberty and the First Amendment.* Westchester, IL: Crossway Books, 1987.

Edel, Wilbur. *Defenders of the Faith: Religion and Politics from the Pilgrim Fathers to Ronald Reagan.* New York: Praeger Publishers, 1987.

Everett, William J. *God's Federal Republic: Reconstructing Our Governing Symbol.* Mahwah, NJ: Paulist Press, 1988.

Farrand, Max. *The Framing of the Constitution*. New Haven, CT: Yale University Press, 1913.

————. *The Records of the Federal Convention of 1787*. 3 vols. New Haven, CT: Yale University Press, 1911.

Ferrara, Peter J. *Religion and the Constitution: A Reinterpretation*. Washington, D.C.: The Free Congress Research and Education Foundation, 1983.

Foote, Henry Wilder. *The Religion of Thomas Jefferson*. Boston, MA: Beacon Press, 1947.

Ford, Paul Leicester, ed. *The Works of Thomas Jefferson*. 12 vols. New York: G. P. Putnam's Sons, 1904–05.

Fowler, R. Booth. *Unconventional Partners: Religion and Liberal Culture in the United States*. Grand Rapids, MI: Wm. B. Eerdmans, 1989.

Handy, Robert T. *A Christian America: Protestant Hopes and Historical Realities*. New York: Oxford University Press, 1971.

Healey, Robert M. *Jefferson on Religion in Public Education*. New Haven, CT: Yale University Press, 1962.

Hensel, Jaye B., ed. *Church, State, and Politics*. Washington, D.C.: The Roscoe Pound-American Trial Lawyers Foundation, 1981.

Hertzke, Allen D. *Representing God in Washington*. Knoxville, TN: The University of Tennessee Press, 1988.

Hook, Sidney. *Religion in a Free Society*. Lincoln, NE: University of Nebraska Press, 1967.

Howe, Mark DeWolfe. *The Garden and the Wilderness: Religion and Government in American Constitutional History*. Chicago: University of Chicago Press, 1965.

————. *Cases on Church and State in the United States*. Cambridge, MA: Harvard University Press, 1952.

Hudson, Winthrop S. *Religion in America: An Historical Account of the Development of American Religious Life*. New York: Charles Scribner's Sons, 1965.

Huegli, Albert G., ed. *Church and State Under God*. St. Louis: Concordia Publishing House, 1964.

Hutcheson, Richard G., Jr. *God in the White House*. New York: Macmillan, 1988.Katz, Wilbur G. *Religion and American Constitutions*. Evanston, IL: Northwestern University Press, 1963.

Kauper, Paul G. *Religion and the Constitution*. Baton Rouge, LA: Louisiana State University Press, 1964.

Keller, Robert H., Jr. *American Protestantism and United States Indian Policy, 1869–82*. Lincoln, NE: University of Nebraska Press, 1983.

Kerwin, Jerome G. *Catholic Viewpoint on Church and State*. Garden City, New York: Hanover House, 1960.

Kik, J. Marcellus. *Church and State: The Story of Two Kingdoms*. New York: Thomas Nelson and Sons, 1963.

Koch, Adrienne. *Jefferson and Madison: The Great Collaboration*, New York: Oxford University Press, 1950.

Kurland, Philip B. *Religion and the Law: Of Church, State and the Supreme Court*. Chicago: Aldine, 1962.

————. *Church and State: The Supreme Court and the First Amendment*. Chicago: University of Chicago Press, 1975.

Kommers, Donald P., and Michael J. Wahoske, eds. *Freedom and Education: Pierce v. Society of Sisters Reconsidered*. Notre Dame, IN: Center for Civil Rights, University of Notre Dame Law School, 1978.

Konvitz, Milton R. *Religious Liberty and Conscience: A Constitutional Inquiry*. New York: Viking Press, 1968.

————. *Fundamental Liberties of a Free People: Religion, Speech, Press, Assembly*. Ithaca, New York: Cornell University Press, 1957.

Lehmann, Karl. *Thomas Jefferson: American Humanist*. Charlottesville, VA: University Press of Virginia, 1985.

Levinson, Sanford. *Constitutional Faith*. Princeton, NJ: Princeton University Press, 1988.

Levy, Leonard W. *Constitutional Opinions: Aspects of the Bill of Rights*. New York: Oxford University Press, 1986.

————. *The Establishment Clause: Religion and the First Amendment*. New York: Macmillan Publishing Co., 1986.

Lipscomb, Andrew and G. Bergh. *Writings of Thomas Jefferson*. 20 vols. Washington, D.C.: Issued under the auspices of The Thomas Jefferson Memorial Association, 1903–1904.

Littell, Franklin H. *From State Church to Pluralism: A Protestant Interpretation of Religion in American History*. Garden City, New York: Doubleday, 1962.

Loane, Marcus L. *Makers of Religious Freedom in the Seventeenth Century*. Grand Rapids, MI: William B. Eerdmans, 1961.

Loder, Lawrence. *Politics, Power and the Church: The Catholic Crisis and Its Challenge to American Pluralism*. New York: Macmillan, 1987.

Madison, James. *Letters and Other Writings of James Madison, Fourth President of the United States*. 4 vols. New York: R. Worthington, 1884.

Malbin, Michael J. *Religion and Politics: The Intentions of the Authors of the First Amendment*. Washington, D.C.: American Enterprise Institute for Public Policy Research, 1978.

Malone, Dumas. *Jefferson and His Time*. 6 vols. Boston: Little, Brown, and Company, 1948–81.

Marnell, William H. *The First Amendment: The History of Religious Freedom in America*. Garden City, New York: Doubleday, 1964.

McBrien, Richard P. *Caesar's Coin: Religion and Politics in America*. New York: Macmillan, 1987.

McGrath, John J., ed. *Church and State in American Law*. Milwaukee, WI: Bruce Publishing Company, 1962.

Mead, Sidney E. *The Lively Experiment: The Shaping of Christianity in America*. New York: Harper and Row, 1963.

Miller, Glenn T. *Religious Liberty in America: History and Prospects*. Philadelphia, PA: Westminster Press, 1976.

Miller, Perry. *Errand into the Wilderness*. Cambridge, MA: Harvard University Press, 1956.

————. *Roger Williams: His Contribution to the American Tradition*. Indianapolis, IN: Bobbs-Merrill Company, 1953.

Miller, Robert T., and Ronald B. Flowers. *Toward Benevolent Neutrality: Church, State, and the Supreme Court.* Rev. ed. Waco, TX: Markham Press Fund, 1982.

Miller, William Lee. *The First Liberty: Religion and the American Republic.* New York: Alfred A. Knopf, 1986.

Morgan, Richard E. *The Politics of Religious Conflict: Church and State in America.* 2nd ed. Washington, D.C.: University Press of America, 1980.

———. *The Supreme Court and Religion.* New York: Free Press,1972.

Murray, John Courtney. *The Problem of Religious Freedom.* Westminster, MD: The Newman Press, 1965.

Nelson, Frank C. *Public Schools: An Evangelical Approach.* Old Tappan, NJ: Fleming H. Revell Co., 1987.

Neuhaus, Richard John, *The Naked Public Square; Religion and Democracy in America,* Grand Rapids, MI: Wm. Erdmans, 1984.

Niebuhr, H. Richard. *The Kingdom of God in America.* New York: Harper and Row, 1937.

———. *We Hold These Truths: Catholic Reflections on the American Proposition.* Garden City, New York: Doubleday, 1964.

Nye, Russel B. *This Almost Chosen People.* East Lansing, MI: Michigan State University Press, 1966.

Oaks, Dallin H. *Religious Freedom and the Supreme Court.* Reprint ed. Washington, D.C.: Ethics and Public Policy Center, 1981.

———, ed. *The Wall Between Church and State.* Chicago: Chicago University Press, 1963.

O'Brien, Francis William. *Justice Reed and the First Amendment: The Religion Clauses.* Washington, D.C.: Georgetown University Press, 1958.

O'Neill, James M. *Catholicism and American Freedom.* New York: Harper and Brothers, 1952.

———. *Religion and Education Under the Constitution.* New York: Harper and Brothers, 1949.

Parsons, Wilfrid. *The First Freedom: Considerations on Church and State in the United States.* New York: Declan X. McMullen, 1948.

Pfeffer, Leo. *Religious Freedom.* Skokie, IL: National Textbook Company; American Civil Liberties Union, 1977.

———. *God, Caesar, and the Constitution: The Court as Referee of Church-State Confrontation.* Boston: Beacon Press, 1975.

———. *Church, State and Freedom.* Boston: Beacon Press, 1953; rev. ed., 1967.

———. *Creeds in Competition: A Creative Force in American Culture.* New York: Harper and Row, 1958.

———. *The Liberties of an American: The Supreme Court Speaks.* Boston: Beacon Press, 1956.

Reichley, A. James. *Religion in American Public Life.* Washington, D.C.: The Brookings Institution, 1985.

Riemer, Neal. *James Madison.* New York: Washington Square Press, 1968.

Rushdoony, Rousas John. *Christianity and the State.* Vallecito, CA: Ross House Books, 1986.

Sanders, Thomas G. *Protestant Concepts of Church and State.* New York: Holt, Rinehart and Winston, 1964.

Sandford, Charles B. *The Religious Life of Thomas Jefferson.* Charlottesville, VA: University Press of Virginia, 1984.

Schaeffer, Francis A. *A Christian Manifesto.* Westchester, IL: Crossway Books, 1981.

Schaeffer, Franky. *A Time for Anger: The Myth of Neutrality.* Westchester, IL: Crossway Books, 1982.

Schaff, Philip. *Church and State in the United States.* New York: Papers of the American Historical Society; G. P. Putnam's, 1888.

Schall, James V. *Reason, Revelation and the Foundations of Political Philosophy.* Baton Rouge, LA: State University Press, 1987.

Schulz, Constance Bartlett. "The Radical Religious Ideas of Thomas Jefferson and John Adams: A Comparison." Diss., University of Cincinnati, 1973.

Smith, Elwyn A., ed. *Religious Liberty in the United States: The Development of Church-State Thought Since the Revolutionary Era.* Philadelphia: Fortress Press, 1972.

———, ed. *The Religion of the Republic.* Philadelphia: Fortress Press, 1971.

Sorauf, Frank. *The Wall of Separation: The Constitutional Politics of Church and State.* Princeton, NJ: Princeton University Press, 1976.

Stedman, Murray S. *Religion and Politics in America.* New York: Harcourt and World, 1964.

Stokes, Anson Phelps. *Church and State in the United States.* 3 vols. New York: Harper and Brothers, 1950.

Tussman, Joseph, ed. *The Supreme Court on Church and State.* New York: Oxford University Press, 1962.

Tuveson, Ernest L. *Redeemer Nation: The Idea of America's Millennial Role.* Chicago: University of Chicago Press, 1968.

Wald, Kenneth. *Religion and Politics in the United States.* New York: St. Martin's Press, 1987.

Walton, Rus. *One Nation Under God.* Washington, D.C.: Third Century, 1975.

Weber, Paul J., and Gilbert, Dennis A., *Private Churches and Public Money: Church-Government Fiscal Relations,* Westport, CT: Greenwood Press, 1982.

Williams, David R. *Wilderness Lost: The Religious Origins of the American Mind.* Cranbury, NJ: Susquehana University Press, 1987.

Williams, Roger. *The Complete Writings of Roger Williams.* Vol. 1. Providence, RI: Providence Press, 1866.

Wilson, John F., ed. *Church and State in America: A Bibliographical Guide.* Westport, CT: Greenwood Press, 1986.

Wood, James E., Jr., ed. *Religion and the State: Essays in Honor of Leo Pfeffer.* Waco, TX: Baylor University Press, 1985.

Wood, James E., Jr., Robert T. Miller, and E. Bruce Thompson. *Church and State in Scripture, History and Constitutional Law.* Waco, TX: Baylor University Press, 1958.

LAW REVIEW AND SCHOLARLY JOURNALS

Alfange, Dean, Jr. "On Judicial Policymaking and Constitutional Change: Another Look at the 'Original Intent' Theory of Constitutional Interpretation," 5 *Hastings Constitutional Law Quarterly* 603 (1978).

Antieau, Chester James. "Religious Liberty Under the Fourteenth Amendment," 22 *Notre Dame Lawyer* 271 (1947).

Arons, Stephen A. "The Separation of School and State: *Pierce* Reconsidered," 46 *Harvard Educational Review* 76 (1976).

Baker, John S., Jr. "The Religion Clauses Reconsidered: The *Jaffree* Case," 15 *Cumberland Law Review* 125 (1985).

Beaver, R. Pierce. "Church, State, and the Indians: Indian Missions in the New Nation," 4 *Journal of Church and State* 11 (1962).

———. "The Churches and President Grant's Peace Policy," 4 *Journal of Church and State* 174 (1962).

Bellah, Robert N. "Civil Religion in America," 96 *Daedalus* 1 (Winter 1967).

Berman, Harold J. "Religion and Law: The First Amendment in Historical Perspective," 35 *Emory Law Journal* 777 (1986).

———. "The Influence of Christianity Upon the Development of Law," 12 *Oklahoma Law Review* 86 (1959).

Beth, Loren P. "The Wall of Separation and the Supreme Court," 38 *Minnesota Law Review* 215 (1954).

Bird, Wendell R. "Freedom from Establishment and Unneutrality in Public School Instruction and Religious School Regulation," 2 *Harvard Journal of Law and Public Policy* 125 (1979).

Boorstin, Daniel J. "The Founding Fathers and the Courage to Doubt," in *James Madison on Religious Liberty*, ed. Robert S. Alley. Buffalo, New York: Prometheus Books, 1985.

Borden, Morton. "Federalist, Antifederalist, and Religious Freedom," 21 *Journal of Church and State* 469 (1979).

Boyd, Julian P. "On the Need for 'Frequent Recurrence to Fundamental Principles,'" 62 *Virginia Law Review* 859 (1976).

Brann, Eva T. H. "Madison's 'Memorial and Remonstrance,' A Model of American Eloquence," 32 *St. John's Review* 55 (1981); reprinted in *Rhetoric and American Statesmanship*, eds. Glen E. Thurow and Jeffrey D. Wallin. Durham, NC: Carolina Academic Press, 1984.

Brant, Irving. "The Madison Heritage," 35 *New York University Law Review* 882 (1960).

———. "Madison: On the Separation of Church and State," 8 *The William and Mary Quarterly* 3 (3rd series, January 1951).

Brest, Paul. "The Role of Original Intent," Conference on Original Intent and the Bill of Rights, Charlottesville, VA., May 1, 1986.

———. "The Misconceived Quest for the Original Understanding," 60 *Boston University Law Review* 204 (1980).

Briceland, Alan V. "Thomas Jefferson's Epitaph: Symbol of a Lifelong Crusade Against Those Who Would 'Usurp the Throne of God,'" 29 *Journal of Church and State* 285 (1987).

164   Bibliography

Brown, Ernest J. "Quis Custodiet Ipsos Custodes?—The School-Prayer Cases," 1963 *The Supreme Court Review* 1.

Brown, Richard D. "The Founding Fathers of 1776 and 1787: A Collective View," 33 *The William and Mary Quarterly* 465 (3rd series, 1976).

Brownfield, Allen C. "The Constitutional Intent Concerning Matters of Church and State," 5 *The William and Mary Law Review* 174 (1964).

Butler, Paul F., Jr. "George Washington and Religious Liberty," 17 *The William and Mary Quarterly* 486 (3rd series, 1960).

Butler, Paul M., and Alfred L. Scanlan. "Wall of Separation—Judicial Gloss on the First Amendment," 37 *Notre Dame Lawyer* 288 (1962).

Cahn, Edmond. "On Government and Prayer," 37 *New York University Law Review* 981 (1962).

———. "The 'Establishment of Religion' Puzzle," 36 *New York University Law Review* 127– (1961).

Calisch, Edward N. "Jefferson's Religion," in *The Writings of Thomas Jefferson*, eds. Andrew A. Lipscomb and Albert Ellery Bergh. Washington, D.C.: The Thomas Jefferson Memorial Association, 1905.

Cherry, Conrad. "Nation, Church, and Private Religion: The Emergence of an American Pattern," 14 *Journal of Church and State* 223 (1972).

"*Church v. State* and the Supreme Court: The Current Meaning of the Establishment Clause," 5 *Oklahoma City University Law Review* 683 (1980).

Cochran, Clarke E. "Public-Private-Secular-Sacred: A Context for Understanding the Church-State Debate," 29 *Journal of Church and State* 113 (1987).

Cohen, Charles L. "The 'Liberty or Death' Speech: A Note on Religion and Revolutionary Rhetoric," 38 *The William and Mary Quarterly* 702 (3rd series, 1981).

Cord, Robert L. "Church-State Separation: Restoring the 'No Preference' Doctrine of the First Amendment," 9 *Harvard Journal of Law and Public Policy* 129 (1986).

———. "Neo-Incorporation: The Burger Court and the Due Process Clause of the Fourteenth Amendment," 44 *Fordham Law Review* 215 (1975).

Cornelius, William J. "Church and State—The Mandate of the Establishment Clause: Wall of Separation or Benign Neutrality?" 16 *St. Mary's Law Journal* 1 (1984).

Corwin, Edward. "The Supreme Court as National School Board," 14 *Law and Contemporary Problems* 3 (1949).

Costanzo, Joseph F. "Thomas Jefferson, Religious Education and Public Law," 8 *Journal of Public Law* 81 (1959).

———. "Federal Aid to Education and Religious Education," 36 *University of Detroit Law Journal* 1 (1958).

———. "Religion in Public School Education," 31 *Thought* 216 (Summer, 1956).

———. "Religious Heritage of American Democracy," 30 *Thought* 485 (Winter 1955–56).

Crain, Christopher A. "Free Exercise of Religion and Indian Burial Grounds," 12 *Harvard Journal of Law and Public Policy* 246–251 (Winter 1989).

Curry, Patricia E. "James Madison and the Burger Court: Converging Views of Church-State Separation," 56 *Indiana Law Journal* 615 (1981).

Curtis, Michael Kent. "Judge Hand's History: An Analysis of History and Method in *Jaffree v. Board of School Commissioners of Mobile County*," 86 *West Virginia Law Review* 109 (1983).

―――. "The Bill of Rights As a Limitation on State Authority: A Reply to Professor Berger," 16 *Wake Forest Law Review* 45 (1980).

Dillon, Michael R. "Religious Liberty, Common Law, and the Supreme Court," 14 *Journal of Church and State* 211 (1972).

Drakeman, Donald L. "Antidisestablishmentarianism: The Latest (and Longest) Word from the Supreme Court in *Marsh v. Chambers*," 5 *Cardozo Law Review* 153 (1983).

―――. "Religion and the Republic: James Madison and the First Amendment," 25 *Journal of Church and State* 427 (1983).

Drinan, Robert F. "The Novel 'Liberty' Created by the *McCollum* Decision," 39 *Georgetown Law Review* 216 (1951).

Dunsford, John E. "Prayer in the Well: Some Heretical Reflections on the Establishment Syndrome," 1984 *Utah Law Review* 1 (1984).

Emerson, Thomas I. "Colonial Intentions and Current Realities of the First Amendment," 125 *University of Pennsylvania Law Review* 737 (1977).

Esbeck, Carl H. "Five Views of Church-State Relations in Contemporary American Thought," 1986 *Brigham Young University Law Review* 371 (1986).

―――. "Establishment Clause Limits on Governmental Interference with Religious Organizations," 41 *Washington and Lee Law Review* 347 (1984).

―――. "Religion and a Neutral State: Imperative or Impossibility?" 15 *Cumberland Law Review* 67 (1984).

Fahy, Charles. "Religion, Education, and the Supreme Court," 14 *Law and Contemporary Problems* 73 (1949).

Fairman, Charles. "Does the Fourteenth Amendment Incorporate the Bill of Rights? The Original Understanding," 2 *Stanford Law Review* 5 (1949).

Fink, Nancy H. "The Establishment Clause According to the Supreme Court: The Mysterious Eclipse of Free Exercise Values," 27 *Catholic University Law Review* 207 (1978).

"First Amendment Religion Clause: Historical Metamorphosis," 61 *Northwestern University Law Review* 760 (1966).

Fleet, Elizabeth, ed. "Madison's 'Detached Memoranda,'" 3 *The William and Mary Quarterly* 535 (3rd series, 1946).

Flowers, Ronald B. "A Selected Bibliography on Religion and Public Education," 14 *Journal of Church and State* 475 (1972).

Forkosch, Morris D. "Religion, Education, and the Constitution—A Middle Way," 23 *Loyola Law Review* 617 (1977).

Frankfurter, Felix. "Memorandum on 'Incorporation' of the Bill of Rights into the Due Process Clause of the Fourteenth Amendment," 78 *Harvard Law Review* 746 (1965).

Gaffney, Edward McGlynn, Jr. "Biblical Religion and Constitutional Adjudication in a Secularized Society," 31 *Mercer Law Review* 422 (1980).

―――. "History and Legal Interpretation: The Early Distortion of the Fourteenth Amendment by the Gilded Age Court," 25 *Catholic University Law Review* 207 (1976).

Gaustad, Edwin S. "A Disestablished Society: Origins of the First Amendment," 11 *Journal of Church and State* 409 (1969).

Giannella, Donald. "Religious Liberty, Nonestablishment, and Doctrinal Development. Part I, The Religious Liberty Guarantee," 80 *Harvard Law Review* 1381 (1967).

———. "Religious Liberty, Nonestablishment, and Doctrinal Development. Part II, The Nonestablishment Principle," 81 *Harvard Law Review* 513 (1968).

Giffin, Frederick C. "John Locke and Religious Toleration," 9 *Journal of Church and State* 378 (1967).

Goldstein, Nancy B. "A Strategy for Satan: Maintaining Neutrality in Religion Clause Challenges to Public School Curricula," 23 *New England Law Review* 321 (1988).

Gould, William D. "The Religious Opinions of Thomas Jefferson," 20 *Mississippi Valley Historical Review* 191 (1933).

Graham, John Remington. "A Restatement of the Intended Meaning of the Establishment Clause in Relation to Education and Religion," 1981 *Brigham Young University Law Review* 333 (1981).

Grey, Thomas C. "Do We Have an Unwritten Constitution?" 27 *Stanford Law Review* 703 (1975).

Hammett, Harold D. "The Homogenized Wall," 53 *American Bar Association Journal* 929 (1967).

———. "Separation of Church and State: By One Wall or Two?" 7 *Journal of Church and State* 190 (1965).

Handy, Robert T. "The American Tradition of Religious Freedom: An Historical Analysis," 13 *Journal of Public Law* 247 (1964).

Harris, Troy. "Neutral Principles of the Law and Church Property in the United States," 30 *Journal of Church and State* 463 (1988).

Haskins, George L. "Representative Government and the 'Bible Commonwealth' in Early Massachusetts," 9 *Akron Law Review* 207 (1975).

Henkin, Louis. "'Selective Incorporation' in the Fourteenth Amendment," 73 *Yale Law Journal* 74 (1963).

Hirsch, Elizabeth. "John Cotton and Roger Williams: Their Controversy Concerning Religious Liberty," 10 *Church History* 38 (1941).

"The History and Utility of the Supreme Court's Present Definition of Religion," 26 *Loyola Law Review* 87 (1980).

Hitchcock, James. "The Supreme Court and Religion: Historical Overview and Future Prognosis," 24 *Saint Louis University Law Journal* 183 (1980).

Horowitz, Gregory. "Accommodation and Neutrality under the Establishment Clause: The Foster Care Challenge," 98 *Yale Law Journal* 617–637 (January 1989).

———. "Accommodation and Neutrality under the Establishment Clause," 98 *Yale Law Journal* 617 (1988).

Howard, A. E. Dick. "James Madison and the Founding of the Republic" in

James Madison on Religious Liberty, ed. Robert S. Alley. Buffalo, New York: Prometheus Books, 1985.

Hutchins, Robert M. "The Future of the Wall," in *The Wall Between Church and State,* ed. Dallin H. Oaks. Chicago: University of Chicago Press, 1963.

Ingber, Stanley. "Religion or Ideology: A Needed Clarification of the Religion Clauses," 41 *Stanford Law Review* 233–333 (January 1989).

Ives, J. Moss. "The Catholic Contribution to Religious Liberty in Colonial America," 21 *The Catholic Historical Review* 283 (1935).

"Jaffree v. Board of School Commissioners: An Interpretivist Challenge," 34 *Alabama Law Review* 657 (1983).

"Jefferson and the Church-State Wall: A Historical Examination of the Man and the Metaphor," 1978 *Brigham Young University Law Review* 645 (1978).

Katz, Wilber G. "Freedom of Religion and State Neutrality," 20 *University of Chicago Law Review* 426 (1953).

Kauper, Paul G. "The Supreme Court and the Establishment Clause: Back to *Everson?*" 25 *Case Western Reserve Law Review* 107 (1974).

———. *"Everson v. Board of Education:* A Product of the Judicial Will," 15 *Arizona Law Review* 307 (1973).

———. "Separation of Church and State—A Constitutional View," 9 *Catholic Lawyer* 32 (1963).

———. "Church and State: Cooperative Separatism," 60 *Michigan Law Review* 1 (1961).

———. "Released Time and Religious Liberty: A Further Reply," 53 *Michigan Law Review* 233 (1954).

———. "Church, State and Freedom: A Review," 52 *Michigan Law Review* 829 (1954).

Kessler, Sanford. "Locke's Influence on Jefferson's 'Bill for Establishing Religious Freedom,'" 25 *Journal of Church and State* 231 (1983).

Ketcham, Ralph L. "James Madison and Religion—A New Hypothesis," 38 *Journal of the Presbyterian Historical Society* 65 (1960).

Kirk, Russell. "We Cannot Separate Christian Morals and the Rule of Law," 4, no. 4 *Christian Legal Society Quarterly* 21 (1983).

Kirven, Gerald. "Freedom of Religion or Freedom From Religion?" 48 *American Bar Association Journal* 816 (September 1962).

Klinkhamer, Marie Carolyn. "The Blaine Amendment of 1875: Private Motives for Political Action," 42 *The Catholic Historical Review* 15 (1955).

Knoles, George Harmon. "The Religious Ideas of Thomas Jefferson," 30 *Mississippi Valley Historical Review* 187 (1943–44).

Konvitz, Milton R. "Separation of Church and State: The First Freedom," 14 *Law and Contemporary Problems* 44 (1949).

Kruse, Clifton J. "The Historical Meaning and Judicial Construction of the Establishment of Religion Clause of the First Amendment," 2 *Washburn Law Journal* 65 (1962).

Kurland, Philip B. "The Irrelevance of the Constitution: The Religion Clauses of the First Amendment," 24 *Villanova Law Review* 3 (1978–79).

———. "Of Church and State and the Supreme Court," 29 *University of Chicago Law Review* 1 (1961).

LaFontaine, Charles V. "God and Nation in Selected United States Presidential Inaugural Addresses, 1789–1945," 18 *Journal of Church and State* 39, 503 (1976).

Laycock, Douglas. "Equal Access and Moments of Silence: The Equal Status of Religious Speech by Private Speakers," 81 *Northwestern University Law Review* 1 (1986).

———. "'Non-Referential' Aid to Religion: A False Claim About Original Intent," 27 *William and Mary Law Review* 873 (1986).

Leedes, Gary C. "A Critique of Illegitimate Noninterpretivism," 8 *University of Dayton Law Review* 533 (1983).

"Legislative Free Exercise and Conflict Between the Clauses," 61 *Northwestern University Law Review* 816 (1966).

Levinson, Sanford. "'The Constitution' in American Civil Religion," 1979 *The Supreme Court Review* 123.

Lider, Michael D. "Religious Pluralism and Education in Historical Perspective: A Critique of the Supreme Court's Establishment Clause Jurisprudence," 22 *Wake Forest Law Review* 813 (1987).

Littell, Franklin H. "Federal Common Law or National Ideology?" 14 *Journal of Church and State* 187 (1972).

Little, David. "Thomas Jefferson's Religious Views and Their Influence on the Supreme Court's Interpretation of the First Amendment," 26 *Catholic University Law Review* 57 (1976).

Louisell, David W. "Does the Constitution Require a Purely Secular Society?" 26 *Catholic University Law Review* 20 (1976).

Luper, Ira C. "Where Rights Begin: The Problem of Burdens on the Free Exercise of Religion," 102 *Harvard Law Review* 933–990 (March 1989).

Malone, Dumas. "The Madison-Jefferson Friendship," in *James Madison on Religious Liberty*, ed. Robert S. Alley. Buffalo, New York: Prometheus Books, 1985.

Mauney, Constance. "Religion and First Amendment Protections: An Analysis of Justice Black's Constitutional Interpretation," 10 *Pepperdine Law Review* 377 (1983).

McClellan, James. "Congressional Retraction of Federal Court Jurisdiction to Protect the Reserved Powers of the States: The Helms Prayer Bill and a Return to First Principles," 27 *Villanova Law Review* 1019 (1981–82).

———. "The Making and the Unmaking of the Establishment Clause," in *A Blueprint for Judicial Reform*, eds. Patrick B. McGuigan and Randall R. Rader. Washington, D.C.: Free Congress Research and Education Foundation, 1981.

McCloskey, Robert G. "Principles, Powers, and Values: The Establishment Clause and the Supreme Court," in *1964 Religion and Public Order*, ed. Donald A. Giannella. Chicago: University of Chicago Press, 1964.

Mead, Sidney E. "Religion, Constitutional Federalism, Rights, and the Court," 14 *Journal of Church and State* 191 (1972).

———. "Neither Church nor State: Reflections on James Madison's 'Line of Separation,'" 10 *Journal of Church and State* 349 (1968).

Medhurst, Martin J. "From Duche to Provost: The Birth of the Inaugural Prayer," 24 *Journal of Church and State* 573 (1982).

Meiklejohn, Alexander. "Educational Cooperation Between Church and State," 14 *Law and Contemporary Problems* 61 (1949).

Meiklejohn, Donald. "Religion in the Burger Court: The Heritage of Mr. Justice Black," 10 *Indiana Law Review* 645 (1977).

Merel, Gail. "The Protection of Individual Choice: A Consistent Understanding of Religion Under the First Amendment," 45 *University of Chicago Law Review* 805 (1978).

Meyer, Alfred W. "The Blaine Amendment and the Bill of Rights," 64 *Harvard Law Review* 939 (1951).

Meyer, Hermine Herta. Statement Before the Senate Judiciary Committee on S.J. Res. 199, The School Prayer Amendment, 16 September 1982.

Miller, Arthur Selwyn. "An Inquiry into the Relevance of the Intentions of the Founding Fathers, with Special Emphasis Upon the Doctrine of Separation of Powers," 27 *Arkansas Law Review* 583 (1973).

Miller, Justin K. "Damned If You Do, Damned If You Don't: Religious Shunning and the Free Exercise Clause," 137 *University of Pennsylvania Law Review* 271 (1988).

Miller, Perry. "Religion and Society in the Early Literature: The Religious Impulse in the Founding of Virginia," 5 *The William and Mary Quarterly* 492 (3rd series, 1948); 6 *The William and Mary Quarterly* 24 (3rd series, 1949).

———. "The Contribution of the Protestant Churches to Religious Liberty in Colonial America," 4 *Church History* 57 (1935).

Moehlmann, Conrad Henry. "The Wall of Separation: The Law and the Facts," 38 *American Bar Association Journal* 281 (1952).

Moore, Leroy. "Religious Liberty: Roger Williams and the Revolutionary Era," 34 *Church History* 57 (1965).

———. "Roger Williams As an Enduring Symbol for Baptists," 7 *Journal of Church and State* 181 (1965).

Morris, Richard B. "The Judeo-Christian Foundations of the American Political System," in *James Madison on Religious Liberty*, ed. Robert S. Alley. Buffalo, New York: Prometheus Books, 1985.

Mott, Royden J. "Sources of Jefferson's Ecclesiastical Views," 3 *Church History* 267 (1934).

Murphy, Walter F. "Constitutional Interpretation: The Art of the Historian, Magician, or Statesman?," 87 *Yale Law Journal* 1752 (1978).

Murray, John Courtney. "Law or Prepossessions?" 14 *Law and Contemporary Problems* 23 (1949).

———. "The Freedom of Religion," 6 *Theological Studies* 229 (1945).

"Nineteenth Century Judicial Thought Concerning Church-State Relations,"40 *Minnesota Law Review* 672 (1956).

Nussbaum, L. Martin. "*Mueller v. Allen*: Tuition Tax Relief and the Original Intent," 7 *Harvard Journal of Law and Public Policy* 551 (1984).

O'Brien, Francis William. "The States and 'No Establishment': Proposed Amendments to the Constitution Since 1798," 4 *Washburn Law Journal* 183 (1965).

O'Neill, James M. "Nonpreferential Aid to Religion Is Not an Establishment of Religion," 2 *Buffalo Law Review* 242 (1952–53).

Paulsen, Michael A. "Religion, Equality and the Constitution: An Equal Protection Approach to Establishment Clause Adjudication," 61 *Notre Dame Law Review* 311 (1986).

Peeler, David P. "Thomas Jefferson's Nursery of Republican Patriots: The University of Virginia," 28 *Journal of Church and State* 79 (1986).

Perry, Barbara A. "Justice Hugo Black and the 'Wall of Separation' Between Church and State," 31 *Journal of Church and State* 55 (1989).

Pfeffer, Leo. "The Deity in American Constitutional History," 23 *Journal of Church and State* 215 (1981).

———. "Uneasy Trinity: Church, State, and Constitution," 2 *Civil Liberties Review* 138 (1975).

———. "Religion-Blind Government," 15 *Stanford Law Review* 389 (1963).

———. "Released Time and Religious Liberty: A Reply," 53 *Michigan Law Review* 91 (1954).

———. "No Law Respecting an Establishment of Religion," 2 *Buffalo Law Review* 225 (1952–53).

———. "Church and State: Something Less Than Separation," 19 *University of Chicago Law Review* 1 (1951).

Plöchl, Willibald M. "Thomas Jefferson, Author of the Statute of Virginia for Religious Freedom," 3 *Jurist* 182 (1943).

Rattin, Daniel. "Save Your Local Church or Synagogue: When Are Taxpayer Contributions to Religious Organizations Deductible Under Section 170?" 63 *New York University Law Review* 890 (1988).

"Rebuilding the Wall: The Case for a Return to the Strict Interpretation of the Establishment Clause," 81 *Columbia Law Review* 1463 (1981).

"Religious-Holiday Observances in the Public Schools," 48 *New York University Law Review* 1116 (1973).

"Restoring School Prayer by Eliminating Judicial Review: An Examination of Congressional Power to Limit Federal Court Jurisdiction," 60 *North Carolina Law Review* 831 (1982).

Rodes, Robert E., Jr. "Religious Education and the Historical Method of Constitutional Interpretation—A Review Article," 9 *Rutgers Law Review* 682 (1955).

Roelofs, H. Mark. "Church and State in America: Toward a Biblically Derived Reformation of Their Relationship," 50 *The Review of Politics* 561 (1988).

Rutland, Robert Allen. "James Madison's Dream: A Secular Republic," in *James Madison on Religious Liberty*, ed. Robert S. Alley. Buffalo, New York: Prometheus Books, 1985.

Sandler, S. Gerald. "Lockean Ideas in Jefferson's Bill for Establishing Religious Freedom," 21 *Journal of the History of Ideas* 110 (1960).

Schmidt, Godfrey P. "Religious Liberty and the Supreme Court of the United States," 17 *Fordham Law Review* 173 (1948).

"The Secular State," Editorial, 7 *Journal of Church and State* 169 (1965).

"Secularism in the Law: The Religion of Secular Humanism," 8 *Ohio Northern University Law Review* 329 (1981).

Serra, Theresa M. "Invocations and Benedictions—Is the Supreme Court Graduating to a Marsh Analysis?" 65 *University of Detroit Law Review* 843 (1988).

Shepherd, Michael S. "Home Schooling: Dimensions of Controversy, 1970–1984," 31 *Journal of Church and State* 101 (1989).

Shoke, Kiply S. "Public Education in Shreds: Religious Challenges to Curricular Decisions," 64 *Indiana Law Journal* 111 (1988).

Singleton, Marvin K. "Colonial Virginia as First Amendment Matrix: Henry, Madison and the Establishment Clause," 8 *Journal of Church and State* 344 (1966).

Sky, Theodore. "The Establishment Clause, the Congress and the Schools: An Historical Perspective," 52 *Virginia Law Review* 1395 (1966).

Smith, Michael E. "The Special Place of Religion in the Constitution," 1983 *The Supreme Court Review* 83.

Smith, Rodney K. "Getting Off On the Wrong Foot and Back On Again: A Reexamination of the History of the Framing of the Religion Clauses of the First Amendment and a Critique of the *Reynolds* and *Everson* Decisions," 20 *Wake Forest Law Review* 569 (1984).

Smith, Ronald A. "Freedom of Religion and the Land Ordinance of 1785," 24 *Journal of Church and State* 589 (1982).

Smith, William French. "Some Observations on the Establishment Clause," 11 *Pepperdine Law Review* 457 (1984).

Snee, Joseph M. "Religious Disestablishment and the Fourteenth Amendment," 1954 *Washington University Law Quarterly* 371 (1954); reprinted 1 *Catholic Lawyer* 301 (1955).

Stone, Jeffrey Dean. "The Equal Access Controversy: The Religious Clauses and the Meaning of 'Neutrality,'" 81 *Northwestern University Law Review* 168 (1986).

"The Supreme Court, the First Amendment, and Religion in the Public Schools," 63 *Columbia Law Review* 73 (1963).

Taylor, T. Raber. "Equal Protection of Religion: Today's Public School Program," 38 *American Bar Association Journal* 277 (April 1952).

Thompson, Kenneth W. "The Religious Transformation of Politics and the Political Transformation of Religion," 50 *The Review of Politics* 545 (1988).

Toms, Robert L., and John W. Whitehead. "The Religious Student in Public Education: Resolving a Constitutional Dilemma," 27 *Emory Law Journal* 3 (1978).

Toscano, Paul James. "A Dubious Neutrality: The Establishment of Secularism in the Public Schools," 1979 *Brigham Young University Law Review* 177 (1979).

Toulouse, Mark G. "Pat Robertson: Apocalyptic Theology and American Foreign Policy," 31 *Journal of Church and State* 73 (1989).

"Toward a Constitutional Definition of Religion," 91 *Harvard Law Review* 1056 (1978).

Tushnet, Mark V. "The Constitution of Religion," 50 *The Review of Politics* 628 (1988).

————. "Following the Rules Laid Down: A Critique of Interpretivism and Neutral Principles," 96 *Harvard Law Review* 781 (1983).

Unmack, Fred. "Equality Under the First Amendment: Protecting Native American Religious Practices on Public Lands," 8 *The Public Land Law Review* 165–176 (Annual 1987).

Van Alstyne, William. "Trends in the Supreme Court: Mr. Jefferson's Crumbling Wall—A Comment on *Lynch v. Donnelly*," 1984 *Duke Law Journal* 770 (1984).

Van Patten, Jonathan K. "In the End Is the Beginning: An Inquiry into the Meaning of the Religion Clauses," 27 *Saint Louis University Law Journal* 1 (1983).

Waite, Edward F. "Jefferson's 'Wall of Separation': What and Where?" 33 *Minnesota Law Review* 494 (1949).

Weber, Paul J. "James Madison and Religious Equality: The Perfect Separation," 44 *Review of Politics* 163 (1982).

Welch, Don D. "The State as a Purveyer of Morality," 56 *George Washington Law Review* 540 (1988).

Whitehead, John W. "Accommodation and Equal Treatment of Religion: Federal Funding of Religiously Affiliated Child Care Facilities," 26 *Harvard Journal of Legislation* 573 (1989).

Whitehead, John W., and John Conlan. "The Establishment of the Religion of Secular Humanism and Its First Amendment Implications," 10 *Texas Tech Law Review* 1 (1978).

Wilcox, Clyde. "The Christian Right in Twentieth Century America: Continuity and Change," 50 *The Review of Politics* 659 (1988).

Williams, J. D. "The Separation of Church and State in Mormon Theory and Practice," 9 *Journal of Church and State* 238 (1967).

Witheridge, David E. "No Freedom of Religion for American Indians," 18 *Journal of Church and State* 5 (1976).

Wood, Jame E., Jr. "Religious Pluralism and Religious Freedom," 31 *Journal of Church and State* 7 (1989).

Wyndham, Mark. "The Historical Background to the Issue of Religious Liberty in the Revolutionary Era," 3, no. 1 *Journal of Christian Reconstruction* 152 (Summer 1976).

NEWSPAPERS, RELIGIOUS JOURNALS, AND OTHER MAGAZINES

"ACLU Lawsuit Blocks Hanukah [sic] Ceremony in Public Park," *Washington Post*, December 28, 1986, Sec. A, p. 3.

Ascik, Thomas R. "Congress and the Supreme Court: Court Jurisdiction and School Prayer," *Backgrounder*. Washington, D.C.: The Heritage Foundation, June 25, 1980.

Bauer, Gerald. "The Quest for Religious Freedom in Virginia," 41 *Historical Magazine of the Protestant Episcopal Church* 85 (1972).

Bernardin, Joseph. "Religion and Politics: The Future Agenda." Speech, Georgetown University, Washington, D.C., October 25, 1984.

Blumenthal, Sidney. "The Right's Quest for Law From a Mythical Past," *Washington Post*, November 3, 1985, Sec. C, p. 1.

Bork, Robert. "The Struggle Over the Role of the Court," *National Review* 1137 (September 17, 1982).

Bowen, Ezra. "Radicals in Conservative Garb," *Time* 71 (11 August 1986).

Brennan, William J. "The Constitution of the United States." Remarks made at Georgetown University, Washington, D.C., October 12, 1985.

Buckley, Thomas E. "Church-State Settlement in Virginia: The Presbyterian Contribution," 54 *Journal of Presbyterian History* 105 (1976).

Coleson, Edward. "The American Revolution: Typical or Unique?" 3, no. 1 *Journal of Christian Reconstruction* 172 (Summer 1976).

Cord, Robert L. "Understanding the First Amendment," *National Review* 26 (January 22, 1982).

Dencer, F. Tayton. "The Revolution in Constitutional Theory." Speech, The Rutherford Institute Seminar, Dallas, Texas. May 17, 1986.

Donovan, Teresa L., and Patrick B. McGuigan. "Defining the Separation Between Church and State by Reconnoitering With the Framers: A Judicial Reform Proposal," 2 *Cogitations* 65 (Winter 1984).

Gow, Haven Bradford. "Religious Liberty and the First Amendment," no. 207 *Chalcedon Report* (November 1982).

Green, Jesse C., Jr. "The Early Virginia Argument for Separation of Church and State," 11 *Baptist History and Heritage* 16 (1976).

Hall, J. Leslie. "The Religious Opinions of Thomas Jefferson," 21 *The Sewanee Review* 163 (April 1913).

Hentoff, Nat. "The Case of the Godless License Plate," *Washington Post*, 8 November 1986, Sec. A, p. 23.

Hodge, A. A. "The Christian Foundation of American Politics," 5, no. 1 *Journal of Christian Reconstruction* 36 (Summer 1978).

Hood, Fred J. "Revolution and Religious Liberty: The Conservation of the Theocratic Concept in Virginia," 40 *Church History* 170 (1971).

"How Would the Founding Fathers Vote on the School Prayer Case?" 41 *Michigan Educational Journal* 12 (December 1963).

Huntley, William B. "Jefferson's Public and Private Religion," 79 *South Atlantic Quarterly* 286 (1980).

"Intent of the Framers," *Newsweek* 97 (28 October 1985).

Jones, Archie P. "The Christian Roots of the War for Independence," 3, no. 1 *Journal of Christian Reconstruction* 6 (Summer 1976).

Klenk, John. "President Reagan's Proposed Voluntary School Prayer Amendment," *Backgrounder*. Washington, D.C.: Republican Study Committee, 1982.

Magnuson, Roger P. "Thomas Jefferson and the Separation of Church and State," 27 *The Education Forum* 417 (1963).

Mead, Sidney E. "Thomas Jefferson's 'Fair Experiment'—Religious Freedom," 23 *Religion in Life* 566 (1953–54).

Meese, Edwin, III. "Toward a Jurisprudence of Original Intention," II, no. 1 *Benchmark* 1 (January-February 1986).

Moore, John S. "The Struggle for Religious Freedom in Virginia," 11 *Baptist History and Heritage* 160 (1976).

Pearson, Samuel C. "Nature's God: A Reassessment of the Religion of the Founding Fathers," 46 *Religion in Life* 152 (1977).

Rees, Grover. Statement before the Senate Judiciary Committee on S.J. Res. 199, The School Prayer Amendment, September 16, 1982.

Robbins, John W. "The Political Philosophy of the Founding Fathers," 3, no. 1 *Journal of Christian Reconstruction* 52 (Summer 1976).

Rushdoony, Rousas John. "The Freedom of the Church," no. 16 *Chalcedon Position Paper* (1980).

———. "The Myth of an American Enlightenment," 3, no. 1 *Journal of Christian Reconstruction* 69 (Summer 1976).

Smylie, James H. "Madison and Witherspoon, Theological Roots of American Political Thought," 22 *Princeton University Library Chronicle* 18 (1961).

Sobran, Joseph. "Brennan's View of the Constitution," *Washington Times*, 17 October 1985, Sec. D, p. 3.

Taylor, E. L. Hebden. "The Rock From Which America Was Hewn," 3, no. 1 *Journal of Christian Reconstruction* 178 (Summer 1976).

Taylor, Stuart, Jr. "Who's Right About the Constitution?: *Meese v. Brennan*," *The New Republic* 17 (January 6 and 13, 1986).

———. "Brennan Opposes Legal View Urged by Administration," *New York Times*, 13 October 1985, Sec. A, p. 1.

Index

About the Editor and Contributors

PAUL J. WEBER is Distinguished Teaching Professor at the University of Louisville, Chair of the Department of Political Science and Executive Director of the Grawemeyer Award in World Order. He is co-author of *Unfounded Fears: Myths and Realities of a Constitutional Convention* (Greenwood, 1989) and *Private Churches and Public Money* (Greenwood, 1981), as well as numerous articles and reviews in scholarly journals.

JAMES M. DUNN is Executive Director of the Baptist Joint Committee on Public Affairs in Washington, D.C. He is author of several books, including *Roots of Hope* and *An Approach to Christian Ethics*, and coauthor of *Poltics: A Guidebook for Christians*. He has also published numerous articles in scholarly and religious journals.

ROBERT M. HEALEY is Professor of Church History at the University of Dubuque Theological Seminary. He is the author of a number of books, including *Jefferson on Religion in Public Education* (1962) and *The French Achievement: Private School Aid, a Lesson for America* (1973). His articles have appeared in such journals as *Church History, Journal of Church and State* and *American Jewish History*.

DEAN M. KELLEY is Director for Religious and Civil Liberty of the National Council of Churches of Christ in the U.S.A. He is author of *Why Conservative Churches Are Growing* and *Why Churches Should Not Pay Taxes*, editor of the two-volume work *Government Intervention in Religious Affairs*, and author of numerous articles in scholarly and popular journals.

MARTIN E. MARTY is The Fairfax M. Cone Distinguished Service Professor of the History of Modern Christianity at the University of Chicago. He is the author of more than thirty books, including *Pilgrims in Their Own Land, A Cry of Absence, The Public Church and Religion*, and *Awakening and Revolution*.

WILLIAM R. MARTY is Professor of Political Science at Memphis State University. He has contributed to numerous books and journals, including *Interpretation, Logos, Thought, Journal of Politics* and *Journal of Interdisciplinary Studies.*

STEPHEN V. MONSMA is Professor of Political Science at Pepperdine University and a former state legislator in the state of Michigan. Dr. Monsma is author of *The Unraveling of America* and *Responsible Technology* and editor of *Pursuing Justice in a Sinful World.*